The
Amazing Story
of
Highland Beach

8,000 Years of Change

Town of Highland Beach

3614 SOUTH OCEAN BOULEVARD • HIGHLAND BEACH, FLORIDA 33487

Palm Beach County, Florida

561-278-4548
FAX 561-265-3582

Mayor:
Thomas J. Reid
Vice Mayor:
Michael W. Hill
Commissioners:
John J. Sorrelli
Robert L. Lowe
Rachael Scala-Pistone
Town Manager:
Ben Saag

Welcome to the "Amazing Story of Highland Beach." This is a truly amazing community by the sea on the southeast coast of Florida.

As mayor of Highland Beach, I am proud to bring you a documentary of our history that began so many, many years ago. Our magnificent beaches and extraordinarily high ocean dunes have attracted residents from the ages of the Paleo-Indians to the very present. Our community has been able to provide the highest quality of life to all who have chosen to live here.

Our past is incredible, and its legacy must be preserved. Our future is very bright. We will continue to preserve our natural environment, our archaeological sites and our quality of life.

Representing our town commission and all our residents, I invite you to read this book of fascinating history, part of our fiftieth anniversary celebration.

Sincerely,

Thomas J. Reid

The
Amazing Story
of
Highland Beach

8,000 Years of Change

Sandy Simon

The Cedars Group
Delray Beach, Florida
2003

Library of Congress Control Number 2002117084

ISBN 0-9669625-4-0

Printed in the United States of America

Dedicated
to
all those who came to the Highlands
to live,
to enjoy,
to share their bounty,
and left this wonderful legacy
and to
all those who call
the Town of Highland Beach home.

Other books by Sandy Simon:

REMEMBERING:
A HISTORY OF FLORIDA'S SOUTH PALM BEACH COUNTY:
1894-1998

A STROKE OF GENIUS:
MESSAGES OF HOPE AND HEALING
FROM A THRIVING STROKE SURVIVOR

BEYOND THE CEDARS, a romantic novel (to be published 2004)

The Cedars Group
P.O. Box 201
Delray Beach, Florida 33447

Acknowledgements

I am most grateful to anthropologist Dr. Ina Jane Wundram, Professor Emerita of Emory University, for directing my extensive research of the pre-Columbian period in preparation for writing this book. She allowed me to use her manuscript, "Clovis Points to Temple Mounds: A Prehistory of the American Southeast," based on years of anthropological and archaeological studies. It will be published by the University of Florida Press. She also suggested additional readings by other scholars, starting with the end of the last Ice Age, which provided the essential information for the first parts of the book.

To Mayor Tom Reid for his love of history, his community and his desire to preserve its past, and to the people of Highland Beach, I extend my deep appreciation for their commission of this book, their pride in their community, their willingness to share their stories and their visions and sense of the importance of their history. Those to whom I am very grateful include Vice-Mayor Michael Hill, Commissioners Robert Lowe, Rachael Scala-Pistone and John Sorrelli, Police Chief Anthony Cervasio, Highland Beach Historical Society Chairman Leonard Bell, town attorney Tom Sliney, ex-Mayors Betty Jean Stewart and Arlin Voress, and the management staff of the Holiday Inn.

Many thanks to these people of Florida who shared their family stories of the early days of the settlements including, but not limited to, Gertrude Brownley, Harold Butts, Tom Butts, John Byrd, Arthur Eypel, "Mim" George, Richard George, Bill Koch, Jr., Helen Farrow Long, Jimmy Love, John Miller, Sam Ogren, Jr., Linda Oxford, Harvey Oyer III, Al Petruzzelli, Bud Priest, Jr., Ernie Simon, Roy Simon, Jake Webb, Dodee Weir, Joan Battin Weir, and Tom Woolbright.

I am also grateful to Paul Davis, Environmental Supervisor of the Palm Beach County Department of Environmental Resources Management, Dottie Patterson, Delray Beach Historical Society Historian, Peg McCall, Boca Raton

Historical Society Historian and to Dr. Donald Curl, Professor of History, Florida Atlantic University.

I thank Tamotsu "Tom" Kobayashi, Hoichi Kurisu, and Larry Rosensweig, Director of the Morikami Museum and Japanese Gardens, and Tom Gregerson, Curator, for their expert advice and verification of those portions of the book relating to Yamato Colony, George Morikami, and the Museum and its gardens.

And many thanks to Elfriede Lynch, Florida Atlantic University, for her early encouragement to pursue a career in writing following my severe stroke.

I am grateful to my father and mother for the many wonderful stories they shared with their sons.

Thanks again to my exacting, lovable but demanding editor, Jean Goode, to my dear nephew Christopher Simon, and to Sarah Collins for her expert design of this book and its cover.

I take this opportunity to thank my vital colleague, typist, co-editor, research assistant and confidant, Christy Collins, without whom this book could never have been completed.

Contents

Part Three
1894-1949

Part Four
1949-2003

Preface

When Mayor Thomas J. Reid invited me to meet with him for the purpose of authoring a history of Highland Beach, I was surprised, and not sure that he was serious. Being a native of neighboring Delray Beach where my family has resided since 1912, I knew a lot about that small parcel of oceanfront land between my hometown and Boca Raton, and how sparsely it was populated up to the middle of the 20th century.

I laughed and said, "You're kidding?"

"No," he responded quickly. "I've read your book *Remembering* on the history of South Palm Beach County from 1894. I like your writing style and I think you could do a good job for us."

I smiled and thanked him. "But Mayor Reid…"

He interrupted, "Before you decide, come to my office and see the abundance of historical information we have on our town. We have found seven pre-historic Indian mounds, middens. All are now under condominiums. The most important one was found in 1980. It included more than 100 human skeletons. Members of Florida Atlantic University's Archeology Department came out and researched the site. We understand the skeletons have been dated at more than 2,500 to 3,000 years old."

Now he had my attention. I was intrigued and became so fascinated by the offer that in two days, I was in Mayor Reid's small office, where he described that this book should be part of the recognition of the 50th anniversary of the Town of Highland Beach.

Tom Reid, I discovered, is a visionary, a history aficionado, and an expert in Chinese painting. He is irresistibly engaging. I fell victim to his enthusiasm and his disarming charm. Here, I thought, was an Irishman who convinced me that this story I was hearing was not blarney. I was challenged, yet unsure that there was actually a story of this relatively new town and whether its history would be of interest to anyone but a few of the town's residents and me. To most people who grew up here in the 1930s and 1940s, Highland Beach was called "Jap Rocks," in honor of the first Japanese colonists who came here in 1904, and was mostly an unpopulated dune area overlooking the Atlantic Ocean where teenagers and their dates liked to go.

At first, I thought that page one would say something like this: "Highland Beach, also known as 'Jap Rocks,' had a beautiful beach, a coral outcropping, lots of swampland, billions of mosquitoes, millions of large blue land crabs, and no people." Page two would read: "After the 1970s, Highland Beach now has a beautiful beach, a coral outcropping, some remaining mangroves, lots of cement and stucco high-rise condominiums, lots of people—and no more blue land crabs." "The End."

There's got to be more than that, I thought. Who were the people whose bones were found? Where did they come from? So, I devoted myself to extensive research and situated Highland Beach as a "way station" or "intersection" through which over the centuries people came to hunt for food, to settle and live in peace in the southern part of Florida.

This book is the culmination of hundreds of hours of historical research. Part One addresses the peopling of South Florida some 10,000 years ago by Paleo-Indian big-game hunters. Part Two describes the Spanish Occupation, or, as it is known, the European Contact Period through the arrival of the Flagler Railroad. Part Three brings us from the late 19th century to the early settlements of Delray Beach and Boynton Beach, Boca Raton's creation in the 1920s by Addison Mizner, and World War II. Part Four traces the amazing transformation of the Town of Highland Beach, starting with its incorporation in 1949, from a sparsely populated oceanfront area less than three miles long into an extraordinary, luxurious oceanfront community now identified as the eighteenth wealthiest town in America.

This book is written as a series of stories that are based on facts and the latest anthropological consensus. They have been corroborated covering some 15,000 years of history since the last Ice Age when, it is believed, the first people came to the Americas. I decided to dramatize events in a light-hearted and humorous style. Those dramatizations are set in italic print.

I was also fascinated with the people I interviewed for insights into the more contemporary years from 1904 to 2002. I was impressed with the urbane cultures that blend in this sophisticated community, the striving, particularly by Mayor Reid, to ensure a sense of community and a culture of "ownership" of itself and the region by its citizens, most of whom chose the town for their retirement years.

I appreciate the dedication and co-operation of Mayor Reid, his loyal staff, and other officials and friends of the town in this endeavor. I am not skeptical anymore and am vicariously enjoying the pride of home ownership in this wonderful community of the Town of Highland Beach.

Prologue

The history of Highland Beach and most of southeast Florida could easily and mistakenly be declared to have begun in 1894 when the Flagler Railroad reached Palm Beach or in 1896 when construction of Henry Flagler's railroad passed through what is now Delray Beach and west of Highland Beach to Miami, bringing the first settlers from the North into the immediate area. But the unique and much earlier history of Highland Beach and the surrounding areas of South Florida manifested itself and became apparent and confirmed when one of several prehistoric Indian burial mounds were unearthed on August 8, 1980, evidencing human habitation centuries earlier.

By that year, Highland Beach, already a beautiful and coveted oceanside resort community of upscale homes and condominium towers, was highly developed, and construction was about to begin on yet another high-rise condominium, Parker Highland East, 4605 South Ocean Boulevard, which would be comprised of twenty-six oceanfront, luxury apartments on the Highlands dune. In the Sun-Sentinel of 1984, there was an article stating that while clearing the underbrush so a parking ramp could be built, a construction worker operating a bulldozer accidentally damaged an ancient Indian burial mound that contained hundreds of human bones. While up to eight other pre-Columbian burial sites in the immediate area had been uncovered earlier, few, if any, bones or other artifacts had been found. This particular discovery was, in contrast, profound because pieced together, the bone pieces formed about 160 human skeletons in this mound on the ocean dune at this particular site. The find was important and significant enough to archeologists that members of the archeological faculty from Florida Atlantic University in nearby Boca Raton rushed to the site. After negotiating with the enlightened developer and obtaining an agreement to permit an archeological dig, a team began to inspect, codify, date, and identify the discovery. The ultimate findings were time-tested and it was determined that the human bones were probably pre-Colombian Indians who were buried between 500 and 1500 A.D.

Some believe that the settlement found in the "Highlands" was a part of other human occupation throughout the region, later, perhaps coinciding with the settlements found in Miami that have now been identified with the "Miami Circle," although evidence indicates there was no relationship between the two. Yet, these discoveries have led some archeologists to reckon that the Miami settlement may have been the commercial center of a myriad of early Paleo-Indian communities in the South Florida region, including Highland Beach.

As a result, it is incumbent that this text considers these revelations and pursues the following questions that this 1980 discovery presents:

Who were these early inhabitants?

Where did they come from?

How and when did they get here?

How did they live?

How long did they actually live in the Highland Beach area?

Where are their descendants now?

This book hopes to successfully answer these fascinating, historic questions.

Introduction

The 20th century has been an amazing, logic-defying century of change, reconfiguration, and massive population growth in southeast Florida. Very little change occurred in the area from the 1st century until the 16th century when the first Spanish arrived. Then little happened until 1894 when the Flagler Railroad finally reached Palm Beach. In 1896, it terminated in Miami, completing the East Coast rail system from Jacksonville to the southernmost populated settlement of South Florida at that time.

Highland Beach, known then as the Highlands because of its extraordinarily high ocean dunes, was a direct beneficiary of this rail connection to the rest of America. In 1895, at the time of settlement of Delray, the area was mostly settled by sparse bands of ex-slaves from the Florida panhandle and a few friendly natives called Seminole Indians.

At the same time, Boynton Beach, just north, and Boca Raton, to the south, had perhaps one family each. Boca Raton's first settler was Captain Thomas Moore Richards, Flagler's local representative. Boca Raton did not really become a settlement until 1922 when Addison Mizner came to town to develop "The Greatest Resort in the World."

The Highlands were comfortably nestled between opulent Palm Beach, twenty miles to the north, Delray Beach, immediately to the north, Boca Raton immediately to the south, and Miami, forty-five miles to the south. Consequently, Highland Beach was exquisitely poised to experience all the blessings and astronomical population growth ever seen in its long history. It was also so located as to witness the sometimes-tumultuous periods and often eventful times occurring in the area. It witnessed the arrival of the first human beings to the peninsula, the coming of the Carib Indians, the passing by of Spanish galleons and English adventurers, the passing through of "runaway slaves" and

Confederate Army veterans. It was on the route of the "Barefoot Mailman" who walked the beach from Miami to Jupiter, and in the target area of the terribly destructive hurricanes of 1926 and 1928. It participated in the unprecedented "Land Boom" of the early 1920s and the "Land Crash" of 1927. Its residents witnessed the offshore World War II German submarines torpedoing sixteen "Liberty Ships" headed for England, and they witnessed the population boom that began in the late 1960s and continues to this day.

As a frame of reference, in 1900, at a time of vibrant industry in the North, when New York City boasted a population of two million, Chicago one million, where trolleys, cinemas, and multimillionaires were in abundance, and at a time in history when the average American life span was 40 years, only 500 people lived in all of Palm Beach County, one of the largest counties east of the Mississippi River. That same year, local coastal settlements were just beginning to grow, especially in Delray Beach and Boynton Beach. In 1900, Fort Lauderdale had only seven registered voters, mostly trappers, hunters, and fishermen who had come to the swampy frontier to "get lost while still living in America." And, as significantly, there were only three single women in Ft. Lauderdale. Boca Raton had perhaps 18 citizens; Boynton Beach had 70 residents. Linton (Delray Beach), the commercial center of the South Palm Beach region, was bustling with a village population of 125. There is no recorded population for 1900 in the area of Highland Beach which was no more than a desolate narrow stretch of land between the beach and the "canal," now the Intracoastal Waterway. For many years, Highland Beach was only a place one had to travel through from Delray Beach south to Boca Raton if one wanted to use the "Beach Road," now known as Ocean Boulevard or Highway A1A. The entire beach road at that time was along the top of the ocean dune. The dunes were blanketed with sea oats, seagrapes, thickets and impenetrable underbrush until the influx of post-World War II domestic immigrants from the Northern states. From about 1910 until 1949, and in local circles until the 1970s, the area was affectionately called "Jap Rocks."

Highland Beach Today

On January 1, 1900, Highland Beach was comprised of a magnificent beach, a small coral outcropping, and high dunes covered with gracefully swaying sea oats, gently responding to the almost constant ocean breezes. There were thick forests of seagrape trees, vines, and tangled underbrush. Tall pines grew down the west slope of the dunes toward that fresh water stream then known as "the canal," now the deeper, wider, navigable Intracoastal Waterway. The stream was bordered by a veritable jungle of swamp, underbrush and the fertile black soil of a meandering shoreline.

If we could photograph Highland Beach on January 1, 2000, we would agree that this town is extraordinary. It is unique in all of southeast Florida in that, aside from one oceanfront motel, the 115-room Holiday Inn, the town is virtually 100%

luxury residential. It is bounded on the east by the Atlantic Ocean, on the west by the Intracoastal Waterway and is literally bisected by Highway A1A through its entire 2.9 mile length.

This whole area of South Florida is the nearest of America's coastline to the warm waters of the Gulf Stream. The Gulf Stream is an underwater river that travels north from the western Gulf of Mexico, past New Orleans, around the Florida Keys, alongside Dade, Broward and Palm Beach Counties and then heads northeast at seven knots until it reaches the environs of England.

In Highland Beach, there are now 3,500 residences comprised of high-rise buildings, each of up to fifty condominium apartments as tall as 150 feet, and 200 magnificent single-family homes. Values of opulent Highland Beach homes ranged from $500,000 to $10,000,000, with luxury condominiums valued from $200,000 to $2,800,000. Prices of these coveted dwellings have been increasing at a long-term rate of 7% annually, sometimes doubling in value about every ten years. On January 1, 2000, almost all the residents in Highland Beach were human beings, where as recently as 50 years ago, the principal residents were millions of fierce, large blue land crabs, and small animals…raccoons, rabbits, deer, bears, silver foxes, opossums, various rodents, lots of snakes, alligators of every size, and maybe even crocodiles. Until the Indian mounds were found in 1980, there was no evidence of humans inhabiting Highland Beach prior to about 1900. The Everglades, the enormous swampland and environmentally rich region which extends west of Highland Beach across the southern region of the Florida peninsula, is the only known place on earth where both alligators and crocodiles co-exist. Until government flood control began in the 1880s, Highland Beach was on the eastern edge of the Everglades. Because of its sub-tropic locale, there were millions, even "gazillions," of free-breeding insects—mosquitoes, stinging flies, and "no see-um" gnats, multiple varieties of snakes, bears, panthers and other bothersome "critters" that could drive turn-of-the-century pioneers insane.

While there were virtually no human inhabitants in the immediate area from the 1600s until 1900, today, there are an estimated 3,800 year-round residents, and 7,500 residents and tourists during the wonderfully temperate winter season, all of whom enjoy the magnificent beaches and sunny tropical weather of Highland Beach for as little as a weekend or as much as four months.

Most modern American towns and cities began as rural or pioneer settlements with storekeepers, innkeepers, farmers, and other poor, hard-working residents who endured the difficult incubation years of little or no community infrastructure. In sharp contrast, Highland Beach exploded as a luxurious residential community from the moment of its incorporation as a town in 1949. Along with its neighboring towns, it has experienced among the highest land values in Florida since 1924, during the incredible "Land Boom" of the "Roaring Twenties" until today. There were periods of extremely low land valuations, such as the Great Depression of the 1930s. Beginning with the stock market crash in 1929 until World War II, Highland Beach land was very "cheap," almost a giveaway at less than $50 per acre for oceanfront lots.

Today, the value of homes or vacant land, if you can find any in South Florida and Palm Beach County, is at its highest peak. Homes have reached the most incredible heights in value and unprecedented size...area condominiums valued as high as $4,000,000, oceanfront mansions, as large as 50,000 square feet with eight bedrooms, sixteen bathrooms and six-car garages full of expensive cars valued at about $10,000,000.

Highland Beach is a beautiful, carefully manicured, copiously landscaped oceanfront resort residential community. Without shops, a commercial downtown, and, only recently, its own fresh water source and sewerage facility, residents have had to rely on the infrastructures of its neighbors, Boca Raton and Delray Beach. But there are modern community infrastructure and facilities today, including handsome buildings housing its efficient Town Hall, the well-equipped Town Library, the Post Office, the Town Police Station, and the Town Fire Station, all manned by experts in their fields. Even without schools or retail shops, the town has almost all the facilities of a major city. Tom Reid, the mayor, told me, "Our town has all the facilities as any major city except for schools. We have no students!"

To the many longtime residents of its neighboring towns, for decades Highland Beach was simply the home of tens of thousands of large, blue, threatening land crabs that committed mass suicide each spring by dodging car tires while trying to traverse A1A as they sought the sea to lay their eggs. But, by the 1970s and 1980s, observers in neighboring towns noted with apparent elitist disdain that Highland Beach was "the place between Boca and Delray with nothing but high-rise condominiums, no community, nothing but tall buildings blocking the sea breezes." Or, "if you stretched all those condos atop one another, they would reach to the moon."

Highland Beach wasn't always just a small strip of barrier island along the beach densely covered with high-rise condominiums. In fact, it has its own unique history and its own archaeological evidence that early natives may have lived in the Highlands as long ago as 8,000 B.C.

PART ONE
15,000 B.C. to 1492 A.D.

The Peopling
of the
Americas

Based on the preponderance of research and analysis of evidence now available, it is agreed that human beings did not originate in the Western Hemisphere. Rather, humanity, it appears, began on the continent of Africa. From there, they migrated northward into the European and Asian continents over millions of years, evolving and spreading across much of the "Old World," Europe and Asia. This is known as the Pleistocene Epoch, or what is commonly called the Ice Age, when much of the Northern Hemisphere was covered in ice in the form of glaciers, a period that is believed to have taken place over a two million year period.

While it is generally agreed that the first humans who inhabited North America in general, and South Florida in particular, did not necessarily migrate directly to Florida from Asia, and some might even have come from the European continent, most historians agree that it is more likely the ancestors of Native Americans came from Asia. But from where in Asia? Did they come in one wave? Or did they come over several ages? Did some sail from southeastern Asia, as did the early Hawaiians? Or did they island-hop from northern Asia or Japan to the Aleutian Islands of North America by boat as some anthropologists agree? Did they then sail or walk south along the west coast, and spread south and east? Or did they locate first along the west coast of South America, then sail or walk northward?

Where did the first Americans come from? For most of the 20th century, most anthropologists and archeologists have agreed, based on an abundance of credible discoveries, that the first "Americans" followed herds of game east from areas of eastern Asia across a land bridge, now the Bering Strait, which connected eastern Siberia in Asia to western Alaska in North America. This probably occurred at the end of the last Ice Age, about 12,000 to 15,000 years B.P. or 10,000 to 13,000 B.C. (Note: B.P. is a date designation meaning "Before Present." Since A.D. was 2,000 years ago, B.P. must necessarily be 2,000 years longer than A.D. Adjusting B.C. to B.P. is the same.)

Recently there have been new discoveries that are causing experts to rethink this singular possibility, and to consider instead that over many centuries, perhaps thousands of years, the earliest Americans also came directly from Japan. Possibly Caucasian in appearance, they island-hopped northward to the Aleutian Islands. There are good reasons to support this theory.

It is necessary to remember that there are no absolute answers to any of these pre-Colombian historical questions. Most opinions are based on available artifacts, relics, and other archeological findings, utilizing expert deduction, extrapolation and logic. Still, there are several possibilities to consider, some of which will be included here for the readers' enlightenment and pleasure.

If one considers the most popular theory, that is, the wandering and crossing of the ice-free land bridge, then one must understand what conditions existed at the time and how rudimentary the existence of human beings actually was at that time.

By the end of the last Ice Age, about 13,000 B.C., much of the earth's moisture was trapped in the massive glaciers and ice sheets that covered most of North America and northern Europe. Those bodies of ice in many areas were several miles deep. As a result of the amount of moisture captured in the ice, the earth's seas were lower than at the present by an estimated 300 feet.

Even if the Caucasian-appearing Japanese or Siberian Asians of prehistorical periods had migrated to America between 10,000 and 13,000 B.C., consider the potential barriers to proceeding eastward across the North American continent at the end of the last Ice Age. To traverse the land bridge of the Bering Strait, or sail north from Japan's islands, they would have had to contend with lower seas, swampy areas, fierce, huge animals, and the glaciers, which must have presented enormous barriers to prehistoric man.

At the same time, with seas lowered and much smaller, most of the Caribbean and Bahama Islands would have been hills on the large exposed landmass, perhaps even connecting with Florida's body of land. The Florida Keys, probably actually part of then Florida landmass, would have been the tops of the southern portion of a much larger peninsula of Florida. Perhaps the beaches of Florida extended hundreds of miles to the east, south, and west so that most of the Gulf of Mexico could have been more appropriately named the "Flats of Mexico" or the "Prairie of Mexico."

The land bridge itself was about 1,000 miles wide, and over time was, as a result of its fertile soil, a tree-covered habitat for all kinds of wildlife, including mammoths, saber-toothed tigers, giant armadillos, deer, bear, behemoths, and birds of all kinds.

From ancient Asia, as their population grew, people slowly migrated east and south by the pattern of fission or splitting. Groups of perhaps five to one hundred people left the existing village or band to seek food and remove themselves from adversaries or crowded areas short of food and shelter to a more hospitable area where they could establish a new village or band. They were far enough away to be independent, but near enough to enjoy the safety of numbers. Perhaps the breakaway was caused by a power struggle between a young leader and the existing chief and his followers. Democracy had little to do with tribal leadership and migration, for democracy is a recent phenomenon. Anthropologists agree that the peopling of North America was not accomplished by a mass exodus like the ancient Israelites leaving the only civilized society in the world en mass. Rather, the migration of the people from Asia was a "leap-frogging" means of transfer from one continent to another. People of a village, community or tribe simply followed or stayed with the leader who had exhibited exceptional bravery in the hunt or made the best decisions. In the early human social structure, people did not vote. They simply grunted. It took hundreds of fissions to ultimately move long distances, whether crossing the land bridge or island-hopping from Japan. Once on the American continent, people probably continued their migration southward down the west coast of North America, following herds of animals, their food supply. Likely, over the many years, no single person ever knew they were actually crossing a continent, and, just as likely, none ever travelled more than fifty miles in his lifetime.

At that time, human beings, remarkably able to adapt to changes in the climate, kept warm by wearing heavy animal skins. Daily they had to look for food: herds of animals or vegetation to gather. They had to withstand the ferocious animals, killing them with the crudest of weapons: stones, spears, and their hands. It wasn't a place for wimps, to be sure.

"We think we don't want to climb those tall mountains," exclaimed Kantukah, Lazy Deer. "We think we go south to Puget Sound. Many fish there and most of us really like salmon. The bears are smaller, and in Seattle maybe we can get good jobs in high tech."

Manganwat, Galloping Turtle, looked at Lazy Deer dubiously and laughed out loud. "Lazy Deer, don't you know it rains all the time in Seattle? You are going to hate it there. But if you want to go south, continue until you reach San Francisco-by-the-bay. They tell me it's always 72 degrees there. But beware, there is fog everyday, we are told. Must be nice though, especially in February. Anyway, do what you want, we wish you well. We will not fight you - you know we are always peaceful and will be until the Europeans come and mess up the neighborhood. So, go in peace. But remember, if some of the others want to continue south, don't stop them. Maybe they will reach Los Angeles. It's much warmer there. And some may want to go into show business, maybe even be Indians in Western movies!"

"Ugh, good advice," replied Lazy Deer. "And thanks for it. We've traveled together a long time, and while I hate good-byes, good-bye dear friend."

Once they reached the western edge of the four-mile high glaciers successfully, how did they cross them? And better yet, why even try? Likely, they didn't since animals, their food, didn't venture up the barren ice. So, chances are that they migrated, still in a process of fission as they did, south as far as Texas and South America, then east and northward. There is conclusive evidence that Paleo-Indians lived in many areas of North America 11,500 years ago. These have been labeled Clovis people because of their distinctive stone points that were first discovered in Clovis, New Mexico.

Since the first discovery in New Mexico, these same distinctive stone points, tools with which they worked, dated around 11,500 B.P. (9,500 B.C.), have been discovered over much of North America. Pre-Clovis sites have even been discovered in Virginia and, in 1986, on the coastal areas of South Carolina. New, deeper digs by archeologists have resulted in discovering stone tools, tools for working wood, bone, antlers, and other such items. The radio carbon dating of these discoveries actually established pre-Clovis American habitation as early as 15,000 to 19,000 years ago. Perhaps then, the land bridge, which may not have been passable 19,000 years ago, was not the first avenue of access to North America.

There is substantial evidence from recent discoveries that earliest American human habitation took place on the western coast of Chile in South America, possibly before the end of the last Ice Age, indicating these people may have crossed the South Pacific Ocean before the crossing of the land bridge. That is a fascinating possibility to consider.

As yet, there is no universal agreement on whether the first Americans came across the Pacific Ocean to South America before the last Ice Age, then traveled north from South America, or if, in fact, they first headed east across the land bridge connecting Siberia to Alaska, and then south. For the purposes of this book, the idea of several routes over different periods of time is acceptable, as is the possibility that pre-Ice Age humans first inhabited the coastal areas of Chile in South America. These hypotheses are not mutually exclusive, and it is very possible that at least four different routes and periods could have occurred.

Our research, study, and conclusions in this book lead us to accept that position and view that the first humans of South Florida came from South America, whether originating from the Bering Strait land bridge or not.

We can safely accept the position that most of the early humans who inhabited most of North America came across the land bridge, traveled south around the enormous glaciers and, over thousands of years, dispersed across the continent as far as the eastern seaboard, and, possibly as far south as Peru. In any case, it would seem that there is no such thing as "Native Americans." More accurately, they were "First Americans."

We can hypothesize that something like the following occurred circa 11,500 B.C., or 12,000 B.P.

The First Human Conclave of North America, 12,000 B.P.

The strongest, biggest, bravest man stood on the hill overlooking Puget Sound and looked down to the gathering of thousands of early human beings.

"Gather closer," he yelled in their native language, "gather round. I have something important to tell you."

In the far reaches of the crowd, an elder, around thirty years old, and possibly an early ancestor of a South Florida condominium resident, yelled, "We can't hear you!"

"Come closer. I will speak louder," he replied with a shrug and louder series of grunts.

As he swept his arm across his body, seeking to gather the people, he yelled, "We have become a very large group of people. We are now too large to call ourselves a band. I think we should call ourselves a tribe with a new country."

"USA! USA! USA!" the crowd cheered.

A man nearby who knew, liked, and feared the leader turned to the human next to him and said with a smile, "I like it. The word tribe has a nice ring to it. Don't you think Big Indian Guy, Killer of Large Mammoths, is right on, Antler Man?"

Nodding his head in agreement, "Ugh," responded Antler Man, his companion in many attacks on caribou, "I like it, but what is he up to?"

"Let's listen," said Big Salmon Catcher as he looked back at their leader, Big Indian Guy.

The crowd grew quiet. With all attention focused on him, Big Indian Guy sensed the opportune moment and seized it.

"It is time we separated, formed smaller groups and dispersed across this great North American continent. We cannot travel as one group this big any longer."

"Yes!" someone yelled to the leader, "four thousand years together is long enough."

"So, I have spoken with the bravest in our tribe and each has chosen what he wants to do, where he wants to go, and who will go with him. Some want to stay here. We will call them Puget. Others who want to stay nearby will call themselves Yakima, Chinook, and Paiute. Those who want to go slightly east toward the rising sun will be called

Dakota, Chippewa, Sioux, and Cheyenne. The Utes can go to Utah. And," he continued with a smile, "the crowd that always walks in the mud wants to be called the Blackfeet tribe. And those peoples over there obviously will be called Flatheads."

"There are some who hate the cold weather and want to go as far south as possible. I have warned them, the summers are very hot and long. But noooo....they know better. So, we will call them Aztec, Navaho, Shoshone, Hopi, Apache, Havasupia, Kiowa, and Taos. Sure, there will be others, but for now we'll let them go and still consider them brothers."

"But, Big Indian Guy, there are still some of us left. How about them?"

"Well," replied Big Indian Guy, "some want to go to Chicago, Montreal...even New York. So, we'll call them Winnebago because most of them like to ride on their wives' backs. The others we'll name, oh, hmmm," scratching his chin while thinking continued, "how about Mohawk, Algonquin, Illinois, Huron, and Seneca."

"Yeah, Big Indian Guy, that just about takes care of most of them."

Then, in conclusion, Big Indian Guy stretched out both his muscular, hairy arms and yelled, beseeching his people, "Go now, and populate this great land of America."

As he watched the thousands walking in all directions, happy and optimistic in their decisions, he heard in the distance a cacophony of chanting that continued for a long time, "USA! USA! USA!"

"Hey, Big Indian Guy," yelled Deer Chaser, "there's one fella left. He's over on the other hill all by himself. See him? He has his arms folded in front of him. He looks angry. What about him?"

"Huh. Bad body language," grunted Big Salmon Catcher, with a sneer of disdain.

"I didn't see him. Bring him to me."

After cajoling the frowning lone human sitting by himself, Deer Chaser brought the last human left in the entire first native nation.

Big Indian Guy spoke to the single man, "Who do you want to be, my man?" He smiled, putting his powerful arm around the man's slumped, hairy shoulders, "And where do you want to go?"

"Well," replied the last person to decide his destiny, "my name is Changachgook and I want to cross this great continent so I can live near Cooperstown, in upstate New York. My great wish is that I become...the first of the Mohicans. Is that okay with you, Big Indian Guy?"

"Oh sure," was the reply, "I don't really care. Just be careful and stay away from Cooperstown, New York. The Hurons want to live in the same area."

As Changachgook thanked Big Indian Guy, pleased with his leader's blessing, he turned and tied a feather in his long hair. Then, with a solemn wave goodbye, he took the first of his abundant steps to come, and walked briskly to the east.

As he turned to go back to his cave overlooking the magnificent Pacific Ocean, Big Indian Guy put his arm over his companion, Big Salmon Catcher, and said, "It wasn't as easy as it sounds, but everybody seems happy. Now, if they can just get along."

"I think most of them are crazy," spoke Big Salmon Catcher. "First, they will never find fish anywhere as good as the salmon we get in Puget Sound. Second, those guys who want to go down to San Francisco have no idea what they're getting into. And the ones heading for Los Angeles…wait till they hit that commuter traffic."

They laughed together, bent over at the sight they knew would surely come.

Then, pondering the day's events, they sat down and cooked a giant salmon that weighed about three hundred pounds. After a long silence, Big Indian Guy turned to his friend and said, "How about that last guy? What's his name? Changachgook? Boy, what a weird guy. He says he wants to be the first of the Mohicans. Well, brother, we are all first of something. That's our job, our destiny. The real question, I think, especially for him, is what will be the name of the last of the Mohicans?"

"Something like his name, I suppose," replied Big Salmon Catcher. "Something like Chingachgook."

"Wow! Those are some names!" replied Big Indian Guy as he put his head back on a large mound of moss and went to sleep.

❧❧❧

And so, that's possibly how the first Americans found themselves becoming Puget, Anasazi, and later, as they went east from Los Angeles (the smog wasn't there yet, but the traffic was getting worse by the day), Apache, Navajo, Hopi, and Taos.

On the other hand, that is quite possibly how it didn't happen.

The first immigrants to North America spread across the expansive, magnificent, fertile, thickly wooded terrain of the continent and were satisfied with plenty of food to hunt, fish to spear, berries to pick, and small game to trap. They continued their cultural, physical, and societal migration again by means of fission to extend their presence eastward. They also brought about an enormous evolution of culture, reaching the Bronze Age just in time for the Spanish invasion. Many seemed to enjoy the "change of seasons," just like new residents of South Florida claim that is what they miss most "back home up North." And since these early settlers had no idea that South Florida's warm beaches even existed, they stayed in what is now Canada and northern areas of the United States for thousands of years. They too enjoyed the colorful autumns, the rebirth of springtime, and summer sports like early lacrosse, soccer, and a primitive form of swimming, mostly a dog-paddle rhythm. And they too hunkered down during the cold winter seasons.

Those who sought to travel east beyond the Canadian Rockies soon found the fertile prairies that today are among the most prolific wheat fields in the world. While some stayed, others continued their search east and north as far as Quebec, and some went south to Cape Cod for "lovely summers on the cape."

They were named, over time, Huron, Iroquois, Mohawk, Algonquin, and Mohican Indians.

Others traveled southward along the western coastline reaching California and Mexico, then South America, bypassing the Rocky Mountains of Colorado, Utah, and Wyoming. They later migrated to lands as far to the east as Virginia, New York, and Massachusetts.

During the ensuing hundreds of years, these "Native Americans" (Anasazi, Navajo, Apache, Arapaho, Sioux, Cherokee, and Creeks) continued eastward and southward. In the 19th century, thousands of years later, the Seminoles would finally settle in South Florida.

Others on the West Coast, seeking more tropical climates, continued southward into what is now Mexico and Central America. Anthropologists believe that some ultimately became Aztecs and, later, in the Yucatan and southern Mexico, Mayans. Both groups may have ended their migration there and built enormous cities with sophisticated, urban lifestyles, and cultures. Some other tribes continued the trek southward as far as Peru and were known as Incas.

To fulfill history, they had to hurry, because by the sixteenth century A.D., they had to have become a civilization comprised of more than six million highly cultured, sophisticated people. By 200 A.D., the three nations had produced excellent engineers, astronomers, and became advanced societies. By 900 A.D., it is believed that while the Aztecs thrived and grew in population, the Mayans began to disappear. No one really seems to know why. Similar to the Aztecs, the Incas became a civilized, sophisticated society.

All the tribes were totally vulnerable to European diseases, and peacefully naïve enough to smile broadly as they welcomed the famous conquistador, Señor Francisco Pizarro. The Spaniard brought the most illiterate, meanest, diseased men he could find as long as they could fire a gun. By 1550 A.D, the Spaniards, abusing the name of Christianity in the search for treasures of gold and silver, wiped out the entire peace-loving, intelligent, but unprepared Inca population.

Some anthropologists believe there were other natives, known as the Taino, who didn't stop in Peru, but rather spread again by fission eastward beyond the forbidding Andes Mountains to the Amazon headwaters and down to the Amazon Basin. Some of their progeny live there today, holding on by their fingertips as the "civilized" world pushes them from all directions claiming their trees, their land, and their river.

There are different timetables of when people came to North America. Today, there is growing acceptance of new evidence that indicates humans settled the coastal area now known as Monteverde, Chile prior to the possible crossing of the Bering Strait. New archeological discoveries of these settlements predate the end of the last Ice Age (about 15,000 B.C.).

Should this explanation be adequately supported, it could solve the questions surrounding the difficulties caused by enormous sheets of ice that covered most of North America at the time the Bering Strait was actually exposed land. Who were these people? Where did they come from? How did they manage to cross the entire Pacific Ocean? In canoes? Sailing boats?

It may be possible that the original "Native Americans" first settled on the west coast of South America. If so, it is therefore possible that these people were the ancestors of the Inca nation that lived in sophisticated cities until the 15th century. When the Spanish conquerors arrived in 1520, there were an estimated 6 million Incas thriving on the west coast of South America.

A logical extension of this theory is that these were the ancestors of those people who traversed the Andes Mountains and settled in the warm, relatively hospitable Amazon Basin, perhaps 12,000 years ago.

It is believed that the tribes located in the Amazon Basin migrated again by means of fission northward, ultimately reaching the northern shores of South America. Then, perhaps drawing on their ancestral sailing talents, they began traveling by canoe and crude sailboats across the Caribbean and to the north.

Adventurous generations found their way. Since there are always young men and women in any society willing to brave the unknown, it is considered likely that these tribes of the Amazon who first traversed the enormous Pacific Ocean, crossed the Andes, and set off northward from the familiar jungles to the shores seeking the hospitable islands.

They most likely first ventured north to the offshore islands of Aruba, Bon Aire, Curaçao (the ABC Islands), and the Windward Islands. Then, in time, they settled virtually all the islands of the Caribbean. These tribes were later labeled the Arawak and Carib Indians by the Spanish.

Or, if they sailed to the west, they may have settled in the Cartegena, Colombia region with its magnificent protected harbor, before venturing north to Panama, the Central America region, and the Yucatan.

Anthropologists believe that they eventually reached the Florida Keys, and then, the lee side of the Florida peninsula at the mouth of the Caloosahatchee River near Fort Myers. They were known as the Caloosa or Calusa. Now, one may assume that the river was named after the Indians. If not, the Indians were named after the river. But who named the river? Who was there first?

Years after the Caloosa settled, another tribe, the Taino, which came north from the Amazon Basin, settled on the southeast coast of Florida near Biscayne Bay and migrated north to Palm Beach County. They became known as Tekesta (People of the Good Earth).

That is how the first inhabitants could have arrived at Highland Beach. It could have been as early as 8,000 or 9,000 years ago. In could have been as recently as 1,500 years ago when the early natives settled Mayahmah (Miami) at Biscayne Bay, the main population center of southeastern Florida.

Over time, the Indians spread over most of the peninsula, as far north as St. Augustine and Jacksonville, and as far west as the Florida Panhandle. The number of tribes grew and were called "Bimini" Indians. "Bimini" was the name given to Florida by the Taino and Tekesta Indians. Taino refers to "the sense of common heritage and culture of the natives of the Caribbean" and the historical tribes of Florida, such as the Caloosa, Timucua, Tekesta, Ais, and Jeaga, according to the Tekesta Taino tribunal band of Bimini and Miami, Florida.

Paleo-Indians, the earliest humans to arrive in South Florida, are believed to have been hunters of big-game. If it is true that they arrived in America 12,000 years ago, and in the Florida area 9,000 years ago, the effects of the Ice Age were still apparent, including extremely low seas all over the world. The Pacific Ocean may have been much smaller and interspersed with many islands at the time making it more traversable. It is possible that the first arrivals traveled to Florida by foot from South or Central America. If this is possible, the first Floridians could have come eastward from what is now Yucatan, the land of the Mayans, or from Mexico, land of the Aztecs. If those native lands became crowded and short of food, the most adventurous natives may have set off to find new homes to the east, walking across what is now the Gulf of Mexico.

If, on the other hand, they arrived later, say 8,000 B.C. or even later, the seas would have been somewhat higher. As the ice cap melted, Indians from South America set sail to the north, finally reaching the Caloosahatchee River near Fort Myers, and farther north the Apalachicola River, where they became known as the Apalachee Indians.

For the author and hopefully to you, my dear reader, this is a most fascinating and provocative exercise in anthropological theory as it relates to the original peopling of the Americas and southeast Florida.

And how did these ocean-oriented pre-historic people live? The earliest peoples were hunters and gatherers with the most basic of tools. They had to discover by painful trial and error, foods that were not poisonous, when to trap fish at low tide, or somehow wrestle a turtle to submission. They dug up the earth for roots with their stubby, worn hands until years later when one inventive, less physical, lazy inventor of yore, might have yelled,

"Hey, Kanatoo, try a stick! It's a lot better."

"O.K., Mantuk," he may have replied, "but I refuse to eat what you call an oyster! Yuk!"

The early South Floridians still had to hunt and gather what they could without the benefit of weapons or tools. Until crude bows and arrows first appeared on the scene thousands of years later, around 700 A.D., muscle power, running mile after mile after big-game, hoping the "food on the hoof" would tire and fall over first was their solution. A simpler method was to wait at watering holes and capture the prey. Picking and digging were their other means of gathering food. In southeast Florida, coastal food in the form of fish, crabs, berries, seagrapes, small game and turtles was plentiful, tasty, and easy to capture.

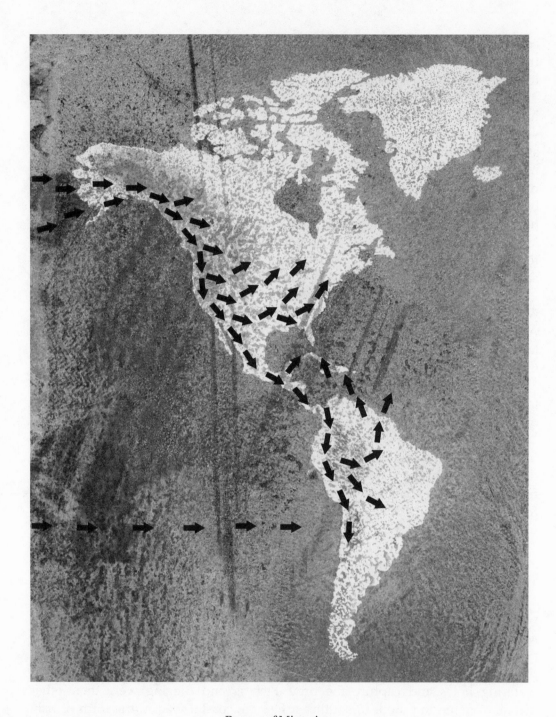

Routes of Migration

The Highlands
3000 B.C.

The three muscular young men in loincloths crouched on the beach and among the softly swaying sea oats and tall grasses on the dune, watching. Lean, tall, muscular, and longhaired, they were anxiously watching the bright, moonlit ocean.

"Shhh, be quiet, my brothers, let us not disturb our sisters, the great sea turtles, as they come to lay their eggs," Takanawah, the leader of the group, spoke as he waved his hand, quieting the other two young men of his village.

Goochkinkah spoke, "Our family will eat well tomorrow."

Kinkactah, the youngest, smiled as he looked to the shoreline, searching the lapping waves for the enormous turtles that would lugubriously stroke their way out of the sea onto the beach and, using their huge flippers, pull themselves up the slopes of the warm, golden sands of the beach, guided by the light of the full moon hovering overhead, spreading its reflection across the sea.

It was time. For days, nearly weeks, these female giant turtles had swam a few hundred feet offshore, bobbing their heads to breathe, lingering until they were ready for the difficult, exhausting trek up the beaches beyond the high tide level toward the dune. They were returning to the place of their birth so many years ago. They knew this was the proper place because it was the location just near the flat rock protrusion of coral that jutted into the sea, breaking the long expanse of uninterrupted sandy, gently sloping beaches of the shoreline.

Yes, it was time. This was a repeat of what Koonkah, the largest and oldest of the Atlantic sea turtles in the area, had performed in her role of this biannual ritual of laying eggs in the sands of this very beach.

"Look!" said Goochkinkah in an excited whisper. "There she is. Let's go and get her now."

"Not yet, my anxious brother," spoke Takanawah as he gripped his younger colleague's arm. "We must wait and watch her as she crawls up the sand toward us. We must not disturb her as she finds her place to dig her nest." He muttered to himself, with a frustrated grunt and frown, "Why am I always chosen to bring the young, impetuous of the camp with me?" Then he smiled and whispered to himself, "Oh well, they are young."

They continued to crouch and wait.

After about five minutes of lumbering up the slope, Koonkah, using first her front flippers, then, alternately her rear flippers, pushed herself up on the soft sand of the familiar beach until she found her spot. Still facing the dune, she began the next step of her two-hour performance. Slightly turning and lifting one side of her body to dig a deep hole in the sand, she reached down with her rear flippers, one after the other, scooped the beach sand, and then tossed the sand to the side, flipping the sand away with each stroke. After awhile, satisfied with the hole's depth and size—about three feet deep and eighteen inches across—she heaved her body as she began laying her eggs, allowing the moist white, pliant, round eggs, resembling Ping-Pong balls, to drop on top of one another to the bottom of the nest she had dug with such labor.

"Now," whispered Takanawah, "now we can go to Koonkah and see what She and the Sea Spirit have for us and our village."

Silently, crouching and straining their thighs as they crept bent-legged, the three nearly naked young men made their way from the dune grasses to the sandy beach where they crouched even lower behind the stoic sea turtle. "Look," whispered young Kinkactah, "see how the eggs drop into the hole. This is amazing, Takanawah. I am glad I came along." And, turning his eyes to the massive turtle's large round head, he said, "Look at her eyes, she is crying from her labors."

"She is crying, my friend, to keep the sand from her eyes, not because she is giving us her eggs and allowing us to feed on her bounty. Yes, we will take the eggs, but we must also take her to the village on the dune so that our village in the Highlands can stay here and eat well."

Then, in a quiet momentary ceremony, he placed his hand on the turtle's shell and spoke, "Thank you, Koonkah, our sister, for providing us nourishment and sacrificing yourself for us. And thank you too, oh, Sea God, for your blessings."

Before the night was over, hundreds of other huge sea turtles had climbed out of the calm sea onto the beaches and there laid thousands of eggs, renewing the life cycle of these enduring prehistoric reptiles, which, even 2,000 years later, repeat the biannual summer laying season at the same spots all along the southeastern coastline of Florida. The 20th century inhabitants of the beaches of Highland Beach still witness what the prehistoric native Paleo-Indian Americans experienced on the same dunes, the same beaches so long ago.

During the warm, often very hot and rainy summer months, the natives, in their animal-skin loincloths, sought the comfort of the ocean dunes where the insects and mosquitoes were fewer, blown into the swamps to the west by soft sea breezes and, occasionally, the stronger trade winds. Frequent frightening electrical storms, and even hurricanes, would blow the insects even further inland. On the dunes, the natives built their crude, four-poster teekee huts with thatched palmetto roofs for those warmer, even hot, months. They were low to the ground those days, mostly like caves or lean-tos of palm fronds. But for the cooler and sometimes cold winter months, the natives created their teekee huts behind the protective dunes to the west several hundred feet, along the shore of the freshwater stream. There the natives would spear fish, catch, hit, grab, or spear small game, including deer, opossum, catamounts, and raccoons as the animals fed along the shore of the stream, catching the small fresh-water crabs, feasting on the plentiful crustaceans. They enjoyed eating the tasty armadillo, and found their shells useful for cooking tools. Their favorite food, available only during the summer months, was, of course, the delectable turtle eggs and the succulent turtle meat itself. And it was abundant. They caught and killed only one giant loggerhead turtle at a time, killing only to eat or to make use of the turtle's shell while thanking their fellow living being, the Koonkah, and their Sea God for sharing their bounty. But during the summer months of May through September, thousands of turtles came out of the sea to lay their eggs. As a result, the natives were assured of plenty of food, though they only captured what they needed to survive. This was their custom.

Young Sea Turtle

Early Native Thatched Hut
1400-1900

In the high lands, with temperate, albeit humid weather, constant breezes off the sea, food aplenty, and no belligerent neighbors, the year-round lives of the early natives were free. Their environment was hospitable and easy. Life was good.

It is consistent with anthropological consensus that Paleo-Indians probably lived in South Florida by 8,000 B.C. Those who lived in what is now Highland Beach and much of Florida most likely came from the south across the Caribbean Sea, migrating from South America.

Perhaps in time, with the use of DNA analysis and investigation, we will learn whether Florida's earliest natives are related to southeast Asia, Polynesians and thus Hawaiians who crossed the Pacific Ocean to Chile, or, instead, to those Paleo-Indians who crossed the land bridge from western Siberia and later settled in the northern and western parts of North America and became known as the eastern American Indians. Or perhaps we will find they are related to those who settled in Mexico or the Yucatan.

In any case, people came to South Florida; they lived in what is now Highland Beach; and they left their mark in the mounds discovered in 1980.

It is likely the natives of southeast Florida lived similarly to their cousins throughout the southeast, specializing in hunting and living nomadic lives at first, then by 4,000 B.C., developing soapstone bowls, shell mounds, and crude pottery.

By 1,000 B.C., early civilization began in the southeastern parts of America and the nomadic lifestyle gave way to a more sedentary culture. As a result, villages became stabilized with clusters of thatched huts built in a circle for protection from animals and enemies seeking their food or possessions. Things remained calm and peaceful as long as food was plentiful and Mother Nature cooperated. As the bands grew in population, food would become scarce, and some would decide to move on. It is possible that in the area of what is now Miami, the population grew very large due to a hospitable climate and plenty of wild game, exotic fruits like mangoes, coco plums, sea grapes, turtles, berries, and roots. But in time, it is likely some decided to look to the north for new territories possibly as a result of battles with other bands, and were attracted to the high lands. Later, it was called the Highlands, and then, much later, Highland Beach, one of the loveliest places in America to live.

About the time of Christ, when the Roman Empire was at its zenith, when the people of northern Europe were still in caves, when Solomon's Temple, the Pyramids and the Phoenicians were already part of world history, Native Americans were just beginning to urbanize, albeit on a much smaller scale. Pottery making and cultivation were becoming part of society. In southern Florida, the Belle Glade pottery was already advanced by natives in the Lake Okeechobee region, at that time called Lake Mayaimi.

⚜

The Highlands 1400 A.D.

"Kinkah," Koochinkah shouted above the blowing wind, "bring me more palm fronds. I must repair the hole in the teekee roof so we can sleep tonight. These winds are too strong. We have to re-tie the fronds to each other or we will be soaked all night."

Kinkah yelled back in reply, "Yes, father, I'll do that, but it is really blowing hard. How are we going to do this? I can hardly hold these now. Shouldn't we join the others down behind the dune by the stream?"

Glatkah, Koochinkah's brother, ran up to the teekee, bowing his body against the wind, "Koochinkah, what are you doing? You'd better come off the dune now. The sea is going to wash your teekee away."

"Look at the white waves! The sea is angry. It is roiling!" Glatkah screamed to his brother. "You are fooling yourself if you think you can save your hut where it stands. I told you after that last hurricane you'd better move down to the stream in the protection of the trees with the rest of us. It's too dangerous up here on the dune."

"Maybe you are right, Glatkah, but the view here is so wonderful most of the time. We love to watch the sunrise each day from here. And we especially like not having those terrible mosquitoes everywhere. The breeze here drives them away. Besides," he added with

a sniff, "I am known as the bravest in the village. How would it look? Still, for a while, I guess we'd better get off the dune until the storm blows over. Besides, right now it's getting very cold up here." As he turned back to his chore tying the fronds, he added, "I can always come back after the storm."

"There are always a few who are courageous and will risk living near the sea, while others prefer the secure high and dry lands to the west," Glatkah shrugged. "But I think you are crazy to stay on the dune. It's too dangerous. You can call it courageous, but I call it stupid!"

❦

For thousands of years, especially during the latter years of the 20th century, there has been a clear distinction between those who will brave the often unpredictable rage and force of the sea, even paying more for the coveted locations and make their homes on the beaches or the dunes, and those who prefer the higher, dryer, "safer" lands to the west. While human life in the subtropical coastal regions of southeast Florida may have begun 8,000 years ago, as they say: "the more things change, the more they stay the same."

Since recorded Western history began with the arrival of the Spaniards, there is no written indication whether Koochinkah and his son, Kinkah, survived the storm. Whether the beaches and, even possibly, the entire dunes, were substantially eroded, even removed, is unknown. But likely any removal that occurs today is similar to what has taken place over the tens of centuries of human habitation in what is now South Florida. And it is just as likely, as it is today and will be for thousands of years to come, the re-nourishment of the beaches will resume after the storm, unless we change the natural flow of sand from north to south. As, for example, the unnatural breakwater at the Boynton Inlet, which prevents that sand migration to the south to replenish the beaches of Ocean Ridge, Delray Beach, Highland Beach, and Boca Raton, while accumulating in abundance at Manalapan, north of the breakwater well on the north side of that inlet. The inlet is an artificial one, built in 1926, the breakwater came later when the inlet was alternately dangerous for fishing boats entering and leaving, and filling totally with sand, as in the 1960s.

The main difference between those ancient peoples and us is that they did not have the capability to restore the beaches quickly, if at all. And likely shrugged their shoulders at the devastation, having no idea what may happen next, and more likely than not, picked up their meager belongings and moved to another place that could provide adequate shelter, game and other food they could gather.

The First Event:
The Fall of Constantinople and the Byzantine Empire
1453 A.D.

The Highlands—A Summer Afternoon

On the evening of the first full moon of May 1453, the pre-Colombian Indians of southeast Florida began their annual ritual celebrating the arrival of the giant turtles from the sea. By the bright glow of the full moon emerging from the sea, lookouts stood on the rugged coral outcroppings at the north end of the pristine beach, later known as "Jap Rocks." They carefully searched the sparkling surface of the ocean for the first female loggerhead to emerge. She would then begin the final portion of her journey up the warm beach sands to lay her eggs.

"There she is, There she is!" the first of many young Tekesta lookouts yelled aloud as he pointed at her. "Koonkah has arrived, and now we will have plenty of food for everyone. Tonight we will celebrate."

Hearing the excited calls from the lookouts, the chief and the village's shaman walked briskly side by side from the lee side of the ocean dune to the rocks to verify the sighting and officially declare that turtle-nesting season had indeed begun. They stood on the coral in their deerskin leggings and moccasins, and smiled as they watched first one football-sized turtle head break the surface and draw in enormous amounts of air before diving, then another and another until the calm, shiny surface, reflecting the bright moon, became full of the heads of turtles.

It should have brought excitement and joy to the shaman.

"Let the celebration begin," declared Hinkawah, the chief.

A young man in a loincloth retrieved the flaming torch from the campfire and ran to the village pole on the high dune where the women had stacked dry wood for days in preparation for the annual fertility bonfire that would challenge the full moon's bright glow.

Young boys gathered near the pile of stacked tree limbs and logs. There were large sun-bleached logs that had washed up on the beaches, broken limbs from the underbrush of seagrape trees and bush. The boys took their places with the men in a circle around the now growing fire. Older men sat cross-legged on the sand and pounded on the hollowed-out music logs lying in front of them. Others played drums to a familiar beat. Singing began as the leader's voice initiated the chant.

"Ah-ya-ya, ooo…oooh…ooo, nah-ya-ta."

The sounds were repeated over and over. The chanting got louder and louder. The drumbeat grew more rhythmic and intense. The event was a celebration of the arrival of the sea turtles and also an inspiration to the young in the tribe. The young women watched the nearly naked young men prance and dance, muscular thighs raised high as they circled the flaming bonfire. This was the night each year the young men and women looked forward to. Hormones surged as the evening's dance and chanting got more and more passionate. The full, round moon was now a beautiful red-orange ball, casting its reflection across the entire ocean.

As the evening wore on, the chanting became sensual in its deep resonance, enrapturing the people with its syncopated vibrations. The young men danced even more energetically as they tried to impress and tease, watching the girls following their steps and seeing their muscular arms move up and down, up and down. The girls smiled and swayed as they watched the young men dance for their attention. It was a wonderful event, treasured and looked forward to by all the villagers throughout the year.

"It is a happy time," Hinkawah yelled to his shaman over the din.

"Perhaps," responded the shaman, with a dubious expression, ever conscious of his role as friend and advisor to the chief, and the one person in all the village who could explain the unexplainable. According to the tribal members, the shaman was endowed with cosmic, super-natural powers. They looked to him for guidance about the unknown: Why is the wind so violent? When will the rains stop? Why am I so sick? What shall I do? Why is there no food? Why doesn't the rain come? These were the constant questions asked of the shaman, questions needing answers that seemed so difficult to find. He was Mayahlah, the "wise one" and had always seen what others could not, even as a young boy. He was Mayahlah, the life-long and closest friend of the chief.

"Hinkawah," Mayahlah spoke to his staunchest ally, "I will throw the shells as I have each year at this time. Always I have seen in the formation of the shells signs of good news. Remember last year when the gods showed me there would be no severe storms like the year before? Also, it told me that your son would have a new son. And it was so. The gods never mislead me, Hinkawah. Let us see what the gods will tell me now."

Mayahlah reached into his deerskin pouch where he carried his sacred shells that were gifts from the sea gods—made from the shells of turtles, claws from the armadillo, and sand dollars from the beach.

"Here. Now," spoke the shaman to the handful of shells. He held his hand high as he prayed, "Anna-ha! Anna-ha! I call you to our celebration. I call you to our people. Anna-ha!" He repeated his chant-prayer over and over until he felt in his heart the perfect moment when he sensed the gods had touched his hand. He shook his hand and arm. His eyes closed as his breathing grew deeper and deeper. His whole body began to shake as his hand and arm poised at the top of his rhythmic motion. And then he stopped, eyes closed, arm raised, feet dug into the sand as if to brace himself against the pull of a powerful mystic force pressing against his vibrating body.

All of a sudden he gasped, took in a very deep breath and chanted once more much louder. "Ah-mana-ha!!!" His whole body trembled as beads of perspiration burst on his forehead. His arm swept downward as he threw the shells, as one would roll dice. With eyes tightly closed, his head bowed toward the shells. He was in a trance.

Chief Hinkawah, sitting opposite the shaman, watched every motion, his eyes fixed on his friend. He did not reach to interrupt or interfere, for he knew his shaman was in full communication with the gods: the sea god, the god of the heavens, the marsh god, the food god, the storm god. All the gods were with the shaman at this moment.

Slowly, the shaman raised his head and, turning, looked up, making eye contact with his chief, his eyes opened very wide. Hinkawah saw fear in his eyes.

"Look! Hinkawah," he implored, "look at the shells. See the messages. They are in two places. And see the five shells over there. Oh, my gods, there are strange things happening."

"What is it, Mayahlah?"

"You see?" replied the shaman, "Can't you see? The message is so clear."

They both turned their eyes to the shells. The shaman pointed for his chief. "I have been given a message by the gods. I do not fully understand the message except to tell you that something very bad is happening across the world, across the sea. Far, far away. It is evil. It is a cataclysmic event that begins a process that is too terrible for me to describe. I do not know exactly what is it or why. I do not know where it is or how it will affect us. But I do know this," the trembling shaman, with eyes so wide and staring, visibly shaken and very worried as he continued in his report to the chief, "I am fearful. Oh, Hinkawah, I am fearful. Something very bad has taken place. By itself, it will not affect us or our people. But the five stones are there," he said, pointing, "confirming what I was told when I threw the shells. This event has set into motion a series of events, five of them that spell doom for all our people. The end of our way of life. These events will not occur now, but over a period of many, many years. But, I tell you, there is nothing we can do. They cannot be stopped by anyone. There will be five critical events and, when the fifth occurs, our way of life will be over, never to return. It will be painful. It will make our lives so awful that we will not recover, I fear. Each will portend the next, making the next inevitable. Each will be worse to our people than the one before."

Hinkawah, suddenly finding himself frightened by this prediction went from joy and happy excitement to fear and grave concern.

"Mayahlah, you have always known more than we. What should we do?"

"Do? Hinkawah, there is nothing to do. Life for us is today, the present. We cannot do anything but live our lives as they continue each day. We cannot comprehend the future. These events will happen, but most will happen after we and our children and our children's children are gone to the 'Great Beyond.' So, do not trouble yourself or your people. Time is short and will get shorter. You must know, however, as the great Hinkawah, leader of our people knows, that these events have begun. And they cannot be stopped."

The shaman had no way of knowing, of course, but events were now in place that would lead to the "discovery of America" by Christopher Columbus, and, ultimately, would lead to the demise of the Native Americans' way of life.

In South Florida, as the shaman urged, the Indians continued their daily occupations of hunting, gathering, picking fruits and berries—bananas, guava, huckleberries, mulberries, cocoa plums, citrus, and sugar cane grasses. By this time, the bow and arrow had improved, making hunting game so much easier by permitting the hunter to wait in stealth, then letting loose the crude arrow to sink into the flesh of a deer or rabbit, rather than having a grueling chase to see who gave up first, the hunter or the hunted. Life was placid and relatively peaceful as the Europeans across the sea went through their difficult and painful warring times.

The natives were unaware that in 1453 A.D. an event of great significance occurred in Europe that would precipitate a cataclysmic change in the lives of all Native Americans. Constantinople (now known as Istanbul), that city of vital importance to world commerce, the world's center of silk production, the crossroads between the East and West had for nearly 1,200 years been under the control of the advanced Byzantine Empire. But in 1453 it was seized and sacked by the Turks from the north, closing off the critically important trade route that facilitated enormous exchange between the European and Asian markets. Trade in spices and silks from the East, linens from the West, and foodstuffs from all directions was blocked, creating economic havoc for millions of people.

During the 40 years after 1453, merchants desperately needed to find another way to re-establish trade between East and West. Empires fell, others became vulnerable. Something had to be done. Many men tried to find a solution. Some ventured overland. Others sought to circumvent Africa. All failed.

Having a day named for him in America centuries later awaited the person who could find a new route to the east.

Only Christopher Columbus figured it out!

The first event, the Fall of Constantinople, and with it, the fall of the great 1,200-year Byzantine Empire, coincided with the rise of the Turkish control of the Eastern trade routes that would endure for 470 years and create the urgent need for new routes to the Indies to acquire spices, silks, riches, and food.

The Fall of Constantinople was a rupture of enormous proportions for both societies. So great was the catastrophe that for the following 50 years societies warred against one another, and anarchy prevailed in many regions. Parts of Europe suffered devastating economic depression, the likes of which they had not known. Rich men became bankrupt and thousands of workers became unemployed. The entire Mediterranean region was turned upside down. The major ports of Venice, Marseilles and Alexandria nearly collapsed. The discipline of the Holy Roman Empire became ineffective and unimportant. As a result, Mongols and Turks invaded the weakened nations from the north and east.

Life went on in the Highlands, for events in Europe would not impact the lives of the people of the New World for another five decades. Meanwhile, the Tekesta Indians continued their summer ritual on the beaches and dunes of the Highlands, feasting on the coastal foods in this beautiful and hospitable paradise.

PART TWO
1492-1894

The Second Event:
The Arrival of Christopher Columbus
1492

Thirty years after the fall of Constantinople, an adventurous, young Italian sailor and sea captain sought the favor of King John II of Portugal to finance an expedition to seek a new trade route to the East. Rather than continue to seek a land route east across the unknown, dangerous mountains and lands likely occupied by unfriendly inhabitants, or exploring south and east around Africa, this adventurer believed that untold riches could be reaped if he were the first to find another solution to the economic chaos of Europe caused by the fall of Constantinople and the end of the vital land caravan trade routes. He would sail west to the East Indies. The King would own all rights to discovered lands and all fees he could levy for certain rights. Portugal would be the most powerful combination of city-states in the world, and the King would reign supreme.

Even with his enthusiastic claims of potential riches, the adventurer could not persuade King John II to grant his request because the cost-estimates seemed too optimistic. It was denied in 1483.

In 1492, Isabella of Aragon and Ferdinand of Castile married, joined their forces in the Iberian Peninsula and defeated the Arab Islamic kingdom there. They established the state of Spain. The King and Queen declared Spain to be Christian only, killing, deporting, or converting all Arabs and Jews to their religion. In the same year this confident Italian adventurer, Christopher

Columbus, came seeking financing from Isabella and Ferdinand who, buoyant in their victories and believing the Spanish Inquisition to be God's will in the name of Christianity, were more than benevolent to this young enthusiastic sailor. They agreed to finance Columbus' voyage and exploration. Of course, they expected to reap untold treasures and riches of gold and silver from Columbus' exploits. With his 90 men on chartered ships, he crossed the ocean in two months. Finding Taino natives on the shore, he declared that he had found Asia and its "Indians." Since the Taino were almost nude compared to the Europeans, he called them "uncivilized savages," a label that haunted American Indians into the 20th century.

⚜

Picture the court of Isabella

King Ferdinand took young Christopher aside and softly spoke to his petitioner, "Señor Christopher, Isabella and I have decided to become incredibly rich by financing your exploration to find a new route to the Indies so that we can rebuild our economy."

He continued, "We will pay the costs of your four ships, the Nina, the Pinta, the Santa Maria, and the Juan Carlos to be captained by Pablo Montezuma, Isabella's handsome young body guard. But you must promise me this, Columbus." The King gestured to young Christopher to come to him at his throne and whispered into Columbus' ear, "Shhh…no one must know that the fourth ship, the Juan Carlos, must be allowed to sail in the lead as you reach the edge of the world. I want Montezuma to fall off the edge of the world, never to be seen again. He has been with Isabella. I believe he is her paramour, and I want rid of him forever. It is time he died."

Thus, Columbus, buoyed by this newfound benefactor, led the expedition to the New World. Long days extended into months on the barren sea, and his crew considered mutiny. As a result, he felt that it was time to signal the Juan Carlos to be the lead ship while he reefed the sails of the Santa Maria, and slowed to three knots. It was nightfall, just off the East Coast of Mexico. The fog was very heavy and no one could see the other ships.

At daybreak, Columbus' lookout woke everyone with the yell, "The Juan Carlos just fell over the edge!"

Everyone raced to the bow to look. Some ran up the rope ladders to get better views, but none could see the fourth ship. It was gone forever. Columbus searched the horizon with his spyglass, and, after due diligence, decided the Juan Carlos had indeed fallen off the world. He went below and wrote his report to King Ferdinand, worried that he had been wrong in espousing that the world was round.

But, alas, later in the day, still sailing west, Christopher found the Juan Carlos' destruction on the eastern reefs of Mexico.

And that is what caused Montezuma, captain of the Juan Carlos, to be so revengeful forever, especially to American visitors in Mexico today, a retribution called "Montezuma's revenge."

❧❖❧

It is also important to note that nearly thirty years later, in 1521, Hernán Cortez, the cruel Spanish conquistador, sailed from Cuba past the Yucatan peninsula and entered eastern Mexico seeking gold. With his superior armed forces, he fought his way inland to the Aztec capitol of Tenochtitlán and brutally killed Emperor Montezuma. After destroying the Aztec city, he founded Mexico City on its ruins. This clearly could be another far-fetched illogical explanation of Montezuma's revenge.

❧❖❧

The voyage of Christopher Columbus was the second event foreseen by Mayahlah, the shaman of the Tekesta village in southeastern Florida in May of 1453. However, by 1492, Mayahlah had passed away to the "Great Beyond," properly cremated in a tribal pyre on the revered dunes of the Highlands in the fashion of the early American Indians.

The religious role filled by the shaman's first born son, as with the leadership role of the chief, was a hierarchy development, similar to Europe's primogeniture, that prevailed in the Americas during the Mississipian Period from about 1000 A.D. until 1500 A.D., assuring in most villages an elite sector. As a result, the chief of the Highlands village was of the same family as Chief Hinkawah in 1453, nearly fifty years earlier. The same was true with the new shaman who descended from Mayahlah, Hinkawah's shaman forty years earlier.

And so, when the sea turtle arrival celebration of May 1492 took place, the elderly shaman, Batankah, the wise, met with Latoonka, the chief. The night of that celebration, he too went into the trance expected of him.

When he threw the shells as had his father so long ago and came out of his trance, he declared, "Oohhh…ahhh…I see and hear many things, oh my chief. My father told your father of an event far, far away that began a series of five events that would bring devastation eventually to all our people of our lands."

"Well, Batankah, I am sad to tell you that after forty wonderful and peaceful years of tribal life, the second event is occurring at this time."

He continued with a fearful look, gesticulating as he pointed to the ocean's horizon, "The inescapable continues. Somewhere, and I do not know exactly where, but somewhere there," he said, pointing to the east, "something is happening that will prove to be devastating to our children's children. It saddens me so."

With furrowed brow, Batankah replied, pleading, and holding out the palms of his hands to his life-long friend, "But what is it? What can we do?"

"Do? We can do nothing," shrugged the shaman. "It is already too late. It is in the hands of the Gods. We must simply wait, prepare, and live."

"Prepare," the chief asked painfully, "how should we prepare?"

"We should find a way to improve our tools. Our bows, spears, and arrows are too feeble, too crude. We must make them even stronger, finer. Prepare our people. But," he continued, "it is going to happen. When, I do not know. And I have no idea what the third event shown to my father will be. All I can tell you by the signs is that all the time it is getting closer and closer. I do not believe we will live twenty-five more years before the third event occurs. It could be years sooner. We shall see," he sighed, shrugging his shoulders in resignation.

The shaman could not know that the second event he told his chief was Christopher Columbus' expedition that would culminate at San Salvador in the Bahama Islands, only a few miles east of the Florida peninsula. And that the landing of Ponce de León on the shores of northern Florida in 1513 would be the third of the series of five events.

❧⚜❧

Columbus's Arrival in 1492

At the time Christopher Columbus and his three ships arrived in the New World, there were thriving native populations in the region extending from Venezuela north into Central America, across most of the Caribbean Sea to Florida, and across the entire North American continent. Although today it is taught in our schools that the Europeans had "discovered" this "New World," the facts are that before the European discovery of the New World, thousands of native peoples were there, quite civilized, living on just these 1,000 islands in the Caribbean Sea. Their milieu consisted of hunting, fishing, gathering foods, raising families, and co-existing with the land. The Mother Earth-given air, water, trees, beaches, land, and food were considered available for all people, and were totally shared. After the arrival of the Spanish, that ethos would change dramatically.

While the exact location of Columbus' first landing is still jealously debated, most believe Columbus landed first on the island of San Salvador in the Eastern Bahamas, where he found what he thought was Asia. Thus, he named the area the West Indies, and the inhabitants "Indians." We know now that the Arawak-Taino Indians who populated much of the western Caribbean were peaceful for the most part, though it is likely there was some raiding of each other's tribe from time to time. They were the predominant peoples of Hispaniola, now the Dominican Republic and Haiti.

On Columbus' second landing at St. Nicholas, Haiti on Christmas Eve 1492, he established his first settlement, which included his crew from the Santa Maria that had sunk off the northern coast of Haiti.

In addition to the Arawak-Taino people, there was another even more dominant group. They settled in the eastern Caribbean for the most part, and, after four voyages to the region over the next several years, Columbus' exposure to these more aggressive, more belligerent natives led him to name them Carib Indians, Carib being Spanish for "cannibal." These Carib Indians, over time, wiped out most of the less-aggressive Arawak and, until the arrival of the Europeans, virtually dominated the Caribbean region.

After Spain's "discovery" of this New World, silver and gold mines were opened, wealth was returned to Europe, and soon, by the mid-1600s, after 150 years of Spanish rule, other nationalities, seeking treasures, began to arrive and fight over these new wealth-laden lands. The islands, including the Antilles, Leeward and Virgin Islands, all named by Columbus, were only an appetizer, inducing the Portuguese, English, French, Belgian, and Dutch merchants to send their ships and lusting crews west to share in the opportunities of this new territory. This place had renewed Spain's wealth, which had been lost following the Inquisition and removal of the Arab/Moorish and Jewish cultural intelligentsia in 1492.

With gusto and determination, sailors from all over northern Europe came to the New World, although Spain owned and controlled most of the entire Caribbean. But more and greater riches awaited the Spanish and the others in the Americas. Treasure troves of gold, silver and semi-precious stones seemed to cover these new lands. Cartegena, Columbia became the busiest port of Spanish disembarkation. Portugal ventured farther south, settling the eastern coasts of Brazil and became a significant challenge to Spanish Western supremacy. The Europeans enslaved the native population and used them as forced labor for their mineral harvests. The Dutch in the Antilles, the French in the Dominican Republic and Haiti, the English in the Bahamas, the Danes to the south, and the Spanish on the much larger islands of Cuba and Puerto Rico established sugar and cotton plantations and rum distilleries worked by the Indian slaves.

After the conquerors had destroyed the Indian populations, they began importing African slaves to do their labor. And thus began 300 years of slavery, and colonization in the New World. The conquered served the conquerors as it has been for most of human "civilization."

Excitement in Europe following Columbus' discovery induced others to join him in his travels. On his second voyage, he took seventeen ships and nearly 1,400 people, including colonists seeking new lives and riches. Legend has it that when Christopher Columbus arrived on the island of Puerto Rico on his second voyage, he named the island San Juan, after John the Baptist, and then named the beautiful, easily defended harbor in which he arrived Puerto Rico, meaning "rich port."

Into the cabin rushed Columbus' assistant. He approached the Admiral's chief cartographer.

"Señor Alejandro de la Garcia-Rodriquez Castilla Castro, I have good news. Admiral Columbus wishes you...no, instructs you to map this area of the Carib Sea. He wants you to start with the three biggest islands of Cuba, the Dominican Republic and this island. And that's what we just discovered. He is calling this island San Juan for Saint John the Baptist, and he wants to name this harbor Puerto Rico, or rich port."

The messenger noticed the cartographer was slumped over the table, his head on its side, his eyes almost closed, his hand holding the empty pewter cup instead of his pen.

"What's wrong, Alejandro de la Garcia-Rodriquez Castilla Castro? What is it? Are you sick?" the messenger shook the man's slumped shoulders.

"Oh, my God, oh Christo," he murmured to himself, "he's gotten into the rum."

"Wake up you fool," shouted the messenger in a panic. "Wake up!'

"Huh?" replied the cartographer, eyes now opening drowsily, "What is your problem? I heard you," he said in slurred speech. "I know what the Admiral wants. Now, please leave me. I will do my work. First, bring me more rum. It's been such a long voyage. Por favor, inmediatamente, amigo... gracias."

"I will get it right away," replied the assistant, turning hurriedly on his heels.

"Si, Señor Alejandro de la Garcia-Rodriquez Castilla Castro, right away," responded the messenger, respecting the chief cartographer with a brisk salute. "Right away, Señor."

"Marcharse, now, and don't talk so much. I don't feel so good."

In just moments, the messenger returned with a fresh bottle of rum.

The cartographer, awakening, ordered the messenger, "Go now. Tell the Admiral it will be complete by sunrise tomorrow. And tell him I am so grateful for his confidence in me."

"Si, Señor Alejandro de la Garcia-Rodriq...."

"Shut up you fool! Enough! Go now!"

The cartographer watched the messenger step through the doorway, turn, shut and latch the door.

"Ahh...peace and quiet, at last," mumbled the drunken cartographer as he took another mouthful of the sweet rum, picked up his feather pen and returned to the navigational map spread before him.

"Now, let's see," he muttered to himself, gazing up at the ceiling, "Admiral Columbus wants to name the island Puerto Rico, and this magnificent harbor San Juan. Yes! That's what the messenger said," he exclaimed confidently, but erroneously.

As his pen went to work, Alejandro de la Garcia-Rodriquez Castilla Castro was pleased with his expert calligraphy. He was renowned across Spain for his magnificent, flowery lettering and his ability to decipher intricate navigational notes and technical information.

"There!" He exclaimed proudly, raising his now half-empty mug of rum to his lips as he gazed on his work. "It is beau-ti-ful," he proclaimed to a cabin empty but for himself.

"Yet, I cannot help but wonder why the brilliant Admiral Christopher Columbus has chosen to name this very pretty, 'muy linda' harbour, San Juan after the saint, John the Baptist, and this huge island," he mused—"he wants to name rich port? Why would he do that?" he slurred to himself as he tilted on the chair.

"Well," he said aloud, "mine is not to wonder why—"coining a new phrase for which he would never get credit, unfortunately.

"What have you done, you idiot?" shouted the Admiral, berating his cartographer. "I did not name this magnificent harbor San Juan. And I did not name this powerful gift of an island from God himself Puerto Rico. How could you make such a mistake, Señor Alejandro de la Garcia-Rodriquez Castilla Castro? May your name never be forgotten, you arrogant jerk!"

"Never mind, El Capitán," replied the proud cartographer, "who's going to know anyway? The Dutch, the English and the Danes can't read Spanish, much less my wonderful calligraphy, Admiral. Don't get so excited. It will be fine, you'll see"

"However," the respected cartographer thought, "maybe we should kill the messenger. He could tell the queen."

"Yes," replied the Admiral, "perhaps we should kill the messenger. Maybe we can set a precedent. Or do you think that's been done already?"

His co-conspirator rubbed his chin, thinking, "Nah," he replied with a sinister smile and replied, "Do it."

No one knows for sure if this is exactly the way it happened, of course, since all records of this incident were lost.

When Columbus and his fellow Spanish conquistadors arrived in the New World, what is commonly called the "pre-history" of southeastern Florida, the Southeast, Central America, the Caribbean, and South America came to an end. Instead, as written accounts of events, of peoples, of explorations, religious activities, social changes, cultural adjustments, observations and experiences were instituted, written history replaced pre-Colombian or pre-history history. Pre-Colombian or pre-history are interchangeable terms used to describe events that occurred prior to the arrival of Christopher Columbus.

The Third Event:
The Arrival of Ponce de León and the Spanish Occupation
1513

The history of the Native Americans was preserved mainly by word of mouth—stories and legends passed on for generations—until the arrival of the Spanish in the early 1500s. It was then replaced by written observations of explorers, priests, and others in the New World. This was the beginning of local history in southeast Florida—and the end of the way of life of the Native Americans.

The landing of Juan Ponce de León and his men in spring of 1513 near St. Augustine signaled the arrival of the Spanish on the Florida peninsula. It is said that they sought the Fountain of Youth, and riches in gold and silver, but they were disappointed. What they did find was a verdant and hospitable place with abundant flowers and tall, peaceful native inhabitants. They named the region Pasqua de la Florida, "feast of the flowers."

❧❦❧

When Ponce de León dropped his anchor offshore, gazing at the verdant forests of moss-draped giant oak trees, towering palm and fruit trees, so unlike the familiar dry Iberian hills scattered with cork trees, olive trees and vineyards, he must have marveled at the pristine beaches, the turquoise waters, and the natives who crowded within the seagrape trees along the shoreline, peering in wonderment at the huge, strange never-before-seen sailing ships that they assumed came in peace.

At that time, the natives who lived in northeast Florida, the Timucuans were muscular and very tall. While the Spanish visitors were very short, shorter than five feet, the Timucuan Indians were over seven feet tall, fully two feet taller than the Spanish conquerors.

The Spanish sailors who climbed down the side of the ship to board a landing craft with oars, wore steel helmets, had fully clothed bodies, and wore chest plates of metal, boots and gloves, but the hidden, gazing innocent Indians were nearly totally naked. The Timucuan men, remarkable physical specimens of outstanding muscular development, wore only loincloths and a headband. The women were topless, wearing either skirts of palmetto fronds or deerskins.

As the Spanish men drew closer to the shore, one can imagine the Indians, friendly in their reception, yelling and uttering sounds unfamiliar to the dregs of Spanish society. The sailors, not having seen women, much less topless, in months, and clearly arriving to "claim their discovery," never anticipating actual people to welcome them at the shoreline. But there they were in all of their longhaired and naked persona, and so much taller, looking down two feet into the faces of these very short visitors.

"Wha'? Who? Come," the Timucuan leader may have said as he grabbed the lead Spaniard by the arm, smiling, then pulling, almost dragging his diminutive new friend.

The visitors somehow communicated that they needed water and fresh food, and the Timucuans, having more than enough water, fruit, and game, gathered more than enough for the Spanish and filled their boat, following their beliefs that air, land, food were for everyone to share. In a way, they were actually demonstrating the Christian beliefs the Spanish professed to possess and used as their raison d'être for coming to the New World in the first place.

The mates returned to the ship and presented the chief to the Admiral. Looking up at the seven-foot Timucuan chief and then over to Admiral Ponce de León, the sailor said, "Sir, I present to you the chief of the Timucuan tribe." Whispering, he continued, "Look at the size of that loincloth, Admiral. If we take them back to Spain, they will steal our wives! As you can see, sir, since all of them are this big, I believe we should forget the whole idea of slavery."

"Hmm," spoke de León, "perhaps you are right, but we do have guns, do we not? El stupido? And what about that fountain of youth, pédro?"

"Well, sir, they said that it's nothing special, but when the chief told me he was about 100 years old and he looks about 30, I figured he was lying. Ain't that right, sir?"

"Si, I think so," Admiral de León replied with a nod. Then, he asked, "Are the women seven feet tall too? If so, they may not find our short sailors very exciting. ¿Es verdad? Maybe we ought to sail south and try to explore the Highlands to the south of Palm Beach. There is a coral out cropping there and perhaps the natives aren't so tall!"

For nearly 200 years, Spain had southeast Florida and the Caribbean Sea essentially to itself. The period, from 1500 A.D. to 1670 A.D., is known as the Contact Period. By its end, the Native American population of the entire region was decimated. The lifestyles of the remaining natives had radically changed and would never be the same. In place of the "freedom of use of land, air and water" ethos of the natives was the European culture of land and water ownership, trade, money, devastating diseases and slavery. An enduring mass cruelty by the Europeans was the decision to label the American Natives "savages," simply because they wore few garments, like loincloths, skin or palm skirts, and were "different". Their people were stereotyped with derogatory labels and considered less than human beings, and were treated as such well into the 20th century some 400 years later.

In 1521, Admiral Ponce de León, on his second exploration of the region, landed on the southwestern coast of Florida near what is now Fort Myers, inhabited by the more aggressive natives he presumably named Caloosa Indians. It is said that they were equally as tall and sinewy as the Timucuans. Ponce de León delivered 250 settlers, and 50 horses, cattle and oxen. Those small and wiry cattle, delivered near St. Augustine and later at the Caloosahatchee River, thrived on the open, grassy fertile lands of central and southwest Florida and became the foundation of the state's cattle industry even into the 19th and 20th centuries, having propagated and grown in abundance even though they were short and spindly compared to today's cattle which are the result of cross-breeding, especially with the Brahman imported from India in the early 20th century.

Ponce de León's second expedition to colonize the area failed, due to attacks by the local natives. The peninsula then was free of new Spanish arrivals until 1539 when Hernando de Soto arrived from his adventures with Francisco Pizarro in Peru, the land of the Incas.

The bubonic plague of Europe during the 14th century, which killed nearly one-third of the entire European population, was passed on genetically to its population who later, by way of the Spanish sailors in the 16th century brought the devastating impact of disease to the natives of America. After 15,000 years of separation, the New World inhabitants had no resistance to any of these diseases. For instance, pneumonia, which may not have been so severe to Europeans, was deadly to the natives. Those illnesses infected nearly all people in the villages at the same time, making nearly everyone critically sick. As a result, there were often no available villagers well enough to help them or feed them. Thousands died of malnutrition or neglect.

The illnesses came in waves, one after the other. Anthropologists believe that beginning in 1519, the Timucuans were hit first with a smallpox epidemic, felling these beautiful, tall, muscular human specimens. Smallpox, which destroyed half the native population, was followed by a gastrointestinal scourge, bubonic plague, typhus, mumps, influenza, and then the bubonic plague again.

It is likely these same cycles of devastation took place throughout the Florida peninsula, even to the reaches of the Tekesta of southeastern Florida, some of whom were living in the High Lands.

The most destructive, most devastating impact on the native population happened when Hernando De Soto arrived in Tampa in 1539 in search of gold and silver. He brought with him an army of 600 heavily armed men, 200 horses, attack dogs, and a herd of pigs. They advanced north through Timucuan country to the panhandle area, brutally killing everyone in their path. Then they progressed up into the Carolinas, Alabama, Tennessee, and Arkansas to the Mississippi River. These people also carried Old World diseases against which the natives had no resistance. They left among their legacy remaining cattle, horses and pigs that still have descendants roaming the Florida peninsula, especially Central Florida.

In 1537, De Soto was named Governor of Florida and Cuba, conditioned on his colonizing the region. He had served with Francisco Pizarro in Peru in 1530, with whom he shared the riches and participated in the decimation of the Incas and their culture.

In 1543, Hernando De Soto's troops finished conquering the American Natives. They called the natives "savages" to justify their own cruelty. De Soto's four years of rampage, devastation and killing had completed their decimation from Florida to Arkansas.

Anthropologists agree that there were four main significant forces affecting the New World with the arrival of the Spanish. They were brutality, the disease epidemics, religious missions with their dogmatic beliefs and the imposition of European cultural practices.

During the early years of the Spaniards' presence, the natives were named by roving bands of Spanish soldiers. At the southeastern tip they became Tekestas, members of the Taino tribe of the Carib/Arawak who migrated northward from the Caribbean Islands. The Tekestas had settled the southeast of the peninsula from what is now Florida City at the very southern shore. Their territory was north to about Jupiter Island. North of the Tekesta, to about Stuart, were the Jeaga. The Ais occupied land north of there to about Daytona Beach and west to Lake Okeechobee. The Mayaimi tribe lived on the north side of Lake Okeechobee where Bartow, Lake Placid and most of Polk County is located today. Timucuans occupied the plains, rivers, forests, and swamps north to Georgia, from the eastern beaches at St. Augustine and Jacksonville, across the peninsula to include what is now Tampa and Cedar Key. They were friendlier and are believed to have spread their language southward down the coast as they roamed the peninsula.

Of the tribes of South Florida, the Caloosa in the southwest were clearly the most dominant. The Caloosa ruled southwest Florida to Lake Okeechobee, having predated the Tekestas of southeast Florida. They were more advanced and had mastered the making of pottery, which became known as Belle Glade pottery. They were also more belligerent than those east coast tribes of Tekesta, Jeaga, Ais, all Taino. Some say the Caloosas practiced human sacrifice, unlike the east coast peoples. They are also believed to have enslaved the Tekestas, forcing them to farm for them and provide food and tools.

Most of the Florida panhandle to the west was settled by the Apalachee, presumably because they first settled at the mouth of the Apalachicola River. A natural assumption? Or was the Apalachicola River named after the Apalachee Indians?

One can only speculate that those natives who first settled along the Apalachicola River in the Florida panhandle, where the finest oysters grow in the blend of fresh water and salt water meet, came across the Gulf of Mexico by canoe or sailboats, having separated from the Carib tribes of the Caribbean, south of Florida. It is also a possibility that they could have migrated across the southern parts of America from Mexico. If so, they could be relatives of the Aztec and not Carib.

Wherever the Apalachee and other natives came from to settle what we now know as Florida's panhandle, it is clear that they and other natives settled the entire peninsula long before the Europeans arrived in the early 1500s. The Indians were living their free-spirited lives hunting, fishing, and paying no taxes.

At the time the Spanish first landed on the shores of the New World near St. Augustine in 1513, estimates are that there were "several" million Native Americans throughout North America. In Florida alone there were from 100,000 to 350,000 Indians. Of these, it is thought that about 40,000 were Timucua, about 4,000 Tekesta, 10,000 Caloosa (Calusa), 5,000 Jeaga, 10,000 Ais, and perhaps 20,000 Apalachee and Miccosukee (north central between the Apalachee and the Timucuan). Historians believe that there were 60 million buffalo in all of America at that time with about six million of them in Florida, mostly in the northern half of the state. The principal diet of the Timucuan in the north was red meat from the grassland-ranging buffalo and prolific herds of deer that still roam that area.

It was the tendency of roving bands of Spanish soldiers to continually name small groups of Indians as they met them. As a result, the Indians often found themselves with several names. One day they may be called Tequesta, the next day Jeaga, Ais, or Caloosa. It was a confusing time for the natives, to be sure. I'm sure they wondered if the Spanish really knew who they were constantly meeting across the peninsula and who these strange people were.

Families among the various tribes of coastal Florida hunted and gathered their food during the years preceding the European arrival. Though they did not face the harsh winter months of their cousins to the north, they were not yet farmers. They gathered their food because it was so plentiful year 'round. But they too had to overcome the challenges presented by nature. They had to co-exist with panthers, bears, alligators, crocodiles, snakes of all kinds, foxes, armadillos, scorpions, and the insects that thrived in the wetlands that covered most of southern Florida. They lived alternately with floods during the summers and drought in the winters.

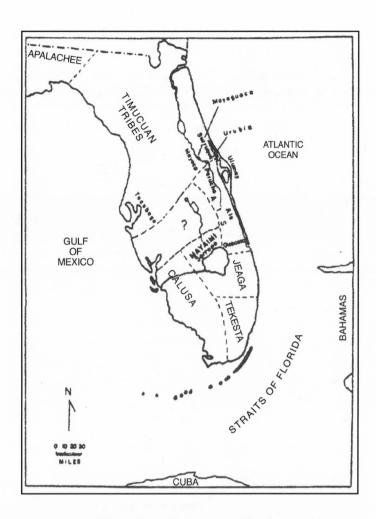

Florida's Indian tribes as named by the spanish,
16th century
Courtesy of State of Florida Archives

They tried and tested various plentiful natural allies like small feathery-leafed plants that, if rubbed on the body, would repel the stinging mosquitoes and gnats. They learned to avoid the shallow waters where the moccasins and alligators dwelled. They slept above the ground in hammocks unlike the natives of northern Florida who slept on the drier ground. Food was extraordinarily plentiful. Fish could be trapped in the small coves along the ocean shore and in the small fresh-water streams that ran to the ocean. Young men would group together, form a human chain, and by splashing the water, corral the thick schools of small fishes, or even larger ones such as tasty grouper and *langostas* (clawless lobsters), that could be scooped and tossed onto the beaches to be boiled at the campfire. Or they could spear the larger fish, especially near the prolific coral outcropping at the High Lands, and capture sea turtles or gather their eggs during the summer months of nesting.

They chased game through the tangles of underbrush capturing deer, armadillos, rabbits, foxes, and opossum. There was food aplenty for the more than 40,000 estimated Native Americans who lived in the south region of the Florida peninsula when the first Europeans arrived in 1513.

Life was good for these early human inhabitants. They were tested at times, but for the most part, they adapted well. And nature cooperated. In the humid, hot summers, for those who lived on the extraordinary dunes in the Highlands, the sea breezes and soft trade winds from the southeast kept the unpleasantness of the insects at bay. It was uncomfortably hot and humid on the west side of the dune near the stream and beyond into the swamps where the breezes never reached, and punishing to the natives when the wind came from the west, bearing the stinging pests. Yet, in the winter months, the cooler air made life comfortable. There were no wintry blasts of icy winds or snows. Alligators and snakes, being cold-blooded by nature, were docile, moribund and, usually, out of sight. Nor were there many visitors from the north. Tourists came much, much later.

The lives of the humans were peaceful for the most part, except when the belligerent Caloosa ventured east. Mother Earth was good to them. There was plenty of food and land; rarely did the bands, or later, tribes, intrude on one another. This was the milieu of the pre-Colombian American Indians.

Florida and other parts of the New World, the "Americas," were becoming attractive to seekers of riches across Europe. In 1562, the French sought to establish a colony in North Florida near the St. John's River, and were intent on claiming the area by establishing a mission of Protestant Christians.

However, in 1565, Spanish adventurer, Pedro Menéndez de Avilés, removed the French and established a permanent Spanish settlement and named it San Augustin.

Even though the English Captain Sir Francis Drake took on the Spanish Empire in the New World, looting tiny St. Augustine, he did little to diminish Spanish rule of the southeastern region of America. These were the days of the English, Spanish, Danish, Portuguese, Belgian, and French competing in their colonization of America and the Caribbean, establishing settlements on the various islands. Cuba was Spanish, the Bahamas became British, and Haiti was French. Aruba, Bon Aire, Curaçao and other islands near Venezuela became known as the Dutch West Indies.

As early as 1586, with seafaring raids by Sir Francis Drake and others, the English began their colonization with settlements in the Carolinas and the French with colonies along the northern shores of the Gulf of Mexico, including New Orleans. Throughout the 17th and 18th centuries, lasting settlements by the English remained in Charleston and Savannah.

By 1650, after a century and a half of Spanish presence, because of the diseases, enslavement, and butchery of the Europeans, nearly 90% of the Florida natives were gone. They had no resistance to the European illnesses or the hostile use of their more advanced weaponry. The same was true throughout the southeast region of America. During that period, the Spanish often attacked the Creek Indian villages in southern Georgia and northern Florida in retribution for harboring runaway slaves of the Spanish landowners. The natives had to learn the European culture of land claim, enforcement and cruelty, but were without the capability to resist the aggressive Europeans.

By the late 1600s, the native population was still reeling from the effects of the European diseases and the harsh treatment of the Spanish. Those who survived were next strongly influenced by the religious missions. After many failed attempts at conversion to Christianity, the best successes in Florida occurred in St. Augustine on the northeastern coast of Florida and in Tampa on the west coast of Florida. There was also some success in the Miami region, perhaps because of the greater successes of the Spanish-backed Franciscan monks in Cuba, the Caribbean, and Mexico.

By then, there were only an estimated 10,000 natives still living in Florida. In the north, the magnificent Timucuans were down from 40,000 to 4,000, most living near their capitol near St. Augustine, but spread across northeast Florida. The Caloosas were now only 1,000, the Ais, with their center in Vero Beach numbered 1,000, and the Tekestas of the southeast, including Miami and 50 miles north to the Highlands, only 400. Their social structures and cultures were shattered. The years under their Spanish rulers was a period of bare survival for the natives of Florida. Eventually, having found no riches on the peninsula, the Spanish became mostly indifferent as they looked to the riches of Cuba and Central and South American gold and silver, particularly of the Incas.

The primitive Tekesta in the southeastern portion of the peninsula still had to cope with the natural elements. Their preferred and abundant diet was still coastal, in contrast to their northern brethren who chased, caught and feasted on buffalo, deer, turkey, bear, and small game.

The greatest challenge they faced, particularly during the volatile summer months now known as "hurricane season," were the fierce and unpredictable storms and hurricanes that originated off the coast of Africa and swept across the Caribbean, destroying most everything in their path.

The Spanish Main
and
Caribbean Pirates
1563-1763

The third significant impact on the Native Americans was the introduction of Europeans and their culture. The Spanish, and later the English, introduced the revolutionary ideas that land could be bought, owned, sold, and protected, even if it meant that only the owners could traverse, cultivate or hunt on that land.

Previously, all the natives could live or hunt, celebrate or catch sea turtles anywhere along the highland dunes. The new concept forever removed the land and waters from universal ownership. Before the Europeans came, all air could be breathed by anyone, all water could be drunk by anyone, all land could be traversed by everyone—all land was for everyone.

Bartering increased, money was introduced, and trade between the natives and the Europeans increased. Skins and pelts, saddles and guns were exchanged. By the early 20th century, the southeastern portions of land along the seacoast, with especial significance to those in the Highlands, beachfront land ownership became an important investment. Its very value exceeded all other areas. The increase in trade, facilitated by the newcomers, did bring the natives some new benefits, including markets for their pelts and manufactured items like blankets.

There was significant competition in exploring and settling the Americas between the nations of the Old World, especially Spain, England, Portugal, France and the Netherlands, in the 16th and 17th centuries. All of them sought their share of the riches, and often fought over territories and wealth. Some reminders of those battles remain in the Caribbean and offshore Florida.

Even until today, Spanish silver coins and even doubloons, the gold coins, have been found washed up on the beaches of coastal southeast Florida. Near "Jap Rocks" in Highland Beach, residents and tourists have been pleasantly surprised as they spot the sparkling reflection of the coins in the sand at the waters edge. Delighted in their good fortune, they ask, "How and where did they come from?"

Here is one explanation.

During the 1600s and into the 1700s, the Caribbean was a very busy and dangerous place. The Spanish were in control of most of the region. Their fleets of heavy-laden galleons carried cargoes of silver bullion, doubloons, and silver coins minted in Mexico, Peru, and Ecuador.

Eventually, as gold and silver were discovered and extracted mainly from the rich hills of Colombia and other northern regions of South America, the transportation of these riches back to Europe became very risky. Fleets of these ships would sail the Spanish Main, the principal shipping route eastward along the northern coastline of South America, bound for ports in Spain. With its extraordinary and protective port configuration, Cartegena, Columbia became the major port of Spanish embarkation. Transport sailing ships, loaded with treasures, and often protected by gunships, sailed eastward bypassing Florida on occasion.

Surreptitiously awaiting them were heavily armed pirate ships ready to attack. They would take all treasures and goods, literally annihilating the crew, and scuttle the empty ships. As the galleons sailed around the southern tip of Florida, they chanced the risk of running aground because so little was known about the shallow reefs in the area, particularly the south end of the peninsula and the Florida Keys. Many of these ships crashed among the rocks and reefs, especially if caught in the unpredictable storms in the region. As a result, the heavy treasures of coins, jewels, and gold and silver ingots sank to the bottom time after time where they have remained, waiting to be discovered by latter-day fortune hunters in the sea or washing up on the shores to be found by lucky tourists while searching for shells.

Most of the soldiers of fortune who plundered the Spanish sailing ships over the decades were English sailors who were carrying out the policies of England. In the 1770s, Spain allied with the American colonies in their War of Independence, and placed a blockade around Minorca and Gibraltar. In late 1782, England attacked and defeated the Spanish garrisons at Minorca. Gibraltar became a Crown Colony and Spain recovered Florida. Most of England's military forces were preoccupied in Europe. England enlisted the aid of renegade mariners who operated with no scruples. Backed by the power of the government, hundreds of mercenaries undertook the profitable "dutiful" adventures of intercepting cargo ships and reaping enormous rewards as they attacked these ships sailing the Spanish Main and the eastern Caribbean.

Pirate Galleon of the 1500's

Among the most active and famous of the pirates who plundered the ships sailing the Spanish Main bearing these rich cargoes were English-speaking Blackbeard, Bluebeard, and, the most dashing of all, New Zealander Errol Flynn of latter-day movie fame.

Edward Teach, born in 1680 and known as Blackbeard, was clearly the cruelest and greediest of the three. He had his base in Nassau, seeking the safety of its magnificent protected harbor. His travels kept him in the Caribbean most of the time until 1704 when England and Spain resolved their differences and Spain deeded over Gibraltar to England, ending Queen Anne's War with Spain.

In 1717, Blackbeard captured the British ship Concorde in the Bahamas, renamed it Queen Anne's Revenge and refitted it to increase its cannons from 26 to 40, making him the most feared British pirate on the seas. He sailed under the heavily armed warships, challenging every ship sailing under the flag of Spain or France.

Bluebeard in contrast, sailed mostly in the eastern Caribbean, using St. Thomas as his island hideaway where he built a stronghold. Even today, Bluebeard's Castle is a tourist attraction. Bluebeard and his men were a constant threat to the enormous Spanish fleet who sought to successfully deliver their treasures to Spain.

Rewards from the Spanish government were quite generous and excellent incentives to the captains and crews of the Spanish galleons, so they were willing to face the menacing pirates. When the valuable cargoes were safely delivered to Spain, captains were given huge land grants in the New World and a portion of the treasures they brought, which they shared with their loyal crews for their bravery and service to the royal family.

❧❖❧

It is not inconceivable that, after a long day of plundering the Spanish ships overloaded with the heavy silver bullion, Blackbeard arrived in Nassau for a weekend of "Rest and Recreation."

Imagine, as his ship docked next to the Straw Market, he looked to the Pilot House, a most popular bordello, and there, emerging with a lovely light-skinned, fully endowed Bahamian woman on each arm, was Errol Flynn, laughing and carousing.

"How did you get here so fast, Flynn?" he called out. "I've been at full sail since you and I attacked that fleet of Spanish cargo ships."

"Hello there, my dear friend, Blackbeard. How good of you to come to my dinner party. Glad you could make it within two days after it transpired." He laughed and continued, "You might have beaten me here, but, my dear greedy friend, you took all the bullion onto your ships and left me only Princess de la Rodriquez Consuella y Palmos Francesca Cortez de Aragon y Seville. As a result, your ships were much heavier than mine. The señorita is on my ship even now, resting while I carouse and plunder these lovely, young Bahamians...or, uh...Lucayans...whatever. But aren't they wonderful? I have only had to promise them roles in my next movie, but it's not scheduled to start shooting...uh, pardon me...filming for another 337 years. But if they don't care, why should I?"

"Well, Flynn, I'll be damned if you don't beat all. Here I am trying to corner the market, driving my ships and men to their limits to gather as much silver as possible, and here you are celebrating Carnivál and smelling the roses, so to speak."

"That's what I've been trying to tell you, Blackie. Chill out. Now, come along, good pirate, and let's have a drink before we try the limbo."

"Har, har, har," roared Blackbeard.

Errol Flynn, the handsome hero of many "pirate movies" in the 1930-50s, also boarded Spanish ships with more flourish than the "Beards," and instead of taking the silver and other jewels, usually charmed the beautiful Spanish royal señoritas, enjoying the fruits of his labor in a different way than the other rascals.

❧❖❧

Blackbeard sailed north along the east coast of the South, stopping in various ports of call including Charleston and Beaufort, South Carolina where he traded with the colonials who found trade with Blackbeard advantageous for them because they could avoid paying taxes to the Crown. Blackbeard is documented to have used the safety of the numerous islands off the coast of North Carolina and found the corrupt local political leaders to be easy to deal with and hospitable to him and his 300 to 400 men. In the end, Blackbeard was killed off North Carolina's shore in 1718 under orders of the governor of Virginia.

While Blackbeard and Bluebeard were just two of the many pirates who searched for under-armed Spanish cargo ships and were extraordinarily successful in their efforts, Errol Flynn was actually a more charming and heroic admiral who never lost a battle. He usually ended up with the Spanish beauty who was being secretly transported to or from the New World. Flynn had a romantic persona envied by Blackbeard and Bluebeard.

There is no recorded documentation of Blackbeard or Bluebeard ever building a residence in Highland Beach, Boca Raton, or elsewhere in Florida.

However, Errol Flynn did visit Boca Raton in 1937. He came on a fishing trip during the height of his movie popularity and visited with my Uncle Carl for several days. He dined at the Arcade Tap Room, hobnobbing with Joe Kennedy, his (not so secret) consort, Gloria Swanson, Bob Hope, Bing Crosby, and Danny Kaye who were wintering in Delray Beach.

But more on this later.

Blackbeard the Pirate

The
Transition Years

Very few of the Indians of southeastern Florida actually survived the European onslaught of the 1500s and 1600s. Thus, there was a gap of time when it appears that almost no one inhabited much of South Florida from the 1500s to the late 1700s.

Their ancestors who lived hundreds, even thousands, of years before in the peninsula left their mark in the at least six mounds found in Highland Beach. Other relics have been found in the Miami Circle, and native pottery has been found around Lake Okeechobee, Boynton to the north, and in the Caloosa region.

Other than those mounds or middens found in Highland Beach, there were a few pre-Columbian mounds discovered in north Boca Raton. During the 1950s, those Boca Raton mounds were turned into a tourist attraction (along with alligator wrestling) recognized by its trademark orange and white cement Spanish galleon. Not much is recorded on these mounds. Since the galleon could have sunk in the local mud, it may have actually become the foundation of its own "mound," highlighted with a mast of cement.

Until 1763, when the British exchanged Havana, Cuba for Florida, which the British had won from Spain during the Seven Years War (1756-63), Florida was under Spanish control. But at the time of the exchange, the Europeans were hardly present in Florida. Only in San Augustin were houses still standing, and Pensacola was a small military settlement. There was little, if any, European presence in southeastern Florida, and little evidence of native habitation in the region. But there were Caloosa still in southwestern Florida. West of Lake Okeechobee, called Lake Mayaimi, were possibly a few remaining Ortona Indians.

The
Seminoles

In 1763, after the British took control of Florida, it created a strategy to establish a significant force south of its Georgia colony in Savannah. It tried to split Florida into two parts: East Florida with its capitol in St. Augustine, and West Florida with its capitol in Pensacola.

The British began mapping Florida's coastlines. They became interested in establishing relations with the new settlers moving into the peninsula from the North. In addition to the white settlers from former colonies were Indians breaking away from the Creek nations of Georgia and the Carolinas. They had been labeled Seminoles by the Spanish, meaning "renegades, breakaways, or runaways."

The British sought to colonize the peninsula, worked with the remaining Indian Natives, and tried to attract colonists from Virginia, Maryland, and the Carolinas. The effort sought to establish new plantations in the northern parts of Florida. The new plantation owners, in turn, bought and settled slaves there to work the cotton and tobacco fields similar to those in South Georgia. The harsh lives of the Africans under their slave-masters drove many of them to run away. Many escaped and sought the refuge of the forbidding swamps of South Florida, knowing the slave-masters would not follow them there. The runaways preferred choosing the unknown to their existing inhumane conditions as slaves.

Runaway Slaves in the Highlands
1860

The shaman gestured with his hand toward the cooking food, inviting the two runaways, a black man and woman, to sit near him, to share his meal. Both were handsome, tall, sinewy and muscular, clearly people who had labored throughout their young lives.

"Hungry?" he asked with a friendly smile, in his own language.

"Yeah, suh, we be hungry," the black man answered, somehow understanding the strange language.

"We's be very hungry," the young black woman replied, rubbing her flat stomach, smiling as she gazed on the pot full of turtle meat and what looked like potatoes or roots of some kind. Typically she would have lowered her head and deferred to the black man. But slavery and running away had equaled them, and she was eager to eat.

Using gestures, the shaman sought to find out what he could about them.

"We's been runnin' away from our slave masters up in th' no'th. We can't take it no mo.' They's be bad to us'ns. I don' want no mo beatin's," he said as he pulled up the back of his shirt to show the lash marks on his back.

The woman added, "They's be keepin' us apart in two differn' plantations. We-uns decided to runaway like them Injuns an' come down to the swamps to git lost. We's done good," she added, "'cause we-uns sho be lost."

The two runaways sat down and ate with the shaman. Getting comfortable with the friendly Indians, they stayed with the small band of Tekestas for nearly two weeks, learning how to capture giant turtles on the beach during the summer egg-laying season. And, when the time was right, they carefully packed what food and other gifts from the Tekestas they could. They were not the first, and the black slave couple would not be the last black or white, slave or free man, who came to the Highlands and South Florida to "get lost." That would continue to be sought throughout the entire 20th century.

The couple resumed their journey and the shaman waved to them as he sat cross-legged on the dune watching them select the easy path along the beach's hard-packed, moist sand near the water's edge. They would easily reach the south end of the barrier island near Miami, assuming they could survive the sometimes treacherous waters and alligators of the Hillsboro Inlet to the south.

Throughout the War of Independence (1776-1782), both East and West Florida remained loyal to Britain. In 1781, Spain, then an ally of France, captured Pensacola, and by 1784, regained control of all Florida, ending twenty years of British control.

After the British left Florida, the Spanish, offering land grants, attracted settlers from the newly formed United States. Slaves from older plantations in Virginia and the Carolinas joined the breakaway Creeks who were locating in South Georgia and North Florida. The Creeks were becoming a problem for the plantation owners by accepting runaway slaves, who became either slaves or family members of the Indians, creating a tribe that became known as "Black Seminoles."

Plantation owners of the new United States grew less tolerant of the Indians' absorption of the runaway slaves. The owners demanded that the Indians be run out of the area by the new Federal Government.

Gold was "discovered" by the Americans in North Carolina in 1799, in South Carolina and then in Dahlonega, Georgia in 1828. Dahlonega was in the middle of the Cherokee nation's four million acres. The Indians knew of the gold for centuries. (Do-la-ne-ga means the color yellow in the Cherokee language.) The discovery of gold and subsequent migration of whites into the area seeking easy riches was the final blow to the existence of the Cherokee and Creeks in the region. The Indians had to be relocated in order for the Americans to claim the gold that was on Indian lands.

In 1838, the U.S. Government removed the Cherokees by forcing them to walk all the way west of the Mississippi to Indian Territory (now the state of Oklahoma). This migration is now called the Trail of Tears, a story of disgrace foisted on those Native Americans whose ancestors had been in the region since 1000 B.C. More than 4,000 Cherokees died on the Trail of Tears.

Some of the Cherokees who managed to escape to the south joined earlier "breakaway" Creeks in northern Florida. By 1775 this group of Indians who had migrated from Creek towns in Georgia into northern Florida had become known by the name Seminole, which means "runaway" in the Creek language. The Seminoles were also joined by Indian and Negro slaves who were chased south by plantation owners in Georgia. Although South Floridians believe that the Seminole Indian tribe has been in Florida for thousands of years, they were not the ancestors of the Tekesta, Carib, or Caloosa Indians of centuries before, but were relative newcomers to the area.

After Florida was traded to England from Spain in 1763, in exchange for Havana, the Caloosa and likely some Tekesta were taken by the British to the Florida Keys as slaves and then shipped to Cuba. It would have been simple to bundle the two groups because the Caloosa and Tekesta spoke the same language and were called Arawak Indians. By the late 1770s, it is believed that virtually all these indigenous Indians of Florida were gone.

During the War of 1812, hostilities between the Seminoles and the United States increased, culminating in the First Seminole War, which began in 1817 when General Andrew Jackson was sent to capture runaway Negro slaves living with the tribe, and to defeat the Seminoles and seize the Florida territory from Spain. In May 1818, he captured the city of Pensacola and deposed the Spanish government.

When Florida became a territory of the United States in 1821, and white settlers resumed colonizing Florida, the Native Americans were forced to move farther south into the swamps of southern Florida, an area very unsuitable for their agricultural needs. Finally, in 1823, the Seminoles were forced to cede most of their tribal lands to the United States.

The Second Seminole War began in 1835 when the Indians, led by Osceola, refused to give up their remaining land and move west of the Mississippi River. Bands of Seminoles migrated deep into the swamps of the Everglades.

Map of Seminole Indian War Battles
Courtesy of William Gwynn

The third and final of the Seminole Wars in Florida ended in 1858 when the United States paid the remaining tribe members to go West.

Following the three Seminole Wars of the 19th century, co-existence between the Seminoles and other residents of Florida settled into a calm period. Most of the Indians in the Everglades resided peacefully on their land. They hunted game, lived in the shelter of teekee huts, over time became a fixture of the state, and, aside from small bands venturing east and north for food, stayed in the southern portion of the peninsula. There were some who ventured into the easternmost areas of what now is known as Broward, Palm Beach, and Dade Counties as late as the early years of the 20th century.

Osceola of the Seminole
Courtesy of Charleston Museum, SC

As late as the 1950s, the last of the Seminole Indian residents near the sea in South Palm Beach County lived in the nearby Everglades, and could be found walking in groups into downtown Delray Beach on Friday.afternoons, wearing their colorful hand-sewn blouses. They came shopping for their week's supply of food from Delray's grocery stores. I remember watching them walk into town from the west on Atlantic Avenue. They were very friendly and would nod their heads and silently smile in greeting to the residents of Delray and Highland Beach who smiled in response to them as they too shopped on Atlantic Avenue, South County's main commercial district. Until the late 1960s and early 1970s, when massive land development took place in southeast Florida, Seminole Indians still lived in the swamps west of Delray Beach and Boca Raton.

Then, when so much residential land development exploded in the area, the Seminole Indians, residents west of "The Range Line," now known as U.S. #441, State Route 7, dispersed westward into the Great Cypress Swamp signaling the end of the presence of the Native Indians in the coastal Highland Beach and the Delray Beach area, not to be seen again except on television during autumn's football seasons at Florida State University. Faux Chief Osceola, with war paint on his face, sitting astride his appaloosa pony, gallops across the football field at full speed, spear in hand while yelling a war chant, in celebration of the beginning of each home game at Doak Campbell Stadium. Then, spearing the school's emblem at mid-field, dramatically challenges the visiting team, inspiring the students and other fans to scream and cheer.

And that is about all one can see today of the treasured Native American presence in South Florida.

We must acknowledge the end of a grand era, the prehistoric and the historic, the age of innocence in South Palm Beach County, the age of the Native American Indians who occupied, ruled, then roamed the peninsula of Florida from, perhaps, 8,000 years ago. During the period from the mid 1600s until after 1820, there were hardly any Indians living in Florida. Then the Seminoles began arriving from Georgia and North Florida, until the development of oceanfront condominiums of South Florida.

Like others, they were seeking refuge in the swamps of South Florida where rarely did anyone else risk the dangers of malaria, wild animals, snakes, alligators, and simply too much fear of the unknown in this menacing region.

Florida Becomes
the 27th State in the Union
March 3, 1845

By the mid-1800s, Florida was still, for the most part, considered simply an appurtenance to America, a mere narrow peninsula jutting into the Caribbean, and essentially of Spanish character. The northern portion of the region was very much like its neighbors to the north, Alabama and Georgia, not only in geographical characteristics, but also socio-economically. South Georgians had extended their plantation lands beyond that state's boundary, created dirt road extensions, farmed their cotton, and along the coast as they did in southeastern Georgia, planted pine trees. They harvested the gum-like sap to produce turpentine and other by-products for the Navy. They also had a close cultural bond with the North Florida settlers.

Over time, North Florida had its own separate and distinct plantations. Farmers from the original colonies were enticed to settle and populate the fertile regions that had good soil, excellent water sources in streams and rivers, and good weather most of the year. With the Apalachicola River in the west, and the St. John's River in the east, there were more than adequate ports for trading with other countries, especially those of Europe, as well as northern cities. It was an appealing new frontier that was still in America.

The southern portion of the Florida peninsula was more forbidding. Its mosquito and malaria-ridden swamps attracted very few people. From what is now the Orlando region, southward on both coasts, most of southern Florida was considered "the last place on earth anyone would want to go." And it was looked on as the most remote and inhospitable place in America. Those who wanted to start a new life and leave a terrible existence found South Florida's swamps to be the best solution and the farthest place in America to get lost.

It's interesting to note that by the latter half of the 20th century, some 150 years later, South Florida had become intensely populated and incredibly developed. It became such an appealing location that many people living in the Caribbean nations, and Central and South America left their homes, risking their very lives in the shark-infested waters, to somehow reach the southern tip of Florida, the closest part of America.

Tens of thousands were escaping their poverty-stricken or politically oppressed nations like Haiti and Cuba. They were willing to risk the lives of their children and themselves to cross hundreds of miles on flimsy rafts so they could "begin again." Florida, with its warm, welcoming beaches, was the closest and easiest spot to enter into America.

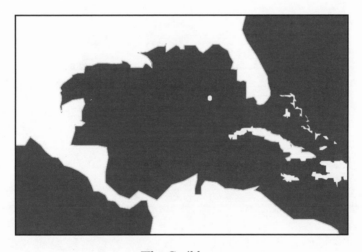

The Caribbean

In 1845, Florida became the 27th state admitted to the Union. It was sparsely populated, with most of the population in and around the cities of Jacksonville and St. Augustine. Of the estimated 87,500 people of Florida at the time of admission, 47,500 were white, and 40,000 black (39,000 were African-American slaves and 1,000 were free blacks). Most of the whites were in the cities. Slaves far outnumbered whites in the rural areas. Large plantations with thousands of slaves occupied most of the northern tier, with very, very few people south of what is now Gainesville. The area south of Thomasville, Georgia was highly populated as well.

Until the Civil War, the Democratic party governed the region exclusively. After the Civil War, most blacks became Republicans following Lincoln's Proclamation. After Reconstruction, the Democrat party, choice of the white population, ruled exclusively throughout Florida until Dwight Eisenhower ran successfully for President in 1952.

Today, the state's capital, by virtue of this historic set of facts, is still located in Tallahassee where today's Florida State University, formerly Florida State College for Women, was established in 1857. In nearby Gainesville, the University of Florida, Florida's largest State University was established in 1853 and located there for similar reasons. It was formerly named the University of the State of Florida, for men only.

Florida's Role in
the Civil War
1863

Northern Florida's population was virtually "Southern or Suthin'" in every way. The economy was agrarian, the social hierarchy was stratified. Dutiful slaves outnumbered the white plantation owners and their slave masters. Florida, like other southern states, was at the mercy of the more populated industrial North which was in control of freight rate structures, shipping tariffs, taxation, and merchandising. As late as the 1860's, steel could be shipped significantly cheaper (almost by half), by rail from as far away as Pittsburgh to Atlanta than from nearby Birmingham to Atlanta. It became obvious to the Southern businessmen and politicians that their Northern Republican counterparts who controlled the House of Representatives and the Senate would do all they could to prevent Southern industry from succeeding. The Southerners refused to give up slavery, insisting on "states' rights" to determine its legitimacy.

Ultimately, the Southern states formed the Confederacy and rebelled against what their political leaders considered "taxation without representation," repressive Federal ("Yankee") laws, and other humiliations and economic oppression.

As a result of their inability to resolve these numerous issues, the Southern states declared that they would secede from the Union. South Carolina was the first to declare its intentions by firing on the Federal garrison at Fort Sumter.

Florida later followed suit, totally committed to the Southern states' cause. It seceded in January 1861, the 7th and last state to do so.

While South Florida was certainly a part of the state, the impetus of secession came from the people of the northern tier, not from the small South

Florida population centers inhabited by handfuls of people. The Miami and Ft. Myers regions, as we know them today, were practically unaware of what was going on "up north," although there were certainly some there who profiteered during the war.

During the early 1800s, those Cherokee and Creek Indians who could escape the U.S. Government edict to walk to Oklahoma in order to leave the gold-rich mountains of North Georgia and North Carolina to the whites fled south to the swamps of Florida. Those Creeks who harbored slaves in Georgia also fled the plantation owners, seeking refuge in the swamps of South Florida. Both were labeled Seminoles for "breakaways" or "runaways."

While the war raged on in Virginia, Maryland, and Pennsylvania, the runaway Creeks, now Seminoles, mostly fished, hunted, ate and slept. And those over in the southeastern coastal area also hunted, trapped, traded, and fished. The people of Florida seemed to be two separate and distinct nations. The Civil War was being won during its early months under the South's brilliant leadership of West Point graduate General Robert E. Lee and its unified people, until that incredible battle at Gettysburg, Pennsylvania when the tide changed in favor of the northern states, the Federal Government, better known as "them damned Yankees."

After the war, the states of the Confederacy were occupied by Federal forces. Slaves, having been freed by President Lincoln's Emancipation Proclamation on January 1, 1863, were now not only free, but free to vote and to hold public office. They became Republican mayors, sheriffs, and notaries public. Within a few years, they became a majority of the several former Confederate states' legislators. As the last Confederate war veterans returned to their homes now occupied by Federal troops, they found that their post-war political positions were occupied by ex-slaves or their benefactors, "Northern carpetbaggers." Most office holders were now Republicans and the Southern whites were all Democrats. Until the Confederate states ratified Constitutional Amendments 13 and 15, they would not be permitted to rejoin the Union. This interim period, euphemistically labeled "Reconstruction," was meant to "readjust the social-political climate of the South to be more like the North in its behavior," especially as it regarded slaves and slavery. The Southern whites were led to believe that Reconstruction meant rebuilding the physical infrastructure, but they were wrong. After President Lincoln's death, Reconstruction took on an entire new meaning. There really was little "reconstruction" of physical infrastructure. Within a short period of time, most of the former Confederacy, now poverty-stricken, was governed politically by mostly undereducated ex-slaves under the auspices of Federal, that is, "Yankee" bureaucrats.

Up to 86% of the Southeastern states' legislatures were comprised of blacks. Most mayors, sheriffs, constables, notary public officials, legislators, and other quasi-government officials were black. Few, if any were white folks. And many returning Confederate soldiers were very, very angry indeed.

In some places, terror, retribution, and fighting ensued. Soon, the birth of the Ku Klux Klan occurred. It was not a good time in the South, and Florida, especially North Florida, was very much a part of the conflict. There were feelings of anger, despair, betrayal, and desperation among the returning Confederate soldiers. There were too many instances of angry retribution against blacks, most of whom were actually innocent of most charges. There were other returning veteran "Johnny Rebs" who dealt with their dilemma differently. Instead of joining post-war gangs, they sought refuge in the remoteness of South Florida.

⨁

The Highlands
Confederate Soldier Runaway
1870

The storm season winds bashing the shoreline of the Highlands told the chief and his band huddled on the lee-side of the high dune that it would be foolish to venture to the water's edge. It would be too dangerous. The Tekesta were not known for their ability to swim. So, the shaman, in his admonitions reflecting the cosmic messages he received, convinced his band to stay away from the high waves and frothy sea. Even so, a few young braves ventured atop the dune, challenging the gusting winds with excited shouts, beating their chests with their tight fists.

"Beat me, oh, gods of the winds if you can," they shouted, trying to impress their fellows and the young girls in the village.

But the boys were obedient enough not to leave the dune. Surely they would not venture near the coral rock outcropping where the waves splashed so high. As they stood braced against the growing fury of the gusts, feeling the cool sea spray on their faces and nearly nude bodies, clothed only in loincloths, they watched the savage churning of the ocean.

"Look!" yelled one youth as he pointed to the sea. "What is it? There! It is a huge canoe, so big. Watch."

"I'll go alert Chief Turtle Slayer, Kahboonkah. He'll tell us what to do."

In very little time, the sea crashed its power against the foundering schooner, ripping its sails and tipping it on its side. In moments, the ship capsized. The chief watched. He had seen this before. He knew about these floating vessels, and for more than three hundred and fifty years these things were seen on the seas by his ancestors. Sometimes food or boxes, timbers or even humans would wash up on the beaches. They utilized and consumed what goods they could; the humans they buried. The Spanish galleons of the 1500s delivered steel helmets, rum barrels, animal and human bodies as they crashed on the reefs, or ran aground in the shallows, permitting the roaring, crushing waves to completely tear the wooden ships apart.

Now, as they watched this day, they saw the sleek schooner that was heading south run aground as its keel slid into the shallow sand bottom. It became still, tipped over on its side, an easy prey for the mighty strength of the unleashed waves as they struck the floundering ship, wave after monstrous, wind-driven wave.

Soon, as they watched, a single survivor washed to the shore. The last monstrous twelve-foot wave carried his body up to its height, then, as the water on the shore swept back to sea under the wave, the hoary crest, like a hammer, curled and drove the human body down onto the beach and crashed on top of him, continuing its last effort before running out of its energy, washing the man up the shore almost to the high dune before receding back to the sea, its work accomplished.

"He is not far. Let's get him," yelled one of the boys. "Maybe he has something for us."

They ran down the dune to the unconscious man. He was fully dressed in a soaked and battered grey leather hat, its strap tight under his chin, a grey army suit, black boots, and around his waist on a wide leather belt was a pistol and holster.

"Bring him to me," yelled the chief. "Maybe he is still alive."

"Be careful," cautioned the shaman.

The villagers took good care of the man. They removed his salt water soaked clothes, placed them near the fire, laid him under a teekee hut near the fire, covered him and fed him turtle soup and waited. One young woman placed warm compresses on the man's face, hoping to comfort him.

Late the next afternoon the man awoke.

"Good treatment, Amanadah," spoke the chief to his shaman. "Your herbs and chanting always chase away the evil spirits. And now, our visitor is with the world again. Grateful thanks, my friend," smiled the chief as he wrapped his arm around the shaman's shoulders.

"Let us now find out what we can," said Chief Kahboonkah. I have learned the language the white man speaks. Let us talk with him now."

As they came to the shipwrecked survivor, the chief squatted on the ground, crossing his legs comfortably, thinking that this could take some time. "Who are you?" he asked.

"My name is Wilbur Monroe. I come from South Jawja, near to Savannah," the man whispered with a drawl, clearing his throat. Patting his empty holster with his hand, he asked, "Whar's m' gun?"

"It is safe with us. We have only one rifle. Your gun is important. Perhaps we will return it to you in good time, depending on who you are and why you are here."

"I need help," replied the man from Georgia. "An' I thank yew for a-takin' good care of me. That was some awful boat ride, ah gotta say," he smiled, holding his head in his hand, remembering. "I'm a farmer, not a sailor anyway."

"Where were you going, and why?" asked the inquisitive chief, realizing this would be a rare opportunity to improve his English.

The soldier responded, "I was headed for Myamah, south a heah, I reckon. Do it be fahr from heah? Do y'know?"

"It is not far, about a day's walk, or a mite more," the chief replied. Then, wanting

to know more, believing his reason for keeping the pistol would disclose itself, asked, "And why were you bound for Miami. There are no soldiers there anymore. Besides, your uniform is grey, not blue. You are a Southerner, not a Federal soldier, isn't it?" he asked incorrectly.

"Yeah. I ain't no damned Yankee," the man stated emphatically. "Mah family's bin in Jawja for nigh onto two hunnert years, and now, things is real bad," he sighed, hanging his head in mock disgrace.

"An now, them Fed'ral troops is all over th' place, a-pushin' an shovin' even the suthin' ladies. It ain't right, I tell ya. An' now them nigras is in charge ev'ry whar! They's thuh sheriffs, thuh mayors, thuh legislators, thuh po-lice, thuh gov'ner. It ain't right I tell ya. Them uppity nigras has taken ovah ev'rythang. An if it ain't them it's the gold-danged carpetbaggers. It ain't right, it wudn't wuth thuh wahr, I tell ya. My daddy wuz sheriff. Now, a nigra's sheriff, my daddy's broke, no job, cain't vote, cain't own property. Them Yankees took ev'rythin.' So, I had to git out. I cudn't stan' it. It were awful, I tell ya."

The man watched the Tekestas gather around as he preached his epistle, assuming he had a sympathetic audience as they smiled, frowned, nodded, and sometimes said, "Uh-huh," not realizing that aside from the chief, none of them understood a word he spoke.

"So, I caught me a schooner, middle o'the night in Savannah for Myamah. Thuh cap'n wuz drunk whin we a-left thuh docks, but I had to go innyhow. Y'see, I kilt a Fed'ral trooper in thuh saloon cuz he was makin' fun of us Rebs. I tell ya, it's awful. Cain't stay in Jawja. I had ta come ta Myamah ta git lost. I niver thought I'd run intah a storm lahk that one. Man! I got sick, oooh, sooo sick. I believe I throwed up from Jacksonville tuh here. I wanted tuh die agin, lahk at thuh battle of Atlanta. Didja hear about that one? Or Chicamauga? Now ther'n were a fight. We beat them Yankees at Chicamauga, but they kicked our asses in Atlanta, f'sure." He frowned, then gesticulated his arm in a way toward the south.

"But now, here I am goin' to Myamah to git lost. An' I thank ya fer yer help. Ah surely do. I don' think they'll come t' git me in th' swamps of' South Florida. Least that's what th' cap'n tol' me."

The man tired himself out getting his story told as the chief and shaman listened attentively. The chief spoke to his shaman in a low voice, "First the black slaves, now the southern soldier, both after the Creeks who ran away and came to South Florida to get lost."

The shaman smiled to his friend and replied, "The Creeks were called Seminoles by the Spanish. I wonder what they will call the next people who come to South Florida to get lost."

"Tourists?" replied the chief, laughing.

"Maybe," smiled the shaman, "or maybe one day they'll call themselves 'Native Floridians.'" He laughed out loud.

"It surely will be a wonderful place to 'get lost,'" the chief said with a smile. "I mean to say, life is good here, it makes you happy with your life and most don't question new arrivals. They become easily accepted by those who live here already. And so, being in a place to welcome those who come here to 'get lost' might actually be part of the destiny of *this land known as South Florida for generations to come."*

"Ah, me," responded the shaman, closing his eyes and turning his head to the heavens. "Perhaps that is part of what my ancestors knew would be our destiny following the first of the five events that began so long ago."

The Fourth Event:

The Coming
of the
Flagler Railroad

As the tribe celebrated the coming of the sea turtles in 1880, the chief and his shaman watched while the young men danced around the village pole and community fire on the ocean dune. The rhythmic beat of the drums was the background as the shaman came out of his trance, began his chant, and threw his shells on the ground. These were a small band of wandering Indians who had walked east and north out of the deep swamps and established their camp on the highest dune of the sea. They found themselves near the coral outcropping at the north end of the pristine beaches described by their forefathers. They were more than comfortable in the familiar area of the early Paleo-Indians.

"Ah," spoke the shaman to his chief and lifelong friend, "you see the positions of the shells?"

"Yes," replied Chief Habanka, "but what does it mean? Dear friend, tell me what the heavenly gods have spoken to you. You look worried. What is it?" the chief pleaded. "Tell me."

The shaman, staring at the shells, reflected on their relative positions, then responded to his chief's request. "Many years ago, our ancestors gathered in this very place. Like us, they celebrated the coming of the sea turtles with the promise of plenty of food for our people. At that time," he said softly as he gazed into the heavens, "there was abundant land, abundant air and plenty of food. Deer were everywhere. The streams and the sea were filled with fishes for our people. Those were glorious and happy times."

"And, my ancestor shaman of the Tekesta and Taino listened to the gods who gave him a new message that there was set in motion in a place on the other end of the sea a

series of events that would affect all of our peoples. He told his chief, your ancestor, there was nothing that could be done."

"That series of events," the shaman continued, waving his hands and showing five outstretched fingers, "totaled five. We can now see by the position of the shells and by what I was told as I prayed in my trance that the third may be over. The third event, the wars with the Spanish invaders and the Americans, and the devastation of those events is finished. The devastation of those events is over. Now, the fourth event is upon us. You can see by the cluster of the shells that many more people, different from us, will come here and change our way of life. It will be soon."

"Well," replied the chief, putting his right hand on the shaman's shoulder, "is that good news or bad news? Most of our people are gone from us, the land for hunting is smaller, yet there are still abundant deer, turkey, and fish. But, at last, the wars with the Spanish invaders and the Americans are over."

The shaman sighed, "Yes, somehow, some of our people survived. And yet, more whites are coming. The shells tell me that an event is happening that will lead to another; together they will be the fourth in that series of five. I do not know exactly what the event is, but it is coming soon. It will affect the Caloosa sooner than we. But our turn will come." Then, he frowned and continued, "It will be very noisy, bigger than a hundred horses, and nothing we have can stop it."

The chief, startled and puzzled at this complete surprise, frowned and asked, "But what should we do? How must we prepare?"

"There is not much we can do at this time," the shaman replied, "but, we are few, and they are many. So we must avoid trouble with them. Perhaps we must hide from these people as long as we can. Stay away, and go back deeper into the swamps, for they will covet these dunes, it is said to me."

"But not yet," interrupted the chief, "not yet. This place is too beautiful, too special to give up before we must."

The shaman rubbed his chin and thought aloud, "We have some time, but not much, my chief."

❧❖❧

The shaman and the chief could not know that the two remaining "events" foreseen so long ago that would complete the series were soon to happen. The "fourth event," the coming of the railroad to South Florida would bring thousands and thousands of whites to that pristine land. Starting in 1895, the impact of the fourth event would be dramatic. In some ways, it would bring pain to the natives, yet, in other ways, it would bring good things like modern medicine and conveniences. Those who adapted to these changes would benefit. Across all centuries, those who could not adapt would likely perish or have their lives become severely impacted. In any case, the area would witness even more extraordinary societal and cultural change.

In 1882, Henry Plant, having been awarded the government franchise to build a railroad from Jacksonville to Ft. Myers via Sanford, Kissimmee, and Tampa, did indeed build his rail system across the peninsula, terminating where the Caloosa Indians had resided for so many generations. By 1886, Hamilton Disston, of Philadelphia, had fulfilled his contract with the state of Florida to drain the swamps of southwest Florida, including widening and deepening the Kissimmee and Caloosahatchee Rivers, opening up enormous tracts of virgin, frontier lands across southwestern Florida. These improvements enabled riverboat shipping down the center of the state from the Kissimmee cattle ranches down the river, across Lake Okeechobee, down the Caloosahatchee to Ft. Myers. Lake Mayaimi, as the Spanish had named it, had become known as Lake Okeechobee. The Seminoles would retreat deeper into the swamps of extreme southwest Florida.

Henry Plant's railroad's successful construction in 1882 from Jacksonville to Fort Myers, with stops in Tampa, Sanford, and Kissimmee accelerated the later venture of Henry Flagler and his Flagler Railroad which, in like fashion thirteen years later, would reach Fort Lauderdale in 1895, and Miami in 1896.

By then, Plant had already built beautiful and successful hotels in Tampa, Sanford, Fort Myers, and Kissimmee.

By fulfilling their contracts, Plant and Flagler were literally given enormous tracts of land by the state to sell, from which to profit, and use to attract settlers to populate this area, one of the last unpopulated frontiers of America.

In Flagler's case, likely similar to Plant's, he received options to purchase at practically nothing several million acres of Florida coastal land from Jacksonville to Miami, more than half of which was under water. But, it held an unbelievable future only decades away.

After the Flagler Railroad arrived in the area, all that was left for the Indians to contemplate by 1899 was the fifth and final event in the series of five as first proclaimed to the Taino shaman in 1453. The fourth of the five, the Flagler Railroad, had reached the South Palm Beach town of Linton (later named Delray) and Fort Lauderdale in 1895. By 1896, the railway would terminate in Miami.

Still, the final of the five events that would forever change the way of life for the natives would not occur until more than sixty years later.

For the Highlands region, later to be known as Highland Beach, the "fifth event," completing the series that had been in motion since 1453 would uniquely define the Highlands forever, and be in stark contrast to the teekee villages of the natives and the neighboring region.

That final event would occur after the middle of the 20th century, nearly 100 years hence, when the pristine, serene beaches and tree-covered land, bordered on the east by the ocean and on the west by the stream (to become the Intracoastal Waterway), would be totally and completely changed by the construction of a new kind of village.

This new community would not be of teekee huts, open fires, and celebration dances by the village bonfire, but would be mostly vertical villages, a community bringing thousands to the favored, coveted dunes in a new way; of people enjoying their lives from a view even higher than the coveted "high dunes" of the Highlands, sharing the same beaches, viewing the sea from high balconies, laughing and creating their own celebrations—not in June to celebrate the coming of the sea turtles, but predominantly during the "winter tourist season" from November through April each year.

That fifth and most irrevocable event foreseen in 1453, some 500 years earlier, that would permanently change the way of life in southeast Florida, and in particular, Highland Beach, would be that high density structure, the high-rise condominium.

Instead of dancing around the bonfire and fertility pole, celebrating the arrival of the first giant sea turtles, these new "vertical villagers" would celebrate the arrival of the "New Year" from their elevated balconies and air-conditioned "Community Rooms." Instead of drinking fresh coconut juice from turtle shells, they would be imbibing in and toasting with thin-stemmed glasses of champagne. Instead of beating on log drums, they would wear silly hats, blow small horns, and shake imported toy rattles. Yes, they too would dance into the night, exhausting themselves. These men, older than the young braves, would wear their best tuxedos and would woo their lovely feminine companions…already selected years before…in their elegant gowns.

Flagler Railroad, circa 1895
Courtesy of Boca Raton Historical Society

The "Barefoot Mailman" Ed Hamilton

Summer 1887

The shaman and his friend, Chief Bahwháktaw, were once again carrying out the natives' early summer traditions of camping near the sea and watching the waters from the dune overlooking the familiar coral outcropping at the north end of the pristine beach for the first of the giant sea turtles to appear for the egg-laying season.

Both were wiser, more aware of events impacting their lives than their predecessors. It was June 1886 in late afternoon, with the sun setting into the swamps to their backs. The soft breezes from the ocean were cooling and reassuring once again. The seas were choppy, but not rough. The rhythmic sounds of the three foot waves splashing on the shore was calming, relaxing the two men following their tiring day hunting a small deer in the nearby woods and palmettos on the west side of the creek.

"There!" the chief pointed. "Look, my friend. There is Koonkah. The first sea turtle! Oh, the sea gods are with our people once again, providing us with abundant food for the summer. We are so fortunate to be here at this special place." Both men smiled. "I believe it is the most beautiful spot in all the world, dear Anawáhah, my shaman. Let us rest awhile, and then capture our first turtle of the year when it is very dark. We will feast later tonight on turtle. But, now we have deer over the fire." As they sat by the flickering flames of the fire, rotating the sticks over the campfire that held the deer carcass, they heard sounds of snapping twigs behind them.

Turning his head toward the sound as his hand instinctively reached for his spear, the chief spoke to the direction of the sounds, "Who are you?"

"Now, don't y'all git nervous over me." The man spoke in "American," which the chief had learned as a boy in the village from the Christian missionary. "I'm jest passin' through," he said, holding both hands in the air.

"I come in peace," he continued with a warm smile and a Southern twang in his speech. He slowly walked up the dune toward them and the welcoming aroma of the dinner over their fire, both hands open, palms up.

"What is your name?" asked the chief abruptly, quickly standing, spear in hand, wary of this strange, clean-shaven unfamiliar-looking visitor, fully clothed but shoeless, with big black brogan shoes thrown over his shoulder. The Indians instantly noticed the black cap on the man's full head of hair, pistol in the holster on his hip, and the leather pack on his back. The chief pointed to the pistol.

"What is that for?"

"It's in case I git too close to a 'gator, or some bad guys, vagabonds they be, git too close to me." He gestured with one hand, "Y'see, I got the U-nited States Mail in this here pouch on m'back," he continued, emphasizing the importance of his affiliation, patting the backpack with his left arm.

"You come from the north," the chief said firmly, looking at the stranger's eyes. "Are you going to Myamah?"

The visitor, with a smile and nod of his head, hoping he was convincing the Indians that he was no threat to them, replied, "Yes sir. I'm the U. S. mailman. I pick up th' mail at the schooner or post office at Jupiter Inlet at the north end of Lake Worth, or on Biscayne Bay, put it in m' pack here, an' then, I walk sixty-seven miles t' d'liver this mail. An' I pick up mail to be sent out while I'm at it. I jus' come from Palm Beach and visitin' with Cap'n Gleason, keeper of th' Orange Grove House of Refuge. I'm on my way to New River by Fort Lauderdale, then to Myamah. Now thar's a purdy place, New River. Been there?"

"No, we stay in this place or in the swamps," replied the chief. "But some of our braves paddle their canoes up the New River. Sometimes, they trade at the Stranahan House. There are good white people there," he concluded, "good people. Not like the Spanish or the English. These people in New River are good to our people. We trade skins for their cloth and things from the Sears catalogue."

"Yep," replied the mailman, "they's be good folks a'right, good folks. Ain't had any trouble from them. But 'tween here and New River, when I have t' walk in th' swamps away from th' rocks an' rough seas hittin' on th' beach. Wal," he paused, "sometimes I have to fight offin' them vagabonds. Now they's mean folk. I tell ya, they's mean! Most of th' time I like walkin' on th' beach, y'know, down by th' water where th' sand's hard. I like t' walk without my shoes. They're tough on my feet! An' it's cooler that way, and m' bunions don' hurt as much. But, in th' summer, it gits awful hot. An' when they's no breeze, or it comes from th' west, th' bugs is as bad on th' beach as in th' shade of th' woods. Then I have to put m' shoes back on t 'walk in these swamps and woods. Snakes, y'know."

"Ugh," the two Indians grunted knowingly with a nod of their heads as the mailman continued talking.

"You must be lonely a lot," questioned the chief, acknowledging that the mailman hadn't stopped talking since he sat down and joined them.

"Yep," he responded with a full laugh. "Heh! Heh! I sure do git lonely bein' by m'self all th' time. It's th' first time fer me. Y'see, I come from a big family back in Ken-tuckee, an' I guess I was more quiet then. M' name's James E. Hamilton, but folks call me Ed. I'm from Trigg County, Ken-tuck-ee. But I couldn't git ahead thar.' Ever since that danged war. They calls it th' Civil War, but I say, they ain't nothin' civil 'bout war. Doncha think?"

"'Sides, I got to be twenny-one years old, an' it was time, I figgered, to start my own life. After all, this Florida frontier holds a lot of promise for a young man willin' t' work."

The Indians grunted and nodded again, trying to fight off sleep as the mailman continued his non-stop monologue.

Hamilton picked up where he left off. "Yep," he said loud enough to get their attention, "I come down here, got m'self a contract with the U-nited States Post-al Service to deliver th' mail from Myamah to Juno. It's a three-day walk each way fer me, 'cause I walk fast. The $50 a month...and it's sure money...beats farmin' enny day, y'unnerstand? Enny day! Then, on Sundays, I stay at my little palmetto hut on Hypoluxo Island.

"Imagine," he smiled, "I git to be on this pretty beach almost all th' time, an' th' gov'ments payin' me ev-er-y month." He laughed as he slapped his lifted knee and said, "I'm a dang lucky man, I am."

"From here, I go no'th to Hypo-lux-o, then, nex' day, I go up to Juno...sure' is busy up in Juno. Juno is gonna be th' county seat of Dade County, y'know. That's 'cause so many people live up thar, all along th' shore of Lake Worth. Purdy lake it is. An' y'know, they ain't one road between Juno an' Myamah. Ever'body travels by boat 'cept me. Can't even use a horse or a wagon."

Then the mailman thought a minute, putting his hand under his chin. "Well," he said, "that ain't the whole truth, 'cause I do use a gov'ment boat to cross the Hillsboro inlet. I have to cross it a-comin' and a-goin'. I better use that boat 'cause they's plenty o' gators in that place. They ain't no roads nowhere."

He paused, "I'm glad they's only one ocean inlet in these parts, believe me!"

"Well, if'n y'all don' mind, I'm all tuckered out. Been a long day fer me, gents."

As he laid back, he shoved his backpack up under his head and slid his cap over his head. In second, it seemed to the two Indians, who looked at each other in bewilderment with slight smiles forming on their lips, the mailman began his nocturnal imitation of a loud, angry panther.

Later that night, when the moon was high, with the sea sparkling in its glow, the two Indians stared at the sea, watching the annual visit of the sea turtles begin.

"Barefoot Mailman" Statue
Courtesy of Town of Hillsboro Beach

Hillsboro Beach
The Postman's Disappearance
Late October 1887

The two Federal Postal Service investigators stood on the coral rock outcropping. They looked down the exquisite beaches of the Highlands and the high ocean dunes covered in gently swaying sea oats. To the two visitors, they seemed to extend undisturbed for miles and miles.

"Yep," said the short one to his colleague, "it sure is pretty down here. Wish I could get a good job here in the winters, 'cause Washington will be too cold for me in another month."

"Yep," responded his friend, "but let's enjoy it while we're here. How much further to Hillsboro do you think?"

The first man pointed straight down the beach to the south and replied, "Not far, I reckon. By the map, it looks to be less than five or ten miles. Let's get started. We've rested long enough. It shouldn't take too long. We've already walked twenty-five miles from Palm Beach. Besides, did you ever think you and I would be walking on a beach this beautiful? And in October? We should walk near the water where it's cooler and the sand is firm. That's where they said the mailman walked barefoot most o' the time. Let's do just like he did till we get to the Hillsboro Inlet. Then," he said with a smile, "let's not do like Ed Hamilton did."

The second man, Elliott Ness, thought a moment, then spoke, "Well, Tom, the telegraph said he disappeared on the 11th, but we need to find out how. If he was killed by vagabonds and they stole the mail, then we got one kind of job to do. We'd have to find 'em. Can't let people do that, y' know. If, on the other hand, he drowned in the inlet, or, like the sheriff thinks, the sharks or the 'gators got him, then it's someone else's problem. Personnel Department, I guess."

"Oh, God" responded Tom Mix, "that makes my skin crawl…I don't like thinkin' 'bout Ed Hamilton getting pulled down by a big old 'gator. Let's get our job done and get back to Washington."

After a couple hours more, the two postal inspectors reached the north bank of the Lighthouse Point Inlet. They stood at the bank of the inlet and stared down into the water.

"The tide must be comin' in," Elliott announced to his colleague, "the water's pure turquoise and you can see clear to the bottom. Wow! This is sure a pretty place, Tom. I'd like to come back here"

"So would I," Elliott replied, nodding his head. "I guess anybody that ever comes here once will decide to come back again. Don't you think?"

Tom, pointing to the opposite shore and to the west, said, "Yep, I sure do, and, Elliott, it's pretty lookin' at the water, the ocean and the dunes. But over there," he said, pointing, "on the shoreline, I see the biggest 'gators I have ever seen or read about! Let's get our work done and leave this place. I'm gettin' the willies."

"Look here, Elliott," he said walking to the casaurina pine tree to his left. "There's a cap on the broken limb. And there, good buddy, on the higher limb is Ed's mail pack. The sheriff said he'd left the pack but took Hamilton's shoes 'cause he was afraid somebody'd steal them. Looks like it may be true Ed Hamilton left his stuff here and tried to swim to the other side to get his boat. And when he did, some big old granddaddy 'gator musta' got him. It's the peak of the rainy season and lots of water from the swamps come into this area bringing lots of 'gators. That's what the sheriff thinks happened. Yep, some 'gator must a-got him."

They spotted the government-owned rowboat on the south side shore of the inlet just where the sheriff said it would be.

Elliott spoke as they completed their local investigation, "I think it's better we wrap this trip up now by visiting with the sheriff and do our report on the train back to Washington. OK with you, Tom?"

⊷⫘⫘⊶

The sheriff addressed his two visitors, "Well, boys, I'm glad you come down here to check things out. Got ever'thang you need?" The sheriff smiled as he sat back in his wooden swivel chair behind his bulky oak desk. He liked his oversized desk with all those drawers. "It's the biggest desk in South Florida, I betcha" he'd always tell any visitor. "It demands respect fer the law, y'see," he would say with pride.

Tom responded, standing at, and admiring, the desk, "Yes, sir, we do. Looks like Ed Hamilton just shoulda not tried to swim the inlet. But we have to ask you, sheriff, we want *you to put up a bigger sign warning people not to use the government's boat. Or at least, if they do, to put it back where they got it."*

Elliott added, "And if they don't, we ask you to put on the sign that there is a $25 fine. We don't need to lose any more postmen. At least 'til we can get the OK to have two boats down here."

The sheriff puffed on his pipe and nodded with a smile, acknowledging the good suggestion, replied, "That's a great idea! Yep, Mr. Ness, I'll surely do that. You're pretty smart investigators. Y'know, we got the man who done that with Ed's boat, but what do we charge him with? Can't be murder. Can't be theft of government equipment 'cause he didn't take it away from the water, now did he? And," he said with a laugh, "we can't name him the 'gator's accomplice, now can we?"

"But y'know, Hamilton's friends from up near his house in Hypoluxo came down here from the Orange Grove House, retraced Ed's steps, and found it just like you did. They's the ones who told me about Ed. We knew somethin' had to have happened but we didn't know what it was, just that we hadn't seen Ed in over a week. Old Charlie Pierce and the Orange Grove House of Refuge keeper, Stephen Andrews, came down here 'cause Ed stayed at the Orange Grove House the night before he disappeared. They came down here on the 18th, two days after Ed shoulda returned from Miami, a week after he'd stayed overnight with them on the 10th. They found his backpack an' clothes in the casaurina pine tree like you did, and they spotted the boat too. We knew Ed was a good swimmer, and strong too, so we never believed he drowned. But we don't know for sure now do we? We do know the rains have been real heavy the past weeks, and that brings a lot of 'gators here. But we jus' don't know f'sure."

Then the overweight, balding sheriff leaned forward and, looking at the inspectors, spoke with a tone of authority, "I do know this; they ain't gonna be another problem around here like this as long as I represent the Dade County Sheriff's office. No sir."

With a flourish, he slapped his hand on the top of his desk. "No sirree, and you can tell your people in Washington I said that. Y'hear, boys? And I'll do my best to keep that feller there," pointing to the prisoner, "in jail for quite a spell. He had no business takin' that boat. 'Tweren't his right, now was it? That's what I aim to tell the judge next month when he comes through here."

Elliott nudged his colleague, Tom, then turned to the door, opened it and stopped. Then he looked back at the sheriff and said, "Y'know, sheriff, the Pony Express lasted only two years out West, and lots of those young boys did good jobs. Lots of 'em got killed too, but our aim is to make sure the mail gets through, no matter what. We don't want to lose any more good mailmen in South Florida. One is too many. We can do a lot on that score, but we sure need your help and all the other lawmen, too. So, thank you for all your support, and let us know if anything else turns up. OK?"

"Yep, gentlemen, sure will. You all come back when y'can, y'hear?" The sheriff still had his Georgia twang and the same way of saying things.

The legend of the "Barefoot Mailman" has been enhanced by the sad but true tragedy of Ed Hamilton's surprise disappearance in this story found in the popular book entitled The Barefoot Mailman, written by Delray resident Theodore Pratt, and published in 1943.

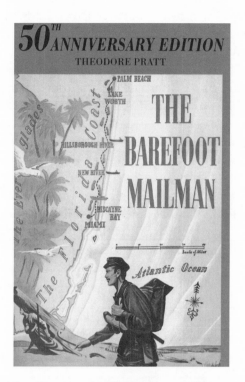

Theodore Pratt's *The Barefoot Mailman*
Courtesy of Florida Classics Library

The above was based on actual records documented by Harvey Oyer III, great-great nephew of Charles W. Pierce who, together with Orange Grove House of Refuge Keeper, Stephen Andrews, retraced Ed Hamilton's steps and told and retold the story. In "Uncle Charlie" Pierce's book, *Pioneer Life in Southeast Florida*, he states that Ed Hamilton was an excellent swimmer, and that Hillsboro inlet was not wide nor a difficult swim, especially since Hamilton was young and in very good condition. Also, it goes on to say that the rains had been heavy, bringing fresh water in from the Everglades, and that hundreds of alligators were in and around Hillsboro Inlet in the days surrounding October 10th when he was last seen leaving the Orange Grove House of Refuge where he had slept that night before.

We'll never know for sure what happened to Ed Hamilton, but his life has indeed been immortalized in many ways. Theodore Pratt wrote of him and named him the Barefoot Mailman in his very popular book of that title. Also, the life-sized statue at Lighthouse Point on A1A is dedicated to this legendary figure.

Job Farrow, father of Helen Long, a longtime resident of Delray Beach, was a "Barefoot Mailman" in the early 1890s. Helen recalls that her father also drove a stagecoach from Palm Beach down to New River, later called Fort Lauderdale, and on to Miami when more and more people began traveling to southeastern Florida during the early 1890s. For a time, the stagecoach service travelled along the route known as Military Trail, the route of military wagon trains which connected Fort Pierce to Fort Lauderdale during the Seminole Wars until 1858. It is the highest inland ridge, and usually drier and more passable than any other, even in the rainy summer season. Earlier, a wayfarer could travel the walking route north or south along the beach with the mailman. His fee ranged from $2 to $5 for the 90-mile trek. They happily paid the price, which was no small amount since ten passengers in a month meant the postman could double his salary. In return, the travelers were provided with a government boat at Hillsboro Inlet and protection from threatening bears and vagabonds, while having a friendly companion familiar with the territory. Traveling alone could be very dangerous in those days—maybe as dangerous as it is today.

The "Barefoot Mailman" served the southeastern Florida coastal area from Miami to Juno, including all settlements in between. There were only two stops during the seven years from initiation in 1886 until 1893. In 1896 the railroad reached its terminus in Miami.

It would be 1914 before Henry Flagler continued his railroad across the Florida Keys to Key West, just ninety miles from the lush, prolific farms of Cuba.

PART THREE
1894-1949

Taming the Swamps
The Arrival of Linton, Swinton, and Boynton

The Beginnings of Delray Beach and Boynton

1894-1900

"Last stop, Palm Beach!" yelled the Flagler Railroad porter.

William Linton, David Swinton, and their new friend, Nathan Boynton, smiled, turned to each other and shook hands.

William Linton spoke first, "We're here; we're finally here. All the way from Saginaw and Port Huron, Michigan."

Swinton spoke next, "You know, gents, we're about to begin an adventure few men ever dream of, much less experience. I mean, look out the window and see what you see."

Linton responded, "Just looking out the wide open window in January is an adventure for me!"

Boynton added, with a smile, "Feel that fresh air!" He sucked in a lung full of South Florida's salty air, reached out both arms and said, "Yeah, smell the sea! That's what I call fresh air. You can actually smell the fish."

"Let's go get to the boat as soon as the train stops."

Just then, the squealing of steel on steel began as the trainman applied the steam driven brakes. The train jerked as the men laughed and grabbed the overhead handles.

"There," pointed Linton to a young man standing with a young woman next to him, holding a sign with "Here Mr. Linton" hand-scrawled on it. "There's Freddy Voss and Missus Voss. They are going to take us to our land. Let's get our bags and get started."

Even though they were tired after their 2000-mile, four-day train ride from Michigan to Palm Beach, they were eager to get started on their new venture in South Florida, one of the best remaining frontiers in America. They wanted to see and walk on the land they had bought, sight unseen.

⚜

By January 1895, smooth-talking William Linton, bookstore owner David Swinton, and determined Nathan Boynton had made their plans to return to South Florida. Swinton and Postmaster Linton advertised their offer to sell five-acre plots of land in Chicago and Detroit newspapers, enticing those wanting to make a new life away from the large, industrial, crowded cities where jobs were scarce at the time. Others, they hoped, wanted to get away from the cold, and still others to start a new life.

The land they advertised and sold had been purchased from Captain George Gleason of Jacksonville at $2.50 per acre. In turn, they sold it for about $25 per acre. Of course, Captain Gleason had bought his large tract, mostly swampland under water, from the government for $1.25 per acre. Thus began the "Buy Low, Sell High" of underwater Florida land that would reap riches for the bold for another 100 years throughout the entire 20th century. South Florida was still known as a raw frontier of wetlands and swamps—too difficult for families. It attracted many single men and was known as a place "where a man could live off the land, hunt for pelts and skins, fish, sell feathers of the abundant birds to the milliners of New York, "and still be warm all the time." They had twelve takers seeking to start new lives in South Florida, America's last frontier.

On the other hand, Nathan Boynton of Port Huron, Michigan was a veteran of the Civil War and still kept the esteemed title of "Major." Boynton, in his newspaper ad, sought workers—carpenters, plumbers, and handymen looking for a job in a frontier "on the sunny beaches of Florida." He too attracted a small band of hearty souls, and even convinced some with families, unlike the men-only Linton's group. The Boynton group would come to his land, live in tents they brought with them, and build the Major's new Hotel Boynton to be located on the ocean dune at the beachfront on the south side of what is now Ocean Avenue. His 160 acres, mostly underwater, were bounded on the east by the Atlantic Ocean, on the west by the meandering "coastal creek," now the Intracoastal Waterway, and parallel south and north boundary lines that connected the two.

Boynton was following the example of railroad magnates Henry Flagler and Henry Plant before him. He wanted to own and operate a luxury beachfront hotel and, over time, become wealthy from his hotel. The city of Boynton Beach was thus initially established as a place of construction workers living on someone else's land, tenant workers as they were called, until their work was done. They loved the weather and beaches, hated the infernal bugs, terrible mosquitoes, raw elements, and the swampland. But, by 1898, they completed the building of Boynton's beautiful white, wood frame, three-story hotel on the ocean dune. It was some feat, using only hand tools and their ingenuity.

In contrast, those adventurous men who bought parcels of five acres from Linton and Swinton just to the south arrived less prepared than Boynton's group. They had purchased the land, sight unseen, on which to build a house, to farm and start a new life. They were landowners, not tenant farmers, and that helped define Delray Beach's character for more than 100 years, indeed, for generations. Some came because they were advised for health reasons to leave the cold climates for sunny Florida, which was being heavily promoted in northern newspapers. Others simply "couldn't get ahead." Jobs were low paying and scarce.

Having no tents or abundant tools, the Linton settlers stayed together in the upstairs room of the Orange Grove House on the ocean dune. They were beneficiaries of the kind Captain Andrews, keeper of the House since 1878. He had taken over after Hannibal Pierce of Fayette, Maine, the first keeper of House of Refuge #3, also known as the Orange Grove House of Refuge departed for Hypoluxo Island a few miles to the north. The Orange Grove House was one of five such houses of refuge built by the government to provide shelter for shipwrecked sailors who would otherwise surely have died from the elements. The 140 miles of raw wilderness between Biscayne Bay (Miami) and Indian River (Vero Beach) was almost totally unpopulated except for roving bands of mostly friendly Indians and adventuresome men who hunted alligators and deer, fished and trapped in the region, living solitary lives like their counterparts in the Rocky Mountains who trapped beaver, hunted buffalo, and fought bears from time to time. Had the second floor of the Orange Grove House not been available to these first settlers, this lonely band may not have survived that first year.

The House of Refuge #3 was nicknamed the Orange Grove House because there was a small grove of sour orange trees nearby. The shelter was located on the dune just north of Atlantic Avenue and A1A intersect in east Delray Beach just north of where today's Marriott Hotel is located. No one seems to know exactly why there was an orange grove near this particular house of refuge. It is generally accepted that in all likelihood, a small band of local Indians camped there, ate their oranges, and left the seeds scattered around their campsite.

The Linton settlers eagerly staked out their parcels and began clearing as much as they could of their land almost completely covered by the nearly impenetrable jungle, underbrush, vines and other unfamiliar tropical growth. They had come to a primal frontier, totally different in almost every way from their homes in Michigan and Illinois. The soil was dry during that first winter, but always wet during the rainy summer months. Most were adventurous and determined to work as hard as necessary to make a new home. After a couple of very difficult years, some of the groups became discouraged. Many of Boynton's workers returned to Michigan when their job was done, particularly after the devastating, unpredictable hard freezes of 1896 and 1898. Some stayed on in Boynton as tenant farmers. It wasn't much better in Linton's small group of farmers. They became terribly frustrated and exhausted by their primitive lifestyles and the infuriating mosquitoes, the rains and the heat. Soon after the freezes of 1896 and 1898, many returned to "sanity" and Michigan.

The Linton-Swinton tract, also 160 acres, went west from the coastal creek, unlike Boynton's, which went east to the sea. The Linton group came to create a farming "village-by-the-sea," where everyone had actual and emotional "ownership," a place where, from its beginning, everyone knew their best interests were interdependent on the other settlers. They came with the intent to stay, fight it out, in this "tropical paradise," this "Garden of Eden," and make a home for their families. But they never anticipated the hardships they would face in the punishing humidity of this sub-tropical frontier.

Orange Grove House in 1895
Courtesy of Delray Beach Historical Society

All the men worked from sun-up to sundown clearing the land with small hand tools, braving the elements. In the end, some could plant only small portions of their five-acre tract because in the summer the land would often flood from the heavy rains. Then, in the winter, rain would not come for weeks and weeks, withering the first crops.

⁂

"Linton, it's nothing like you promised," said one unhappy soul, then another, then another. "These bugs, especially these mosquitoes, are driving me mad. I can hardly stay in the field more than ten minutes before I'm covered with stinging flies, gnats, and mosquitoes."

"Yeah," said another, "and how about those snakes? They're everywhere. A man could get bit ten times in a day. Why, I saw four of them yesterday on my five acres. And the alligators are everywhere. How am I gonna bring my wife and children here, Linton?"

⁂

During the last years of the 19th century, most of swampy South Florida was uninhabited in spite of the State's efforts to attract settlers. Except for a few people living along the shoreline of Lake Worth, with most of those clustered at the north end, the region was virtually without people. That is why, at the time, Dade County included part of Monroe (Key West), Dade (Miami), Broward (Ft. Lauderdale), Palm Beach (West Palm Beach), and Martin (Stuart) Counties. Because it was most heavily populated, Juno, on the north end of Lake Worth, was the county seat of Dade County. The county then stretched from the St. Lucie River south to Key West, and included the land of the Jeaga, Ais, and Tekesta-Taino Indians of the pre-Colombian past.

In the late 1800s, across America, there was little available to cure such illnesses as influenza, pneumonia, tuberculosis, and "consumption." Doctors' favorite prescription was to recommend a move to or at least spend the winter months in "sunny South Florida." Those who had wealth came for the winters. Other adventurous people simply chose to move their families there. It was the farthest south some could travel and still remain in the United States.

And, even today, others relocate from the North to remote South Florida to enjoy their retirement or just their winters in this beautiful place.

Gunrunners to Cuba
The Legend of "The Three Friends"
1898

After the Civil War, South Florida was probably the only region of the Confederacy that didn't experience the "social" reconstruction imposed by Washington. It was also a place that "a fella could find a future, a place where he could get ahead." And Florida, with a short supply of labor, let it be known across the nation and the world that capable workers were more than welcome.

Many Southern young men, feeling stuck in the malaise of the post-war Confederacy, and totally unwilling to move north decided to venture to the frontier of southeast Florida by whatever means they could find.

Young Job Graham Farrow, born after the war in 1871 in Leary, Calhoun County, Georgia, was one of such newcomers to South Florida. Reconstruction, with all its constraints, especially on young white men, was an oppressive period, a time of frustration.

After saying goodbye to his parents, sisters, and cousins, Job ventured south from southwest Georgia. He walked most of the way, a small pack of all his earthly possessions slung over his shoulders.

"I jus' got to go, Mama. I can't seem to git nowhere stayin' here, so, I'm goin' south. At least, they tell me, thar ain't no Yankee troopers all over the place pushin' and shovin,' remindin' us who won the war. So," he said over his shoulder after giving his mother and father a hug, "I'm goin.' An' I'll let you know whar I am whenever I git there."

"Bye, son. An' you be careful, y'hear?"

And so, Job, like many others, fled the occupied Southern states and headed for the new frontier called South Florida "…where a man could hunt, fish, trap, farm, and never have to face another Yankee trooper, a place near the beach where it's sunny all the time. A place that is as far away as you can git and still be in America. South Florida, a fine place to start over again."

Job walked and sometimes caught rides until he reached Juno, the county seat of Dade County where his cousin had homesteaded 160 acres of land and was farming it in fruit trees and tomatoes.

After his long walk and several months "with family," Job began looking for a job. He needed some "spendin' money," even though his family welcomed him, and he helped in the fields. He still wanted "to git on mah own. Y'unnerstan' don't y'all?"

"Sure we do, Job. Jus' keep in touch."

One day, Job announced to his cousin with a proud smile, "I got me a good job as mailman. It pays $50 each month, an' all's I got to do is pick up the mail in Miamah an' carry it to Juno, a-stoppin' along th' way at New River an' Palm Beach. Then, I pick it up agin here in Juno an' carry it back to Myamah. Ain't no big deal, but I figger since all I got t' pay fer is food. I can save me about $40 a month. Why, in no time, I'll have enough put away so's I can homestead me a place like you did, an' build m'self a house."

Thus, Job Farrow became a mailman on the route from Miami to Juno, walking a distance of sixty-seven miles. Every trip, he stopped at New River, picked up and left mail at the Stranahan House, the trading post for that region, passing the especially high dunes in between. He walked three days each way, resting on the "Sabbath" after each round trip. From New River to Palm Beach, Farrow, like the previous mailmen, usually walked along the beach, carrying his shoes over his shoulder and a backpack, passing through what would become Boca Raton, fording the outlet stream to the ocean because there was no inlet at that time.

Helen Long, now 91 years young, chuckles when she comments about her father, Job Farrow, "Daddy told me later that when the stagecoach got so full of newcomers wanting to get to Miami, he'd have to get off the stagecoach and lead the horses until he got tired. Then he'd ask one of the men in the stagecoach to swap places with him so he could ride awhile."

Soon, Job Farrow accomplished his goal. He left his mailman job and homesteaded two sections of land along the south side of New River opposite the Stranahan House, and "set out" citrus trees—lemons, oranges and grapefruit alongside a good-sized parcel of tomato plants. Like so many others, he would ship his products to northern markets, and during the hot summers, when he didn't need to work the land, he would trap, hunt and fish in the Everglades to supplement his income. He hunted alligators, otter, and the prolific deer. After two weeks' time, he could bring pelts and skins worth over $5,000 to the Stranahan Trading Post. Life was good for a young man.

In time, Job Farrow met young Napoleon Bonaparte Broward who had dreams of grandeur. At sixteen, Broward took a job on a small cargo freighter that delivered supplies to the nearby islands of the Caribbean. Soon, however, he decided to go on his own. In 1895, Broward convinced his brother, Montcalm, and George DeCottes to build, own and operate "a powerful tug to carry shipping throughout the Caribbean." Together, they raised $40,000 and had the ship built in Jacksonville. They called it "The Three Friends." They began their business, operating out of New River, later to be renamed Fort Lauderdale. By 1896, they were carrying goods to Nassau. Finding the fledgling shipping business not so profitable, they accepted an offer to smuggle guns to the rebels in Cuba who were fighting the Spanish. The rebels were trying to force Spain out of their island and the rest of the Caribbean.

Job Farrow joined Broward and his partners as a crew member on "The Three Friends," seeking adventure and, it seemed to him, "a way to make some quick money," while staving off the boredom of quiet New River. After all, the settlement was very small, very small indeed, despite the incredible future that awaited the region.

By 1896, "The Three Friends" was running the United States Navy blockade that was enforcing Washington's desire to stay neutral and not engage in a war with Spain. In time, after several successful and profitable deliveries of guns, ammunition, explosives, rifles and other armaments taken aboard in Tampa, "The Three Friends" and its crew were captured by the American gunships.

Helen Long smiles as she repeats her father's stories.

"Daddy told me they really had adventures on 'The Three Friends.' Captain Broward would stand at the bow of the small steamship and warn the crew. 'Men,' he would yell, 'you know we are loaded to the gunwales with rifles, ammunition, and dynamite. If we get caught, they'll probably kill us all, take the ship and its cargo, and no one will ever know what became of us. So, men, let's not get caught.' And with that, they would pull away from the dock and, carefully, warily, making their way through the Florida Keys, staying safely among the islands and in the shallow waters, then crossing the straits to Cuba as fast as possible. They would then deliver their cargo to the Cuban rebels. On their return to Tampa, they would collect the balance of their payment from the Cuban representatives of Simon Bolivar, their leader and major fundraiser in Tampa and the rest of the United States."

"The Three Friends"
Courtesy Rugby America, Inc.
Remembering Eden

In 1896, "The Three Friends" ran aground on a desolate island where "they ate only bananas for days," laughed Helen Long as she reminisced with me. "I guess they were all survivors, weren't they? None of them were killed. That's good, isn't it?"

After several successful supply trips in late 1897, the, "The Three Friends" crew had pushed its luck to the limit. Seeking to run the blockade "one more time," they were found steaming between the Keys and western Cuba, seeking to cross the ninety miles without getting caught.

Suddenly, a shot was fired across their bow. Although loaded with armaments, they were virtually unarmed, facing several U.S. gunships with cannons aimed directly at them. Too close to evade, Broward wisely ordered the white flag of surrender hoisted. Their days of gunrunning had come to an end, and the young men, mostly in their mid-twenties, had to surrender and face the consequences of their deeds. They knew they had broken the law and they could only hope for the best. Their lives were now in the hands of fate. But then, that's where they had been, in actuality, since they started their venture several years earlier.

They were arrested as a group and charged with the crime of supplying guns and ammunition to a foreign nation, although technically, the U.S. was not at war with either Cuba or Spain.

At the time, the nationally respected Hearst and Pulitzer newspapers competed to glorify these swashbuckling young men "fighting for a just cause," in support of the still popular Monroe Doctrine. As a result, the adoring American public, regaling these young heroes, urged the government to release the crew of "The Three Friends" from jail.

The United States. changed its position of neutrality and declared war on Spain when a U.S. ship, the SS Maine, mysteriously exploded and sank in the Havana harbor in February 1898. Although there was no conclusive evidence identifying the culprits, the United States declared war on Spain. Even after 100 years, the U.S. still has never been able to determine exactly how the SS Maine was blown up or who should be blamed. The government still isn't sure whether it exploded or if it imploded, meaning it was dynamited from within and not attacked from the outside. Nonetheless, sometimes, the philosophy of the government often is: *"Ready, fire, aim."* Maybe the Spanish blew up the ship, maybe not. Some say it is very possible the Cuban rebels, seeking to bring the U.S. into their war against Spain, actually found a way into the SS Maine and detonated explosives, perhaps brought to them by the crew of "The Three Friends."

In their adventures, and under the leadership of Napoleon Bonaparte Broward, the crew of "The Three Friends" and their reliable deliveries to the rebels was credited with enabling the daring Cubans to help push the Spanish out of Cuba. After the sinking of the Maine, they became national heroes and, as a result, the crew was released three months later in May of 1898.

During the resulting Spanish-American War, Teddy Roosevelt led a group of cowboys seeking more adventure and called them the Roughriders. He led them up "San Juan Hill," actually Sandover Hill, victoriously defeating the Spanish. Teddy was extended enormous credit, some deserved, and given the mood of America, became a hero too.

The Spanish-American War was fought not in Spain or in America, but in Cuba and in the Philippines. Following the conclusion of peace negotiations between Spain and the U.S., the heroics of Teddy Roosevelt and Napoleon Bonaparte Broward were on the front pages of all U.S. newspapers, led by those owned by Pulitzer and Hearst. As a result, in 1904, Broward was elected Governor of Florida, and Teddy Roosevelt was elected President of the United States.

In May the following year, at a governors' conference in Memphis, Roosevelt and Broward met over cigars and brandy.

﹏❖﹏

"Governor," President Roosevelt asked, leaning forward from his chair, lighted cigar in hand, and looking through his signature spectacles, "do you still have that boat, 'The Three Friends?'"

"Yessir, Mr. President," Broward responded with a proud grin sweeping his face, "I sure do.' The adding, "I love that boat. Built it myself, you know, with my brother and my friend, George DeCottes."

"Well," replied the President, smiling, "Governor, you should be proud of that boat because if it wasn't for 'The Three Friends,' you wouldn't be Governor today."

"Right you are, Teddy," Broward smiled and responded, "and if it wasn't for 'The Three Friends' you wouldn't be President."

"Bully, bully," laughed Teddy Roosevelt.

﹏❖﹏

And that is the legend of "The Three Friends," Napoleon Bonaparte Broward and his crew, including the former "Barefoot Mailman," Job Farrow, who walked the beaches of the Highlands and who helped the Cuban rebels.

But Govenor Broward wasn't through. He was determined to develop that area now known as Fort Lauderdale "into a region that could sustain population growth, farming, and dairy production". Bringing two huge dredges to the New River, he sent one up each tributary, opening drainage canals and passages for the flooded lands' waters to find their way to the sea. It was Broward who "tamed the Everglades" in that area, planned the development, infrastructure, and marketed the lands of that region. He was later recognized as the "developer of Broward County," and, as a consequence, the new county, one of the five that were created when Dade County was divided, was named in his honor. Broward County's northern boundary begins at the Hillsboro canal, the south line of Boca Raton in Palm Beach County, very near Highland Beach.

Yamato Colony's Genesis
1853

The shaman and the chief, continuing the traditions of the past, sat on the coral outcropping at the north end of the beaches of the Highlands. Together, they watched for the bobbing heads of the sea turtles arriving to deposit their eggs on the beaches of southeast Florida.

"It is a good life, my friend," spoke Latakwah, Deerhunter, leader of the Seminole band that had walked from the great swamps of the Everglades north and east to the preferred beaches of the Highlands searching for food. "And, while we have good food in the swamps, there are so many of our people there. It is good we know of this place from our fathers."

"Yes, my chief. Life is good. Especially now that the English are gone. They were different than the Spanish, but their ways are also different than ours."

"And now, our small band awaits the arrival of Koonkah, the first of the giant turtles. Tonight, I think, we will dance on the dunes as our people have done for so long."

They slowly walked up the slope of the beach. When they reached the top of the high dune, they both turned, looked out over the magnificent beaches, enjoyed the breezes in their faces, felt their long hair trailing off their necks as the wind carried their hair almost horizontal, turned to each other and smiled.

"Mother Earth has been good to us, Latakwah," spoke Matankah. "Yes, my shaman, we are blessed to be here in this place."

"Now, my chief, let us see what the gods have in store for us. Let us throw the stones."

"Ahna-na, Ahna-na, Ahna-na," chanted the shaman as he closed his eyes. "Ahna-na," he repeated over and over, eyes tightly closed, with his body swaying to the rhythm

of his voice. "Ahna-na," he continued, as his rhythm accelerated faster and faster. He was now entering his trance. "Ahna-na," he repeated again as the chief watched his mystic communicate with the cosmic universe.

"Ahna-na...Na!"

The shaman stopped abruptly. He raised his right hand, then brought it to his front, clasping his closed hand with his left hand and, with a flourish, cast the ritual stones and shells onto the palmetto mat the chief had laid out.

"How-wan-na!"

The shaman turned his head, and, carefully studying his tossed messengers, stared. He turned his head to his chief and, with a small smile, spoke, "I have interesting news, my chief."

"What is it? What news? Is it like our father's news? The five events that would forever change our way of life here in our land?"

"This news is not bad. It is good," exclaimed the shaman.

"Oh," responded the chief, "what is your good news?"

"You know the legend of our people. It is said that our ancestors first came from across the great sea to this land so long ago. The land was covered in ice sheets, animals were ten times bigger than now, the seas were very low."

"It has been told to us that our people came from there," he continued, speaking louder, pointing to the west, "not from there," pointing to the north.

"And now?" asked the chief, animated but perplexed.

"Now, we are told peoples from the lands of our earliest ancestors will be coming to our land. Here. Not today," he cautioned, raising his hand, "but soon...soon," he said softly. I do not know when; I do not know how many. But something is happening now in the land of our ancestors...I cannot know exactly what or why, but it will change our place here. An event is taking place that will irrevocably affect our land. It will precipitate two other events we cannot stop, or even understand. But they will happen."

"How is this good news?" asked the chief.

"The people who will come here come in peace. They have knowledge. They have serenity. They come to grow things, not take or destroy. I do not know if you and I will see that day, but our children will, for certain."

The shaman could not know that as he spoke, events in another land far away were culminating in extraordinary changes in the Far East.

After decades of efforts by the Dutch, English, and the Russians, the Americans, represented by Admiral Matthew C. Perry, would finally force open the nation of Japan after 200 years in near global seclusion under 700 years of Shogun Rule. The nation had been under the power of the Samurai warrior class for seven centuries.

Commodore Perry, with his squadron of heavily armed warships, men-of-war, entered and anchored in Edo Bay, "Gate of the Inlet," challenging the much smaller boats of the unprepared, xenophobic Japanese nation. He threatened attack, if necessary, to force the Japanese to open their coveted, populated markets to trade on terms favorable to the Americans, terms that, if given to his nation, would become the same for the other trading nations. No one had succeeded after years of efforts except for the Dutch who had a permanent port at Nagasaki from the 17th to 19th century. The English, deeply involved in the Opium Wars with China, had tried to force the right to introduce and powerfully enforce the opium trade in Japan also, but without success.

Under the guise of a commercial and friendship agreement, Perry's Kanagawa Treaty was ostensibly simple and would allow American ships only to rescue lost American sailors who might find themselves picked up by Japanese fishermen, whalers, and others. The treaty also permitted the storage of supplies on Japan's shores to facilitate such a rescue. Perry would force the Japanese, in truth, to open their markets and trade with United States merchants, thus ending two hundred years during which Japanese could not leave Japan, and outsiders, except the Dutch, could not enter Japan. British trade with nearby China—the highly profitable but debilitating opium trade forced on them by the English—had been going on for years, but Japan had successfully kept the British and their cruel trade out.

Perry's arrogance, his forceful negotiations and his display of overwhelming power (he claimed he could call on another fifty warships nearby and another fifty from California if necessary) also forced the culmination of the political conflicts within Japan between the pro-Tokugawa and anti-Tokugawa.

The Shogunate, based in Edo, was determined to maintain the "purity" of the Japanese largely by prohibiting trade and exchange with the rest of the world.

Ultimately, the political infighting continued until Perry forced Japan's leader, Tokugawa Yoshinobu, the last Shogun, to abdicate his power that was first assumed in the obscure village of Edo in the beginning of the 17th century.

Yoshinobu acceded to Perry's demands in 1854 and accepted the treaty. Emperor Mutsuhito moved the capital to Edo in 1868 and named the city Tokyo. He took the name Emperor Meiji, initiating the era known as the Meiji Period—Meiji meaning enlightened government.

Perry's entrance into Edo Bay, with his four men-of-war, 967 men, and six cannons was the event foreseen by the shaman in the Highlands that summer of 1853.

After the Civil War, Florida found itself faced with a chronic shortage of labor. As a result, the state lagged behind the rest of the country in development. The state government enlisted private companies to assist in attracting settlers, workers, investors and entrepreneurs. Together, they even sought to attract foreign immigration to the state. The State Bureau of Immigration was created in the late 1860s to assist and promote the emigration of foreign nationals to undeveloped areas of South Florida. Brochures, mailings, and advertisements in many other countries, including Japan, were part of the strategy of bringing people to South Florida, including the southeastern coastal areas. The thinking was that foreigners would possess talents and capabilities that were not locally available. Japanese, especially, were assumed to have special expertise in farming, and would have extensive and constructive impact on the Florida economy. Jacksonville Board of Trade President Charles Garner stated, "Speaking of the potential Japanese immigrants, they will inaugurate many new methods of cultivation of fruits and vegetables, besides showing our people how to cultivate and prepare tea and other articles not grown here." Other leaders were also enthusiastic supporters of the efforts to bring Japanese farmers to Florida because "…they have had two centuries and a half of practical training in intensive farming."

It is interesting to note that as early as the early 1870s, efforts were being made to attract Japanese to Florida, only two decades after Commodore Perry convinced the Japanese government to trade with Western countries. The growing interest in Japan by the West was intensifying so much during those post-Civil War years that even southeastern Florida was "in the chase."

Internal Japanese political conflict preceding the Perry visit was so severe that Japan came close to its own civil war. Yet the Perry agreement, the subsequent opening of Japan, the post-U.S. Civil War conditions in Florida, and the determination of a 30-year-old Japanese man would all enable the new colony in Boca Raton to become a reality. It appeared that the confluence of several conditions fell into place from the end of the American Civil War in 1864, and the beginning of the modern Japan era, the restoration of the Meiji Period, the era of enlightened rule. Emperor Meiji in 1868 created the first possibility in 200 years that Japanese immigrants could emigrate from Japan. These colonists would live not on land owned by others, but on their own land. They would arrive in what was then Dade County, and actually farm and live on their own property, so unlike the generations of Africans and poor whites who were common laborers, slaves, or tenant farmers. They would fulfill the definition of "colonists" as defined by the founder of the historic Yamato Colony, Mr. Jo Sakai.

Jo Sakai, and that is his true name, not a shortened version of Joseph, is properly credited for searching for and acquiring the land, and negotiating terms and governmental permits, both in Japan and America in order to create the unique and now historic Yamato Colony west of Highland Beach.

Yamato Colony and Jo Sakai

Yamato Colony, first enabled and conceived in the late 19th century in the small fishing village of Miyazu of the Kyoto prefecture in western Japan, was given the name of Yamato, after the ancient name of Japan.

Chronicles tell us that Emperor Jimmu, having established his rule on Kyushu, then led his forces and extended his domain. Eventually, he or his successors continued to reign from Yamato to over all of Japan. Thus, Yamato gave its name to the imperial house and eventually to all ancient Japan.

Jimmu was Emperor of the Ainu, a tribal people of the 2nd and 1st millennium B.C., descendants of the Jomon people who lived in the area from about 10,000 to 300 B.C. and populated all of Japan. Around 660 B.C., Asian peoples began to populate the islands of Japan, forcing the natives to the northern and eastern provinces of Honshu. That is when Emperor Jimmu moved his imperial house to Yamato. Yamato people subjugated "barbarians" to the west and the east.

Coincidentally, this was the same era that the settlements of the Taino of the Amazon and the Caribbean were established in southeast Florida.

Jo Sakai was born of a Samurai family in 1874 during the early years of the Meiji Period. Having graduated from Kyoto's Doshisha University, he sought additional formal studies believing, as did most Japanese, that true self-actualization was best achieved through higher education. He decided to study abroad, reflecting the global perspective young, adventurous Japanese could consider only since 1868. He attended New York University's School of Accounting, Commerce and Finance, graduating only five months before making his historic trip to Florida to locate the land on which he would establish his colony which he would later name Yamato Colony.

Jo Sakai and his wife Sada
Courtesy of Morikami Museum and Japanese Gardens

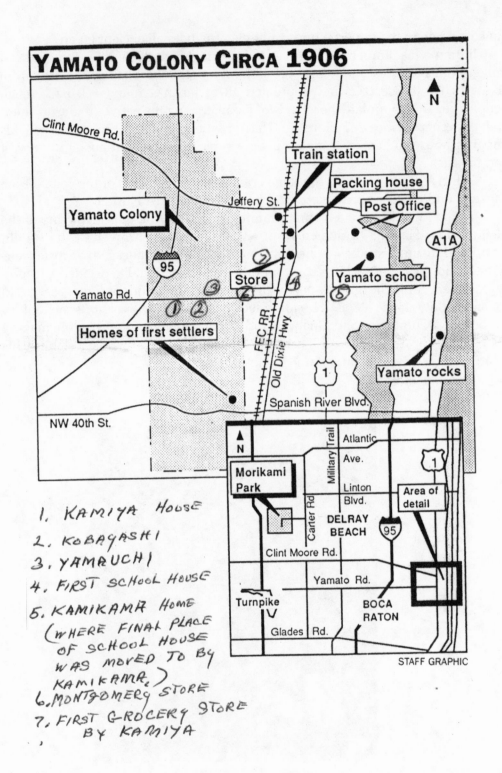

Yamato Colony Map
Courtesy of Tamotsu Kobayashi

Intent on establishing a farming colony for young Japanese immigrants, Jo Sakai, 30, first came to Florida in December 1903 when he landed at Jacksonville aboard a steamship from New York. Armed with only a letter of introduction from Joseph French, Dean of New York University, young, enthusiastic Jo received a surprisingly warm reception in Tallahassee from Florida's Governor William Jennings, and other state and business leaders who eagerly sought to convince Sakai to locate his colonies in their area.

Sakai had already met with James Ingraham, President of Flagler's Model Land Company, and decided to visit the site proposed by Ingraham as soon as possible. He first visited Boca Raton on Christmas Eve of that year, having just arrived from St. Augustine on Flagler's railroad. He wanted to look over the land he was preparing to purchase from Flagler's company.

Jo Sakai had selected this site for his colony even though earlier he had shown interest in locating four colonies in Lee, Manatee and Leon counties near Tallahassee. After meeting with Ingraham, his only written agreement was to locate in Dade County, at Boca Raton, purchasing the land from Model Land Company.

Flagler had received an estimated one million acres in Florida as the quid pro quo for building his railroad, and Model Land Company was charged with the responsibility of marketing, selling, populating, and developing those lands from which Flagler and his investors would reap enormous rewards. Of course, Flagler was already incredibly wealthy from his ownership position in the giant Standard Oil Company. Ingraham, who had been competing for Sakai's favor against Texas, where other Japanese agricultural settlements were already established and large-scale rice cultivation was organized, quickly met with Sakai just before Christmas Day.

On December 27, 1903, two days after arriving in Boca Raton, Jo Sakai boarded a train back to St. Augustine to complete the groundwork for his colony. On December 31st, only four days later, with his purchase under contract, Yamato Colony established and his American work completed, Jo Sakai left Florida for Washington, D.C. and New York. He then sailed across the Pacific Ocean, disembarked in Tokyo Bay, and returned to his home, his family, financial partners, and his friends in Miyazu.

But how did this all come about? The sister of Jo Sakai had married Mitsusaburo Oki, who provided the necessary financial backing of this "American adventure" that became Yamato Colony of South Florida. Oki was a member of a wealthy trading family steeped in generations of successful merchants in Japan. For centuries, Japanese families comprised of successful merchants were the wealthy class. But they were of lower social standing, considered aggrandizers and dedicated to the generating of profits and wealth building. In contrast, the Japanese population highly respected the Samurai, or "warrior" class, as the highest level of social standing. The Samurai, while ruling the provinces across the land, also served as protectors of the communities, of the laws, and of the culture.

During the Meiji Period after 1868, the Samurai class was discredited and disenfranchised. They were no longer able to receive government stipends, thus reducing their wealth base. While their social standing was somewhat lowered, they were still considered very high on the social ladder, and the merchant class continued to seek their elite standing through marriage.

It was the same as in Europe during the 11th and 12th centuries when the populace also trusted The Knights of Templar and The Hospitaliers, who selflessly dedicated themselves to protecting the civilian Crusaders and other travelers to the Middle East. According to their code, they were sworn to poverty, chastity, and honor and were elevated above all but the highest of the clergy. The Samurai, as well as the Knights of Europe were so socially respected, it became necessary, over the years, for those families wealthy in commerce to seek a marriage of their children to those of the Templar. In such a marriage agreement, again, as in Europe from the 12th century, the merchant class of Japan sought to bring social standing to its families by marrying into the Samurai. In turn, it was to the financial benefit of those Samurai families who bore children to induce them to marry issue of the merchant class, bringing the connection of wealth to their families. In this way, as in other societies over the years, both groups would elevate and sustain their wealth and social standing in one way or another.

When Jo Sakai returned to Japan from Florida, he found conditions particularly difficult: his nation was facing a dangerous conflict with Russia. Seeking permission for young single males to leave their country at such a time was not something his government found politically supportable.

After exploiting the inevitable political divisions in the Diet, Japan's legislature, whose leaders were invariably in favor of whatever their political opponents vigorously opposed, Sakai was finally able to achieve the influence needed to obtain exit visas for forty single young men from Miyazu desirous of starting a new life and finding better opportunities in America, rather than staying in their poor fishing village. They were coming as colonists, not as tenant farmers or hired labor for other landowners. They would be free, independent farmers, a concept new to Japan in 1868.

This unique project, Yamato Colony, could not have even been dreamed of prior to Commodore Perry's success which opened Japan for emigration of its citizens, their return, and immigration by foreigners. Without the first, the second could not have conceivably occurred even in one's wildest imagination. It also needed Florida's post-Civil War need and demand for labor, and the fortuitous marriage of Jo Sakai's sister to Mitsusaburo Oki.

Thus, the creation of the first Japanese colony in the State of Florida became a reality, once again displaying what one person, even a 30-year-old student, can accomplish, given a favorable confluence of events and exquisite timing.

After he finally obtained the necessary exit visas, Jo Sakai brought his first Yamato Colony farmers to Boca Raton within just a year following his first visit in December 1903. Quite a determined, resourceful visionary was young Jo Sakai.

But then, one must understand that Jo Sakai came from a strong lineage of Japanese warriors, the admired, sometimes feared, Samurai.

Jo Sakai's visit to this new frontier would have a positive impact on South Florida for decades. His farmers would survive the Cuban pineapple competition, the "Land Boom" and "Bust" of the 1920s, the terrible hurricanes of 1926 and 1928, the Great Depression, and the unfair incarceration of Japanese-Americans during World War II.

"Yamato Rocks"
The Early Days
1904-1912

When the first Japanese colonists arrived in Boca Raton, they received a friendly reception by the sparse farming population in the area. A Boca Raton resident, Frank Chesebro, kept a diary describing Sakai's first visit and a list of the first twenty-one colonists' names, dated January, 1905. In 1906, a second group of Japanese immigrants, including George Sukeji Morikami, arrived and more and more people from the North came to settle in the area.

There were perhaps 16 scattered residents in the area now known as Boca Raton, about 150 citizens of nearby "bustling" Delray, likely no more than a fisherman or two in what is now Highland Beach, and 83 in the Boynton area, most of whom were farmers, or maintenance workers at Nathan Boynton's oceanfront hotel.

As for the hospitality of the "rich, oceanfront farmland" Sakai had described to his prospects, the colony's land was at least two miles from the sea and the pristine beaches. The ground was more than 50% covered in a nearly impenetrable jungle of sharp-edged, thick palmetto bushes on the higher land, with the remaining property mostly underwater, sometimes as much as three feet deep, thick with underbrush, snakes, mosquitoes, and alligators. The palmetto bushes were sometimes two hundred feet in diameter and eight feet high. Their roots extended outward at least six feet, and down four feet into the soil. The best one could say about the palmettos was that their roots made good firewood, and their fronds made fans for brushing away the pesky mosquitoes and stinging horse flies that were everywhere.

True, there were acres of arable sandy open space, but pine tree thickets, scrub oak, bushes, and vines covered almost all the land that wasn't under at least a foot of water. The sandy soil, when accessible, was very dry during the winter droughts, and, in some places, under water during the summer months of heavy rains. There was no drainage or irrigation. The young men, hoping to carve out new and prosperous lives in this very rugged frontier of the New (Western) World, must have been severely tested in their determination, resilience and tenacity. They had virtually nothing with which to build a new colony except themselves, a few tents, some hand tools, and their spirit. When they could not pull out, dig, or otherwise remove the resisting, ubiquitous palmettos, they planted and cultivated their fields *around* them. Some farms, more like gardens, were circular in layout, unlike today's modern long straight lines of planting beds. Everything was done by hand in those days of the early 1900s. There were no tractors, not even mules or horses in the earliest years. Occasionally, they received boxed goods sent by fellow Japanese in Northern U.S. cities.

Often they would walk to Atlantic Avenue in nearby Delray to shop for all their essentials, including the flour and rice that they couldn't grow, and salt, blankets for winter, bolts of cloth, seed, fish hooks, lead sinkers, and fishing hand lines.

The long, hot and humid summers forced these young and hearty men far from home to seek weekend solace on the cooler beaches. Because the coral outcropping of the Highlands was directly east of the Yamato Colony farmlands, it was the easiest beach location for the Japanese. They would walk east along their self-created dirt path, now Yamato Road, to the small canal, now the Intracoastal Waterway, and cross the narrow stream either by floating, swimming, or rowing a boat that they had put together with boards that came from the boxes in which salted pork had arrived by barge from the North. After crossing the canal, the Japanese would continue their weekend trek to the beaches and the ocean where they would swim, wade, and, while sitting on their haunches on the coral outcropping, fish with baited hooks on the ends of their hand lines. These living coral rocks attracted wondrous and abundant fish and other sea life, including snapper, grouper, rockfish, snook, reef fish, *langouste* (Florida lobsters), and even larger fish that fed on the smaller fish. So many fish swam near the beach of the Highlands that grouper up to 300 pounds were caught at the shoreline even until the 1950s. Over-fishing and net dragging of anything and everything from the sea during the latter part of the 20th century nearly wiped out all fishing from the beaches. But, in those pioneer days of the early 20th century, the South Florida coastline, especially at the shoreline of the Highlands, with its rocky outcropping, was a cornucopia of rich, tasty seafood. And the Japanese knew where, how, and when to fish there.

On weekends, locals would pass by the beaches of the Highlands, walking or riding horses, and then later, driving automobiles along Beach Road, the narrow dirt road on top of the dune. As they went by, they would spot the familiar cluster of young Japanese men squatting along the edge of the coral rock as they fished, holding onto their baited hand lines, watching the fish in the crystalline turquoise waters below being tempted by the smaller bait fish or shrimps the men had captured by net in the canal. Sometimes, there might be only four, sometimes up to twenty Japanese men hand-line fishing from the edge of the coral outcropping. Everyone was friendly, exchanging hand waves, smiles, and shouts of "Hello."

The Yamato colony grew in numbers. Some men went back to Japan, married and brought their new wives to South Florida. Children were born in the colony. The Japanese frequented "their" beach area near the coral outcropping in greater numbers. The fishing was always good at the rocks. Americans in the area marveled at the prolific catches, as well as the successful farming of the Japanese. Clearly, in this long stretch of mostly sandy-bottomed shoreline from Boca Raton to Delray Beach, this rocky outcropping was, by far, the best location for fishing. And, to everyone in the region, it was the beach that "belonged" to the Japanese.

"Yamato Rocks," later named "Jap Rocks"

The Japanese in 1904 quickly and proudly extended the name of their ancient homeland and their colony to the protruding coral outcropping that provided a home to so many fish. They called it "Yamato Rocks."

It was too far for Delray residents to travel on the unsure dune dirt road known in Delray as Ocean Boulevard. As a result, during the early years of the 20th century, this locale became known in conversations as "the place where the Japanese go," or "where the Japanese folks fish." No one really recalls when, in some local conversation, someone in Delray first named it "Jap Rocks," certainly not in a pejorative sense, for the Japanese colonists were well received throughout the region and were friendly neighbors to the local townfolk.

By 1910, Delray boasted 250 residents; Boca had perhaps 50 people, mostly black farm laborers; and Boynton, maybe 100. For sure, recollections of pioneers indicate that the only people of the early years who frequented the coral outcropping, squatting along the sharp edges, fishing with hand lines, and swimming nearby, were the Japanese farmers. These were the same beaches where, for hundreds of years, the Paleo-Indian "natives," then later the Tekestas, had captured the sea turtles, studied the thrown foretelling stones and shells by the shaman, lived in palmetto-thatched teekee huts, and marveled at the same magnificent beaches and turquoise waters. Soon, the Japanese too would await the arrival of "Koonkah," the first of hundreds of giant sea turtles arriving to lay their eggs in the warm sands of the Highland's beaches each summer.

※❖※

May 1907

The six Japanese men crouched among the thick sea oat grasses and seagrape trees awaiting the arrival of the first giant sea turtles of the laying season.

"Shhh," whispered Arika, the leader, "keep very quiet, my friends, or we will alert and perhaps frighten away the turtles. We must wait for them to begin laying their eggs before letting them know we are here."

"This is very exciting," whispered another. "I've never witnessed giant turtles deposit their eggs on the beaches before. I have been told it happens every summer in southern Japan, near Yokohama and in Okinawa, but not near Miyazu."

"And wasn't it fascinating to watch from 'Yamato Rock' before the sun set to see them bob their heads as they came nearer to the shore, Tomaya?"

With an excited nodding of his head, he responded, "Yes, Toshio, and now, with the full moon, we can see so many turtles on the beach. Look. Down the sand. There must be hundreds of turtles. They're coming out of the sea. Some are walking up the beach. Others are digging their nests. Some are busy laying their eggs. And still others are covering their nests or making their faux nests to mislead the poachers, like the raccoons, foxes, and opossums. Mother Nature is amazing."

"Keep quiet you two," spoke Arika, as he whispered to himself, Oh why, oh why am I the one who always has to teach the ones who talk the most? Why me, oh Buddha? "Now" he continued, "now let's go to the turtle and get the eggs. We will feast soon on the plenty the seas have brought to us in our new land."

In time, the name "Jap Rocks" became *the* name for the larger immediate area, stretching miles beyond the coral outcropping itself. During the 1920s and 1930s, it was the favorite fishing spot for other fishermen, young and old, from Delray, and later from the Boca Raton area. "Jap Rocks" was always a "must visit, must fish, must see" place.

Yamato Colony's Gift
and
George Morikami's Legacy

Of all the colonists of Yamato Colony and their heirs, the person best known to have left his mark on the life and culture of South Florida is George Sukeji Morikami, who came to Yamato Colony in 1906, two years after the first colonists arrived.

He was just 19, but his mentor Jo Sakai, who had created the colony was only 30 years old. Establishing a new life as a farmer in Yamato demanded all the tenacity, patience and determination that the men could muster. In addition to the sweltering heat and stifling humidity of the summers, the young farmers faced daunting challenges from the thick jungles, palmetto clumps, underbrush, thorny vines, and the incessant attacks from the mosquitoes that were so thick that the men had to wear hats and head-nets to protect their faces. Mosquitoes carried typhoid fever that nearly decimated many workers who only a few years earlier had dug the Panama Canal in Central America.

Driven by the dream of riches that would come from their successful farming efforts, the Japanese were diligent and unyielding in their determination. They fought the disastrous summer floods that often would destroy their carefully tended pineapple farms. Their ability to grow choice pineapples that were so succulent made Northern markets pay dearly for this "bundle of Florida sunshine." Their own railway terminal, proudly lettered "Yamato," was a fulfillment of the promise of the Flagler Railroad from whom Jo Sakai had purchased the land.

George Morikami 1906
Courtesy of Delray Beach Historical Society

George Morikami came to Yamato under the agreement that he would serve three indentured years for his employer, Mitsusaburo Oki. He would also receive a $500 bonus at the end of his service, own his own land, and have enough money to return to Japan—rich enough to marry the girl he had left behind. Unfortunately, Oki perished from typhoid fever in late 1906 just when the colony was becoming a farming village.

When Oki died, George had not yet completed his three years. Consequently, he lost his stipend and his land. He found himself virtually penniless, unable to speak English, and unable to return to Japan and marry the young woman. He was just as poor as when he arrived. But with the generosity of a friend, he began farming a loaned one-half acre parcel that eventually became his first landholding in America. Morikami had now achieved a milestone—land ownership—a concept most unlikely for a poor Japanese resident from the fishing village of Miyazu.

It was a desperate situation for young Morikami. At the age of 22, he struggled to learn English at the Delray Elementary School he attended with children fifteen years his junior. That could have been demeaning but it did not deter his focus. In order to tend his farm, he had to walk the six miles to and from Delray, often carrying on his back the heavy load of fertilize or seed he had bought from Sundy's Feed Store. During harvest season, he carried the crops to be sold. Soon, help came to the colony. Flagler's Model Land Company got the railroad to build the Yamato rail station to facilitate shipping of their harvests.

Over the years, Morikami farmed his land, successfully transitioning from his favorite golden pineapples to vegetables. In 1914, Flagler's Railroad reached Key West on island-hopping bridges and Flagler extended the same low rates to Cuban farmers for their shipments as he gave the American farmers on the mainland some 250 miles north. Flagler's barges carried Cuban produce to Key West and then, by train to Northern markets. In time, to protect their markets, Cuba put an embargo on the export of pineapple shoots that Florida's farmers needed to replenish their crops.

Yamato Colony FEC Railroad Station in 1914
Courtesy of Delray Beach Historical Society

By the mid-1920s, several factors brought an end to the commercial farming of pineapples that seemed to stretch as far as the eye could see from Yamato to Boynton. The State of Florida resumed the drainage of the region, digging canals criss-crossing the swampland. As a result, the water table was lowered too much for the pineapples to survive during the dry season. And, during the "Land Boom" of the mid-1920s, the price of land escalated too high and too fast. Farm workers were no longer available at the price of $1.50 per day. As a result of these factors and Cuba's embargo, pineapple farming in South Florida was history. Vegetable farming was the answer for local farmers, including the Yamato colonists.

Pineapple fields, Yamato Colony 1920's
Courtesy of Tamotsu Kobayashi

Over the years, like most of the other local farmers, the Japanese prospered and continued to buy land when they sold their crops each harvest season. Like my father, they put their profits into more and more land, eschewing the risky stock market and banks. Several colonists accumulated parcels of 40 acres or more. In the early 1920s, George Morikami decided to move out of the Yamato Colony environs. My mother told me that George had purchased a 40-acre tract, like Shiboh Kamikama, from U.S. #1 east to the Intracoastal Waterway's centerline. He convinced my father in 1924 to purchase the adjacent 40 acres immediately to the south. "It's good, rich farm land," said George to my father. "Be my farming neighbor. You are already my good friend." My father did purchase the tract, also extending to the centerline of the Intracoastal, now Lake Wyman, just north of 20th Street in northern Boca Raton. His cost? $2,000 total. Those lands extended to the centerline of the Intracoastal Waterway until the 1940s when the State of Florida confiscated all private riparian rights of all submerged lands in navigable waters.

My father kept 20 acres, but George sold his at the peak of the "Land Boom" for an enormous amount. But, in keeping with the times, he received just 5% in cash with terms to the buyer for the 95% balance. During the months and years later, he bought and sold other parcels the same way. His lands resold several times, eventually doubling, then tripling in price until the bubble burst so dramatically after the 1926 hurricane. My father tended to "buy and hold," and when the bubble burst and land values crashed to almost nothing, in most cases, all was gone except the land, now much lower in value. From "paper" millionaires to penniless, the locals started over once again. Like so many others,

George Morikami, having little to show for those halcyon years of excitement, land auctions and riches, found himself with boxes of worthless mortgages and notes. Properties that sold for $500,000 were now worth, at the most, $500. George was broke once again. Like so many others in the region, his dreams were dashed on the rocks of reality. Even the Mizner brothers went belly-up, declaring bankruptcy after three short, unbelievable years. Perhaps Florida's "Land Crash" of 1927 helped precipitate the Great Depression.

"Brother, have you got a dime?" was the typical question of the American people who went into deep psychological and economic depression—the Great Depression—from 1929, some fourteen long years until America went to war in December 1941.

Even during the 1930s, George Morikami continued to buy land at very low prices, sometimes five acres at a time. He chose to purchase land farther west of Delray because it was cheaper. With his modest amounts of savings, he felt he could buy more acreage if he went into the hinterlands. Some he purchased during the 1930s were at prices from as little as $1.50 per acre to as much as $16. Later, in the 1950s, he likely paid up to $50 per acre. In time, he accumulated 200 contiguous acres of land west of Delray Beach and west of what is now Jog Road. My father, still a farming neighbor of George's, bought the adjacent farmland. My father had also purchased land "out west" after each harvest season, especially during the Great Depression. Our family worked that land by hand and mule, and then by tractor into the early 1960s. People still needed to eat, and Palm Beach County provided more than 90% of all winter vegetables to the nation, a performance that continued until NAFTA in the early 1990s.

Local farmers who did not leave the area for other cities found that their only option, short of giving up completely, was to go back into vegetable farming. Some chose gladioli farming after the war in 1946. They had experienced the local economic disaster fully eighteen months before the stock market crash in October 1929. Some had that year and a half window of opportunity to seek jobs and new starts elsewhere. Many of the Yamato colonists did leave the area, some to Miami, Tampa and Ft. Lauderdale. A few moved to cities like Jacksonville in northern Florida.

Among those few who stayed were the Kamiya and Kobayashi families, and bachelors George Morikami and Shiboh Kamikama.

Tamotsu "Tom" Kobayashi

Tamotsu Kobayashi and his sister, Tomiko, are among the few remaining descendants of the original Yamato colonists. Tamotsu was born in Yamato Colony in early 1927 just six years after his father, Hedio, had returned to South Florida from Japan. Like many others in the colony, he had gone to marry the bride who had been selected for him by his parents.

Hedio Kobayashi first came to the Yamato Colony in 1907 as part of the continuing emigration of young Japanese bachelors from mountain villages near Miyazu on the west coast of Japan. And like the others, he was seeking a fresh start and opportunity in this new American frontier of South Florida. He did achieve all his life's goals in this farming colony of young men totally separated from everything familiar. Like the others, he had to use a grub hoe to remove acres of enormous palmetto roots and trunks by hand in order to clear the land for planting. It was back-breaking hard work, but still, they were not employees, and they were not sharecroppers. They were indentured farmers for only as long as needed to repay the loan that financed their travel expenses. They were inspired and determined people from Japan.

Yamato Colony was established in what would later be called northern Boca Raton, just west of the railroad tracks. Mr. Oki selected the land to avoid wet swampland. Of course, he looked at and bought his land during the dry winter season. Most of the land within the colony was sandy soil, draining well for the most part. There were scattered tall pines and hundreds of resisting palmetto bushes, some as large as 100 yards across.

After thirteen years of a difficult, almost monastery-like existence, Hedio Kobayashi wrote his parents to alert them that he was coming back to Miyazu. So, he urged them to "find a young wife for me."

In 1921, Hedio married young, attractive, and certainly adventurous Umeko Kono. Before he left Yamato for Japan, Hedio had first built a wonderful home for his new bride. After they returned and his family grew, he added to the house, which was elevated on pillars to avoid the waters of the rainy summer months. The outer face was attractively covered with wood shingles.

Heido Kobayashi home 1921
Courtesy of Tamotsu Kobayashi

In late 1921, less than a year after they arrived, Umeko gave birth to their eldest son Sakai. Later, with the help of Ben Sundy, he was given an American first name of Theodore. Ben Sundy had advised them that life would be easier for their son with an American name because at that time U.S. law forbade land ownership by aliens. Eventually, there were four children: Theodore (Sakai), Tomiko, a daughter born in 1925, Tamotsu ("Tom") born in 1927, and the youngest brother, Kiyoshi born in 1935.

Umeko and daughter Tomiko Kobayashi
Courtesy of Tamotsu Kobayashi

Kobayashi family, Las Olas, Ft. Lauderdale, 1940
Courtesy of Tamotsu Kobayashi

Tom Kobayashi spoke with me in length about the Yamato Colony years,

"During the 'Land Boom' of the early and mid-1920s, my father, like a few others in the colony, not really being career farmers, became licensed real estate brokers in Boca Raton. Many bought land and sold it as the prices went up. Some of the local friends we knew and worked with included your father, Alex Simon, John C. Mitchell, Harry Chesebro, Richard and Bill Younger. It was a wild time with land prices going up almost on the hour! Addison Mizner and his brother, Wilson—well, some say Wilson sold a lot of land under water, and some he didn't even own. But the 'Land Boom' collapsed in 1927, and in less than two years the tourists stopped coming. You couldn't sell land, and farming got harder. Most of the Yamato Colony people moved away during the really tough years of the Great Depression. Nobody had any money, and nobody could get a job. All we could do was work in the fields, and since it was too hot to grow anything during the summer, we'd go over to 'Yamato Rocks' to the beach and fish for food. There were lots of fish at the rocks, and it was much cooler there. But we couldn't make a living fishing there. As a result, many left the colony. Most moved to Miami to get jobs. Some became restaurateurs. Others became nurserymen or gardeners there, and some started new companies in the landscape business. Ours was the only family to relocate to Ft. Lauderdale. Oish Kamiya went to Jacksonville in 1930.

When the war started, the only people still living in Yamato Colony were Kazuo Kamiya, Mr. Kamikama who was a bachelor, our family of six and George Morikami, another bachelor. So, there were just two families, a total of only nine people still in Yamato when the war started.

Only nine lived there, but more still owned their land although the government confiscated all our land. Heck, they didn't pay us for the land until years later…and it wasn't much. But what can you do? Could a bunch of Japanese succeed in suing the U.S. Government after World War II? Not likely.

One man, Mr. Kamiya, had two boys and three girls. One of his daughters was in California. He went to visit her in mid-1941 before Pearl Harbor was attacked. He was put in the camps for the rest of the duration. Four years. But it wasn't so bad. After the U.S. declared war, we were guarded by the American government. Two men from the Coast Guard came to watch us at our house. They said they were guarding us for our protection as well as to stop any spying for the Japanese. So, they did two jobs, one was for our protection. A funny thing happened. One of our guards told us his father was a German national, but nobody was guarding him in New Jersey, and here he was, a German's son guarding some Japanese, most of us U.S. natural-born citizens. That was funny, we thought.

Before the war, Mr. Kamikama bought the old Yamato schoolhouse. It was near the Yamato train station, east of Dixie Boulevard. He moved it near the old Indian mounds east of where Yamato road meets Federal Highway. Mr. Kamikama moved there himself and lived near the Indian mounds. I think he bought it for around $15 per acre. Later, in the 1950s, those mounds became a tourist attraction named 'Ancient America.' I believe he finally sold that land for about $15,000 per acre. Mr. Kamakama was a rich man. He made a lot of money on land."

Yamato Colony in 1910
Courtesy of Delray Beach Historical Society

For more than 54 years, George Morikami and my father were best friends and neighbors. They helped one another, were "always there," and found a camaraderie as penniless immigrants who came to South Florida during its earliest days. Morikami came in 1906, and my father in 1920. Both were foreigners. Both had come to an alien land unable to speak the language. Both went into farming. Both were punished by the elements of winter freezes or summer floods when all crops were lost. Through it all they remained devoted friends who shared so much.

That is why I agreed when asked in 1986 to serve as Chairman of the Morikami, Inc., a dedicated volunteer support group formerly known as "Friends of the Morikami," who, with the county, built the foundation of what is now the "jewel" of Palm Beach County's Parks and Recreation Department, the Morikami Museum and Japanese Gardens. I stayed on longer than the one-year initial commitment I had made because I became dedicated to the success of this remarkable cultural oasis. I traveled to Miyazu, Morikami's hometown, with our delegation to seek funding for our new museum. In the end, Miyazu's 26,000 citizens, with the wonderful support of longtime Mayor Toshio Tokuda, contributed over $280,000 of the nearly $1 million we received from Japan.

I reluctantly stepped down at the time of my severe stroke in 1993 after eight years. Yet, my loyalty to the friendship of my father, Alex Simon and his dear friend keeps me involved. I am now in my sixteenth year serving on the Board of Trustees.

In a way, from a personal perspective, my involvement in the museum and the rapidly becoming internationally renowned gardens are my gifts to the legacy of my father's longtime friendship with George Morikami. George felt a warm closeness to the people of Delray Beach who came to his aid in December 1941. In gratitude, in the late 1970s, he gave to the people of Palm Beach County all that he had—his 200 acres.

He said at the time, "I came with nothing, and I leave with nothing. I just hope that the people of my homeland and those of my adopted homeland come together on my land and learn from one another the beautiful cultures of each."

A word of tribute to those who have dedicated themselves to this "Cultured Eden" is appropriate.

In 1976, Palm Beach County accepted the gift of George Morikami's land. Dennis Eshleman, the young visionary Director of Palm Beach County's Parks and Recreation Department, hired a young Harvard graduate and Japanophile named Larry Rosensweig to be Executive Director, and sole employee, of the original, very small museum, Yamato Kan. It was a primitive, unair-conditioned, uniquely Japanese designed facility that for the first time brought the culture of the Japanese people to the South Florida community and its tourists. Larry then wisely hired Tom Gregerson, a Michigan State University graduate who also had traveled and taught in Japan, to become Curator. Together, they have spent their entire careers overseeing the park, the growing collections, and guiding supporters and volunteers. With their intelligent leadership, the loyalty and vision of Dennis Eshleman, contributions from the state and the recreational funding of Palm Beach County, the new, much larger 36,000 square feet Morikami Museum opened to great fanfare in 1993. The team of staff, volunteers, and the Parks Department have together brought forth a veritable miracle of environmental, cultural, and haute horticulture in today's Morikami Museum and Japanese Gardens. And now, the American Orchid Society has located its world headquarters at the park.

At this writing, in 2002, The Morikami Museum and Japanese Gardens, among the loveliest parks in the land, provides in its $5 million museum, $3.5 million gardens designed and built by noted architect, Hoichi Kurisu, an ambience of serenity, peace and cultural nourishment for all its visitors, which now number 140,000 annually.

Thank you, George Sukeji Morikami. We are most grateful for your generous gift of love.

Hoichi Kurisu

The new Morikami Museum experienced success immediately, from the early years of 1993. Everyone in the area felt a sense of great accomplishment. In particular, we all felt that the fabulous dream and gift of 200 acres from a simple Japanese farmer, who came to the area as a young man, was now truly and properly fulfilled. Yet even after its opening, Dennis Eshleman and I, as Chairman of the Morikami, Inc., agreed that something more was needed that would attract residents and visitors alike to this magnificent museum.

We met and discussed our visions of the Morikami. At almost the same time we both thought of the same thing. "Japanese gardens," Dennis said aloud. "That's it," I immediately responded. "Let's build the best Japanese gardens in America." Dennis, ever the watchdog of county funds, responded, "I wonder how much that will cost?" I wondered, "I have no idea, but we can find out pretty fast." We agreed we had to pursue the possibility, recognizing that only about 5% of the population is attracted to certain cultural facilities and activities. For instance, if you offer various words to people like opera, museum, ballet, tennis or orchestra, only a small portion will react with enthusiasm. So, we both felt that to be economically successful by attracting enough visitors, we needed more. We also agreed that if we were going to do this, we needed to continue to maintain the integrity of the reputation of the Morikami Museum. That meant obtaining the best designer and builder of these new ambitious gardens.

As it turned out, just a few months later, I attended the World Conference of Japanese Gardens in Portland, Oregon where I learned about the newest gardens and their prominent designers. I also learned that the essence of Japanese gardens is to be more a nourishment of the soul, an enriching of the human spirit than simply pretty trees, rocks, and flowers. Gardening and garden design are a very significant part of Japanese culture and a revered vocation. Gardens are also vital in the daily experience of Japanese life.

But, what to do about subtropical Palm Beach County? Could it work in our region too? Could our trees and plants be adapted to Japanese sculpture? There were many questions that had to be answered before what turned out to be more than $3 million was invested.

The careful county process of selection began soon after Dennis, Larry Rosensweig, and I met to discuss our plans. We met at the county offices where officials listened to résumés and studied past projects of several world-renowned architects. The various county department representatives met together to insure that the entire process met government requirements of the following departments, including Finance, Construction, Budgeting, Legal, and Parks and Recreation.

In the end, Kurisu International, Inc. of Portland was selected. I was very happy because I had spent a great deal of time with its owner, president and lead designer, Hoichi Kurisu during the course of my stay in Portland. He was a most passionate, highly respected man who had helped design and maintain the local magnificent gardens on four acres of rugged Oregon terrain quite similar to Japan.

I was inspired by Hoichi's grasp of what these gardens were meant to provide to the observer, what they would have meant to our major benefactor, George Sukeji Morikami, and what their gardens mean to the whole of the Japanese culture. I investigated everything he said, designed, and wrote. I felt Hoichi's commitment and talents were extraordinary. The new Morikami Japanese Gardens of sixteen acres is now among the finest and largest Japanese gardens outside of Japan. It also is one of the few gardens composed of six consecutive gardens reflecting garden design from the 8th century to the present. They consist of "Floral, Noble and Scholar Gardens—8th-13th century; Paradise Garden—14th century; Early Rock Garden—16th century; Late Rock Garden or Zen, of the Samurai influence—late 16th century; Flat Garden—17th-18th century; Modern Garden—19th-20th century.

In his poem *Rojien* ("Heavenly Drops of Dew"), which follows, Hoichi metaphorically equates George Morikami, benefactor, to be that "Drop of Dew" that grew into a soft rain that became these new Japanese gardens, fulfilling Morikami's hope that his gift of his only belongings, 200 acres, would be used by the people of his homeland, Japan, and those of his adopted homeland, America, to bring them closer together, to lean on each other's culture, and to build a mutual understanding.

Rojien

Garden of the Drops of Dew
A space of heart and mind
in which to witness and experience...
The coincidence of profound inner stillness
Of dynamic action
Historical perspective
yielding
contemporary insight
The spontaneity of reason...embracing revelation
centuries of cultural evolution...
unfolding understanding
Powerful natural forces...
ceaselessly animating all.

Rojien...Drops of Heavenly Dew...
Refreshment. Hope.

An expressive endorsement of
intelligent, creative, compassionate
thinking sustaining humanity's
21st Century.

Tremendously inspiring...
intuitively transforming.

Hoichi Kurisu   *Rojien. 7/96*

Hoichi Kurisu
Courtesy of Michiko Kurisu

Hoichi Kurisu was born in Hiroshima, Japan in 1939. He spent his childhood there until the fateful summer of 1945. When on a vacation with his parents he was fortunately separated from the city by a high mountain range. At the young, innocent age of six, he witnessed the unbelievable sight of the world's first atomic bomb attack, and it was on his city, his home. He recalled to me almost in a whisper,

> "We were, for some reason, perhaps visiting relatives out of the city, on the other side of the mountain when all of a sudden the noise was so great. We had never experienced such a loud sound. Then, the rush of the wind and the explosions of the buildings which were all blown away in every direction. The cloud of debris rose rapidly into the sky, forming a mushroom cloud. The heat was unbelievable. We looked up stunned. We were all terrified, not understanding. Everyone ran for cover, into hiding. It was beyond anyone's understanding. I believe we witnessed Hell. It was so terrible.
>
> Afterwards, when we went back into the city, there was nothing. Nothing at all. No buildings, no houses, no people, no pets, nothing. Dust was thick on everything. I will never forget that sight, how meaningless human life must have seemed. How can we do this to one another? Instead, I believe we must become better people. We must find in our souls healthy thoughts, a sense of peace all the time. No negative influences. We must feed to one another those positive notions, those influences that bring about the highest levels of humanity from others."

Hoichi has never forgotten, nor could he possibly, those events he witnessed when he was just a six-year-old. Amazingly, within less than ten years, during the U.S. occupation of Japan, the city of Hiroshima was substantially rebuilt. Hoichi attended high school there. He later attended Waseda University in Tokyo, and in 1962, traveled to America to join his father. In 1963 after one year in the United States, this talented young designer returned to Japan to fulfill his self-actualization through education, as the Japanese believe. He feels privileged to have apprenticed under Mr. Kenzo Ogata, one of the most famous and respected garden designers in all of Japan. After five years of tutorial studies and hands-on experience under Mr. Ogata, Hoichi returned to the U.S. in 1968. He settled in Portland where he worked and facilitated the design and construction of later phases, as well as detailed maintenance programs of the prestigious Portland Japanese Gardens, now considered the finest outside of Japan. He also designed and constructed the Anderson Gardens in Chicago, now rated just behind the Portland gardens. Following Portland's experience, he designed and built the Morikami Japanese Gardens. He shared his feelings about these new gardens with me.

> "The remembrance of Hiroshima is why I was inspired to compose Rojien, and why the Morikami Gardens remain so important to me. All of my being is in their design and construction to help bring peace to its visitors.

> He looked into my eyes with sincerity and humility, his trademarks, and, speaking softly, said to me, "I hope I have succeeded, my friend. I pray I have."

Hoichi, shin yu, my dear friend, I watched you design these gardens. I watched you standing in the lake placing each stone by hand and studying each path, each tree. You may never know how much your efforts to accomplish this task have succeeded. But succeed you have. Your work will bring much joy to thousands and thousands of people who visit these magnificent gardens. You have added your talents and genius to the culture of this region just a few miles from the ocean dunes of Highland Beach.

The Woolbright Legacy
1912

People from all over America came to South Florida during the early years of the 20th century, when Delray and Boynton were tiny settlements and little or nothing of human habitation was in Boca Raton or Highland Beach. Some came and left, and some stayed, seeking new lives away from the cold weather of the North, leaving after experiencing the pain of subtropical living in South Florida's crude frontier.

Among those who came early and stayed were the Woolbright family who settled in Boynton. Their pioneering presence is evident by the main east-west corridor named Woolbright Road that intersects with I-95 at the location of their homesite and twenty-eight acres of early pineapple farms.

Tom Woolbright, born in Boynton on May 22, 1914 in a small rented house at the old Merkel Orchid Gardens on the east side of Federal Highway, vividly remembers as a boy riding with his father to visit the farmers in Yamato Colony.

> "Sometimes we'd say to others in Boynton during the early 1920s, 'You ought to see the fish those Japs catch sittin' on those rocks near Boca Raton. They use hand lines, and can sure catch some fine fish. My dad used to meet with the Japs and talk about growing pineapples. He learned a lot from them. I believe that was after the first war, about 1917. I was a little boy then, but you remember things better then than you remember what happened yesterday."

Then, after a moment, I asked when he lived at where I-95 intersects with Woolbright Road today.

"In 1916, Mr. Tasker...Allen was his first name I think...had thirty acres planted in pineapples about where I-95 intersects with Woolbright Road in Boynton. He decided to build a house in that thirty acres just north of the bridge, about where the northbound entrance ramp is today. It was on a hill, probably one of the highest ridges in this part of Florida. My dad helped Mr. Tasker build his house during the summer when there wasn't much to do. My daddy was a carpenter, y'see.

Well, there came a hard freeze in February 1917 that burned all the pineapple blooms. It didn't kill the plant, and the pineapples still grew. But you couldn't sell them. The freeze ruined Mr. Tasker and he plain gave up and left town in the middle of the night. Y'see, he couldn't make his payments to Mr. Fred Leonard. Mr. Leonard, who owned the Lake Ida Pineapple Company, had loaned him the money to build the house. Six years later, my daddy bought the Tasker house and the thirty acres of pineapples. We grew pineapples after that on that land. We were the only folks in the area, so I guess that's why they called our road Woolbright Road in those days. Still is called Woolbright Road, isn't it?

Pineapple farm in 1912
Courtesy of Delray Beach Historical Society

My family first came to Boynton in November 1912, just a few months after your grandaddy came to Delray. They came from Illinois to visit my grandmother who came south earlier because she had tuberculosis. Her doctor told my grandfather she wouldn't be able to survive many more winters, and he'd 'better get her to Florida.' So he did, and my folks liked it so much, they stayed here. It was a real small place, mostly farmers, and all were real nice."

I urged him to continue. After all, my family has known Tom and his family for ninety years. He thought for a moment, recollecting his early years,

"I remember when Mr. and Mrs. Tenbrook ran the Bijou theater on Atlantic Avenue at East First Avenue. 'Course," he smiled, "they built it before I was born, but I remember it cost ten cents to get in. We sat on wooden benches, and when a rainstorm came up, you couldn't hear a thing because the roof was made of metal. Mrs. Tenbrook played the Roller Piano and had to stop during the storms. It was the only theater south of Palm Beach, and the folks who lived from Boynton to Boca Raton would drive up in their Fords or Maxwells to see a movie."

The Intracoastal Waterway

The Intracoastal Waterway, literally the western boundary of Highland Beach, is mainly a recreational waterway for pleasure boating along the eastern coast of southeast Florida. In fact, the Intracoastal Waterway actually extends from the Florida Keys northward through every state that borders the Atlantic Ocean, all the way to Maine, staying inland except in North Carolina where it goes "outside" into the Atlantic Ocean along the Outer Banks.

As for Florida, it provides enormous opportunities for power boating, excursions, island hopping, and picnics. Where it widens dramatically, for example in Miami, Boca Raton, Palm Beach and Stuart, some seventy miles north of Highland Beach, it offers large bodies of water for sailing the larger sailboats. In some places, particularly the highly populated areas in South Palm Beach County, the frequency of bridges makes sailing less than the optimum experience.

Where the Intracoastal joins the ocean by inlets as in Boca Raton, Boynton Beach, Lake Worth, and Palm Beach the murky waters, flushed daily by the ocean tides, are alternately crystal clear turquoise, inviting for skiers and swimmers, and then dark in other areas a significant distance from the inlets. This is a result of the blending of waters draining from the farming hinterlands and the maze of drainage canals. Those waters are not so inviting.

In Highland Beach and Delray Beach, homes and condominiums along the east bank of the Intracoastal benefit from the ocean flushing there and are able to have dockage slips, bulkheads, and spectacular views, boat dockage, popular walkways along their bulkheads, and a rather wide, although brackish, waterway.

It wasn't always that way. It was during the late 1880s that the East Coast Canal was dredged by the Intracoastal Transportation Company by widening and deepening existing streams as a toll waterway that, like the Erie Canal in New

York, was developed as an entrepreneurial venture to be income producing. Given franchise rights by the State of Florida to promote the development of the eastern seaboard, the company built a canal wide enough and deep enough for mostly shallow depth and relatively narrow boats that delivered goods, materials, food stuffs and other needs of the growing populace. This was during a time when roads did not exist in this sparsely populated region. Most people lived along the shores of the bodies of water through which the canal would pass, such as Biscayne Bay in Miami, and Lake Worth in Palm Beach. During that period, the first state efforts at draining both coastal areas were proceeding in earnest.

From the outset of local settlements, the canal was the only solution to removal of, or at least dilution of, the growing amounts of human excrement.

Over the decades, the canal became more and more important for shipping, and as importantly, a route for drainage to the sea of unwanted inland waters that covered much of the land of southeast Florida. While the first effort by the state to drain the swamps of the region began in 1880, including constructing the Palm Beach Inlet (then meant to be an "outlet"), drainage efforts really had not taken hold in the area until Gov. Broward began his drainage program in 1906 of deepening and widening the rivers that flowed into New River. Still, the capacity of the East Coast Canal had to be increased by widening and deepening it just to keep up with the floods of the summer rain season. And new "outlets" had to be built to get the water out to sea.

Waterway cargo boat from Palm Beach on the Intracoastal
1906
Courtesy of Delray Beach Historical Society

As the problem continued to grow with more demands on the canal, the government built more artificial outlets to the sea. The little wash-out stream to the sea in Boca Raton was ultimately widened and deepened into a sizable "outlet" that would, at ebb tide, send the brackish, semi-fresh waters from the flooded hinterlands to disperse into the Atlantic Ocean. As the drainage system continued to expand, opening more and more flooded land to farming, cattle grazing, and homes, more ocean "outlets" were needed. In 1926, the State created the Boynton Beach and Boca Raton "outlets," providing more routes to the sea. The other artificial or man-made outlet of West Palm Beach, created in 1880, made a total of three between Lighthouse Point's natural "outlet" plus Lake Worth's.

Of course, when man "plays with Mother Nature," there can be repercussions. Prodded by land developers, cattlemen in Central Florida, bankers, and local politicians, the State of Florida, together with the U.S. Corps of Engineers, increased its efforts and expenditures on "taming the Everglades." In this effort, the Kissimmee River's meandering and annually flooding route was straightened into a straight manmade canal southward to Lake Okeechobee. This Corps of Engineers' effort opened tens of thousands of acres of land, not only farther south and west of Miami to Palm Beach, but also in Central Florida from Kissimmee to the Florida Straits at the southern tip of the state. Much more land was "dried up" and opened for cattle grazing, housing and development. For awhile, the water table was lowered substantially, deleteriously affecting the farming of the lands. The natural filtering of the slow-paced, shallow, curvaceous Kissimmee River, which for centuries had kept Lake Mayaimi (later Lake Okeechobee) clean of phosphates and other impurities, and not only naturally regulated the flow of millions of gallons of surface water into and through the precious Everglades, but also filtered out the growth-stimulating fertilizers of the grazing lands upstate.

Part of this enormous amount of drainage water seasonally flooded the Intracoastal Waterway to the east that flows through and alongside the pristine, oceanfront communities of Boca Raton, Highland Beach, Delray Beach and Gulf Stream. These communities must stay vigilant in their observations of the quality of the vitally important Intracoastal. As they found out, the "outlets" of floodwaters also had a reverse role—that of being "inlets" which not only benefited the area by "flushing" the Intracoastal, but also permitted ocean waters to enter and, during heavy storms, flood adjacent lands. Additionally, the ocean's water quickly salinated the lands along the waterway, removing farming from that land forever. So, the "outlets" became inlets and the double-edge sword effect became a fact.

During the late 1930s, the Federal Intracoastal Navigation District (FIND) began its widening and deepening of the Intracoastal to afford a greater capacity of inland shipping to augment the Florida East Coast Railway. However, it was not until the onset of World War II that the Palm Beach County coastal communities benefited from FIND's efforts. The channel was deepened to eighteen feet, a substantial increase, and was widened from about forty feet in some areas to a minimum of about 200 feet. By straightening the mud bank shorelines, FIND removed tens of thousands of mangroves and other natural growth...semi-tropical jungles...and fish hatcheries from the banks of the Intracoastal. Breeding areas of shrimp, small fish and crustacean communities were essentially removed.

Still, during World War II, the Intracoastal Waterway, now deeper and wider, provided a "safe passage" for wartime shipping to avoid confrontations with marauding German submarines offshore southeastern Florida.

Until the 1960s, after decades of abuse, the government decreed that no longer could the Intracoastal Waterway...the canal...be the repository of all human waste of the coastal cities. Until that time, all municipal sewage was literally dumped, totally untreated, directly into the Intracoastal. While the financial costs of building regional and local sewerage plants seemed great, and caused taxpayers' outrage, it was obviously a necessary paradigm shift from a rural lack of concern for the environment to an awareness of what destruction was taking place. The Intracoastal had been a cornucopia of fish and other water-life. Soon what we caught was inedible or poisonous or a rare occurrence. Decades later, at the turn of the 21st century, the Intracoastal's quality has returned to a relatively clean state.

Today, the Intracoastal Waterway is clearly—excuse the pun—a recreational avenue for pleasure boating, especially in the wealthy region of the Gold Coast, the southeastern coastal communities from Palm Beach to Miami. Boating has become so prevalent, and waterway shipping so rare, that hundreds of automobiles must now stand still, idling their engines, as numerous pleasure boats of all sizes moving at "no wake speeds" slowly pass through the drawbridges.

South Palm Beach County
1901-1918

Throughout the first two decades of the 20th century, the earliest years of settlements in southeast Florida, there were virtually no roads from Daytona Beach south. There were, of course, sand and hard shell-rock roads within some of the coastal towns, including Boynton and Delray, each of which had a shell-rocked main street. By 1901, Delray had its first sidewalk down its main street, Atlantic Avenue. The Delray Ladies Improvement Association members, weary of walking in mud with their full length dresses during the rainy summer season, and in deep, soft sand during the dry winter months, decided it was time to take matters into their own hands. As their first project, they voted to build a "sidewalk" of two boards attached side-by-side from the dirt road named Swinton Avenue eastward to what is now Fifth Avenue, two blocks past the railroad tracks. Since the property owners couldn't agree on which side to place the boardwalk, the ladies, with the wisdom of Solomon, placed the walkway down the middle of the road.

The Ladies Improvement Association then pressed on and held fund-raising events such as bake sales and ice cream socials, bringing ice down by train from West Palm Beach. They also made leggings for the men to protect their calves from the vines and sharp-edged palmetto thorns. In time, they built the two-story Ladies Improvement Association Building on Atlantic Avenue where, at first, they hosted traveling bands and actors' groups who traveled the coastal areas performing for the new settlers. In 1912, the first bank in Delray rented first floor space in the Ladies' building.

In those days, Delray was considered the most attractive settlement north of Miami. Palm Beach was becoming exclusively a winter haven for the very rich;

Boynton's settlers were mostly workers and tenant farmers, but Delray, begun solely as a farming settlement where everybody owned at least five acres, had its culture based on actual and psychological "ownership." The five-acre parcels originally defined by William Linton and David Swinton have remained essentially intact as "city blocks," most of which today approximate 4.5 acres, allowing for street rights of way. Life in the southeastern Florida frontier was very difficult—harsh, hot, and crude compared to life in the Northern states. But the people in the area were cultured, gentle, God-fearing, kind, and helpful to one another in spite of the hardships. It was during these early years that Delray's unique culture took hold.

Delray Beach Woman's Civic Improvement Association
First phase built in 1904
Courtesy of Delray Beach Historical Society

The Adventures of Joseph Priest, Sr.: 1908

One of the early settlers, Joseph Priest, Sr., wrote to his children,

"After being in Fort Lauderdale a few years, for some reason we drived (sic) to Delray. I think it was my guardian angel that brought me here in 1908. I found this to be one of the best farming sections I had been to. Delray had a small school, two churches (St. Paul's Episcopal and Trinity Lutheran), three grocery stores, one lumberyard and one large canning factory, a post office, a Masonic Lodge and Goodfellows' Lodge. We found the best people on earth. Everyone was ready to help the other fellow. There were no roads then, just a deep sand road...foot trails through the bushes from house to house. The train ran regular, no bridge across the East Coast Canal so we could get to the beach. Just a small barge (lighter) and a footpath from the canal to the beach. There were no roads west to the backcountry—there were lots of pineapples at Delray, hundreds of them in acres...most of the time people got a fair price for them. There were quite a few deer, turkeys, lots of fish and lots of alligator. There were a few who hunted them for a living. Their skins brought a pretty good price. The Everglades had lots of alligators where these men hunted them—they would kill and skin from 200 to 300 on a two week trip.

We made friends in Delray. There was John Sundy, J. Ben Smith, H.J. Sterling, Frank Creco, George Stacy, T.C. Milton Hoffman and W.J. Cathcart. Everybody in Delray was friendly. Mr. Cathcart always helped the other fellow when he couldn't help himself."

Mr. Priest's family continues to reside in Delray Beach, including Dot Baker and R.O. "Bud" Priest, who shared with me their grandfather's diary. They too have been pioneers and civic activists in this area for nearly a century. Mr. Priest's diary went on to say,

"In the early days, the only way we had to travel was with the mule team or work mules. They were higher priced, from two hundred to three hundred dollars. In the early days, here in Delray, money was scarce, common labor one dollar and a quarter per day, carpenters two dollars and a half per day, and, at that, not many jobs."

Mr. Priest, having lived in Ft. Lauderdale, recorded a good deal of the South Florida way of life in the early days of the 20th century.

"I often think of the old days at Fort Lauderdale—I always have a warm feeling for that place. I knew the Ashleys that terrorized this part of the country. I have worked on the same job with them. They were hunted down by Sheriff Baker. They were in hiding for several years, but Sheriff Baker camped on their trail until he got them.

From Delray, some of us would go up to West Palm Beach once in a while if for no other purpose, to get a little firewater. That was the nearest place we could get it. The train was about sixty cents for the eighteen miles...It took John Sundy and me about five hours in mule and buggy.

At that time, Delray was in Dade County. The north line then was the St. Lucie River. Since that time (1908) Broward, Palm Beach and Martin County (and Monroe County) have been taken from Dade County."

In 1900, the population of all of Palm Beach County was just 500. By the year 2000, one hundred years later, the population exceeded 1,000,000. In 1900, when the expected life span of America was 40 years, when New York had two million persons, Chicago more than one million, Fort Lauderdale had seven registered voters, all of whom were men, since women's suffrage did not occur until the 19th Amendment was ratified on August 26, 1920. Of course, more than seven men lived in the Ft. Lauderdale/New River settlement then, but many were there to "get lost" so they deliberately didn't register to vote so they could not easily be located. There were three single women in Fort Lauderdale in 1900. It is claimed they vied for the opportunity to teach dancing to Napoleon Broward and Job Farrow, especially after their publicized heroics and gunrunning days had brought them such notoriety.

In 1900, the population of Delray, the leading community between Palm Beach and Fort Lauderdale, was 150. Boynton had 83 people, and Boca Raton is thought to have had 18. There is no information on the population of the area that fifty years later would be called Highland Beach.

In 1900, there were two trains passing through the region each day—one heading south in the morning and one heading north in the afternoon. That way, the day's harvest could be readied at the railway stations before the afternoon train came to carry the goods to northern markets.

The Linton settlement was named in 1896 for its founder by its initial settlers. But, following the terrible and ruinous freezes of 1896 and 1898, William Linton, now unpopular in the settlement, defaulted on his notes to Captain Gleason, sold land he didn't own, kept the proceeds, and fled the area. He returned to Saginaw, Michigan where he ran for the U.S. Congress. The Linton residents decided that they might bring themselves better luck by renaming their community. In 1901, they selected a special six-member committee, three of whom were from Detroit, including the committee's chairman, Mr. W.W. Blackmer. In a quick vote they renamed their settlement Delray, after a suburb of Detroit.

Tomatoes being delivered by mule team to railroad
Courtesy of Delray Beach Historical Society

It's interesting to note that Swinton Avenue, built and paved during the mid-twenties, was named after David Swinton, Linton's quiet, apparently honest partner, while Linton Boulevard, the town's only recognition of its founder, wasn't named after William Linton until the 1970s, seven decades after he had fled the scene and all who had known him had died.

More and more people came to "the last frontier in America" in the early 20th century. Southeast Florida was the place to go for those who suffered from tuberculosis, consumption, and influenza, those who wanted to start over, and those who wished to escape the cold harsh winters of the North and still remain in America.

Still, there were few comforts and lots of agonies. The only "air-conditioning" in southeast Florida were the trade breezes off the sea. And when that was replaced by western breezes, the gnats and mosquitoes became even more unbearable. While all windows could be shuttered at night to keep out the stinging hordes of mosquitoes, there was no way to enjoy the breezes. So, most of the year, residents had to make a choice of a hot, humid home, or a cool one with mosquitoes everywhere. Screens had not yet evolved, so settlers were at the mercy of living room "smoke-pots," closed shutters, and kerosene-wrapped rags they wrapped around their legs and arms as well as the table legs to keep "the varmints" at bay. It was a harsh existence and no place for wimps. That is why the preponderance of South Florida's population was significantly under forty years old. "Only the hearty need apply" was the byword.

In those days, land had value based on one of two requirements: either you could farm it, or you could build your home on it. Little if any land was purchased for investment. There was so much of it, so little money, and taxes would "eat you up." No one had much interest in being smothered by clouds of gnats and mosquitoes that were so dominant near the waterways and at the beach. Land on the east side of the "canal" was so unattractive that during the first decade of the century, one could purchase oceanfront land east of the canal for $3.50 *per mile*. Today that seems absurd. But in those years, there was no equipment to remove the intensely impenetrable jungle of palmetto bushes, vines, and or to relocate tons of sand. Besides, except for the dunes themselves, nearly all land between the ocean and the canal was under water. In most places on the east side of the canal, between Palm Beach and New River, the water was often at last three feet deep. (Incredible as it may sound, it was that way in Delray Beach south of Casaurina Street even into early 1950s.) In the early years, there was hardly any access to the "east land." Crossing the waterway was only available in Boynton and Delray by small barge or lighter until 1911. Crossings were not available anywhere else between Palm Beach and Fort Lauderdale.

Lighters on Intracoastal at Atlantic Avenue
before the first bridge, 1910
Courtesy of Delray Beach Historical Society

As a result, any desire to venture across the waterway by pulling the public lighter's chains, then walking the footpath to the beach, was limited to Sunday picnics. In Boynton, tourists reached the Boynton Hotel at the end of the Ocean Avenue by walking the footpath and crossing on Boyton's lighter. The "beach area," any land east of the waterway, was especially unattractive for homesites except for a few structures that served as "summer houses" for some of the more prosperous families like the Sundys. At that, their locations were limited to the top of the dunes to capture as much breeze as possible.

In 1902, the post office and McRae's Pharmacy were built in Delray. The Ladies Improvement Association building was constructed in 1904, also on East Atlantic Avenue. By that year, Delray had its cemetery, meeting hall, school, two churches, bazaars and bake sales. It also had a sizable black population with its own churches and schools.

McRae's Pharmacy and General Merchandise
Destroyed for recycling in 2002
Courtesy of Delray Beach Historical Society

The Inn, the first hotel in Delray Beach, was built next to the railroad tracks in 1910 by Frank Chapman. He had bought the land for the hotel from William Linton, but it was later discovered that Linton didn't even own the land. This was another instance of scandal involving land dealings with Linton and his subsequent retreat back to Michigan. The Inn met its demise by fire in 1926. At that time, there was also a small theater built by Mr. and Mrs. Tenbrook named The Bijou, and Sundy's Feed Store.

The Inn built by Frank Chapman in 1910
Destroyed by fire in 1926
Courtesy of Delray Beach Historical Society

In 1911, Delray became incorporated by the State of Florida. It was the first city between Palm Beach and Fort Lauderdale to be chartered.

Electricity came to Delray in 1914 and to Boynton in 1921. Little, if any settlement was occurring south of Delray except for the Yamato Colony, which by 1910 had its own post office and railway station, presumably in accordance with the careful negotiation of Jo Sakai and his requirements of the Flagler Railroad's subsidiary, The Model Land Company.

Delray had its own bank chartered on April 12, 1912. Besides the bank and McRae's Pharmacy, there was Wuepper's Mercantile Store, Sterling's Commissary, and two schools. School Number 4 Delray Colored was a palmetto frond-hatched structure that the colored folks had built in 1894. They were taught by the friendly Seminole Indians in the area. The public school for white folks was located at the northeast corner of Atlantic and Swinton Avenues. Even by 1895 when the first white settlers arrived, the "colored community" had its school and two churches, Greater Mt. Olive Missionary Church and St. Paul African-American Methodist Church.

Delray Pineapple Canning Plant
N.E. First Street, east of the railroad
1909-1910
Courtesy of Delray Beach Historical Society

Sundy Feed and Fertilizer Store built in 1910
Courtesy of Delray Beach Historical Society

Records indicate that by 1910, Delray had a population of 250 people. There are no records available indicating the populations of Boca Raton, or what is now Highland Beach. Likely, Boca Raton's total, including Yamato's 40 residents, approached 70, Boynton's population in 1910 less than 150. It was still a very sparsely populated frontier, to say the least, but times would change for this swampy, bug-infested, alligator haven, whose only attractive period lasted from after Christmas to the end of March.

Sunday picnic on the beach
Circa 1910
Courtesy of Delray Beach Historical Society

By 1910, the principle agricultural crop was the succulent pineapple. It was everywhere in Delray and Boynton, it seemed. Harvest season was in the summer. Sprigs and feeder buds were purchased from Cuban farmers; cabbage was grown during the winter months, as were tasty beans and tomatoes. If the winter could pass without a hard freeze, the local settlements of Delray and Boynton could "do just fine."

Addison Mizner's Boca Raton and the "Land Boom" of 1922-1926

In 1918, Addison Mizner and his brother Wilson arrived at the winter playground for the very rich—Palm Beach. Legend has it that they had sought gold in the Klondike some fifteen years earlier. Having failed in their search for riches, they turned to Palm Beach, home of the truly rich. South Florida , for a century, been a place that, especially during the temperate, winter months, has attracted the very, very rich, the very rich, the modestly rich and, coincidentally, those seeking to become very rich. The latter was the case of the socially correct, gregarious, clever Mizner brothers.

Addison Mizner, much like today's Boca Raton, was "larger than life." At 310 pounds, he was an attention-seeking showman who carried a pet monkey on his shoulder. He was impressive, articulate, ambitious, and drawn to *La Dolce Vita*. But he was not as he seemed to be. For example, during his four years in Palm Beach, Mizner became a most sought-after architect, even though he was not trained in the field. He was a bon vivant, invited to all the important social functions, and admired for his clever, trend-setting behavior. With bravado, he exuded confidence and bluster. He bordered on the arrogant, demanded only the finest, and likely disdained the farming locals, the Indians, and certainly the working class. He was a popular raconteur.

Addison's brother, Wilson, considered by some a charlatan, hyperbolic at the least, and maybe a scam artist to many, also added to the, some say "outrageous mystique of the Mizner Brothers."

To this day, there is an ongoing effort in New York to stage a play about the Mizner brothers and their South Florida escapades during the free-spending "Roaring Twenties." Titles of the proposed Broadway play have included such descriptive names as "Wise Guys" and, more recently, "Gold," both of which are considered to be accurate depictions of the "Mizner Brothers." During their four years in Palm Beach, the Mizners sought out the very rich, attended swank dinner parties and receptions, and sold themselves. In a short time, they had become extraordinarily popular.

L-R: Wilson Mizner, Marie Dressler, Addison Mizner
1926
Courtesy of Boca Raton Historical Society

At the least, Addison had become the Palm Beach society's favorite. He was cultured. His family had lived in Italy, and he had panache, a magnetic *joie de vivre*. He drew the wealthy to him even though his absence of wealth alone would not have past muster. He was a popular designer and builder of luxury homes, Worth Avenue buildings, and even the prestigious Everglades Club. Addison Mizner became an eminently successful social guest among the winter vacationers whose names screamed New York society, including the Vanderbilts, the DuPonts, and the Singers (of sewing machine fame), all in their private railway cars parked near The Breakers, the center of gravity of wealth in Palm Beach.

Addison Mizner demanded the best of design, quality and aesthetics. He sometimes put cleated shoes on his feet to "distress" and age the wood members of his design. He would use hammers to crack tiles to give them a worn Mediterranean patina. He introduced his innovative Moorish-styled rough stucco design into the region.

Convincing some of his wealthy friends, especially Paris Singer, the family scion, to invest in his land development schemes, Addison Mizner obtained the necessary funding to build "The Greatest Resort in the World" just south of Delray Beach.

Addison Mizner
1924
Courtesy of Boca Raton Historical Society

As a result, in 1922, Addison and Wilson moved a few miles south and founded their development company. With the Singer fortune backing their efforts, they purchased 17,500 acres of land, mostly in ten-acre parcels, and began building the waterfront showcase hotel they named the Cloisters Inn. It was at that time the most expensive hotel per room in the world. Addison Mizner had a dream, a grand vision. He wanted to build a magnificent resort for the very, very rich. It would be the most magnificent, the most opulent resort in the world.

His brother, Wilson, in charge of advertising and marketing, wanted to be the best, acquire the best, make the most money, and, essentially, have it all as soon as possible. His national newspaper advertisements declared that the new resort would be "Somewhere between Venice, Italy and Heaven."

Addison, especially in the words of his hyper-marketing brother Wilson, was a visionary, a trendsetter, an artist. Their advertisements declared that the resort would be the "Greatest Resort in the World" because Addison Mizner was the developer! The two brothers paid careful, almost obsessive attention to their publicity, public relations and imagery. In so many ways, both critical and generous modern day Boca Raton still exemplifies nearly all the characteristics of the "Mizner Brothers."

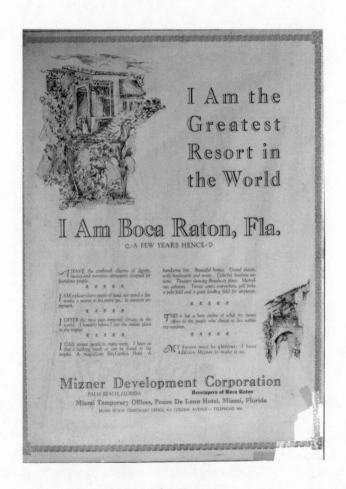

1926 Advertisement
Courtesy of Boca Raton Historical Society

While the design of the Cloisters Inn—so grand, so opulent, so expensive— was of Mediterranean-Moorish influence, some people labeled Mizner's designs, sometimes unfairly, as "neo-Spanish, bastardized Moorish," or Spanish Renaissance. Actually, his designs, especially in the fabulous coveted homes of Boca Raton's Old Floresta and Palm Beach, are still beautiful and with the same sense of harmony and rhythm of the Arabic-Moorish designs of southern Spain, including the Alhambra of Seville, the last grand remaining edifice of the Moors before Isabella and Ferdinand expelled those designers and artisans and other Moors who achieved such remarkable feats in Spain some 700 years before.

It is interesting to note that while Henry Flagler built his hotel and other buildings of Dade pine, and painted them yellow, Addison Mizner chose hollow clay tiles covered with rough, Moorish-style stucco. Moving to Boca Raton, he also used stucco instead of wood and painted his Cloisters Inn beige. The Cloisters Inn, later under the ownership of the Geist family was renamed the Boca Raton Hotel and Club and was painted pink. Later, especially during the 1980s and 1990s, that color was repeated all over town.

Cloisters Inn 1926
Now the Boca Raton Hotel and Resort
Courtesy of Boca Raton Historical Society

Part of Mizner's ambitious design was a large Venice-like canal connecting the Cloisters Inn, now the five-star Boca Raton Resort, with the Flagler Railroad Railway station. He envisioned gondolas from Venice, Italy to elegantly shuttle wealthy tourists to and from the station to the hotel. Regrettably, Addison Mizner's dreams came only partially to reality. The Cloisters Inn did open grandly in 1926, but the residential developments, shops and boulevards did not. Today one can appreciate the wide median strip of Camino Real east of Federal Highway in south Boca Raton, the canal's failed location.

Much of Mizner's influence can be seen throughout eastern Palm Beach County, from the Boynton's Woman's Club, homes, offices, and shops in Palm Beach, to Gulf Stream and Boca Raton. Many neo-resorts use the name Mizner or Addison to their marketing advantage, for, it is assumed, if the name is its identity then it must be of the highest quality. And the name still sells, even eighty years later. There is Mizner Park, The Addison Reserve, Mizner Landings, Addison Meadows—the list goes on and on.

Casa Del Ray in 1925, now Worthing Park
Short term residence of Addison Mizner
during Cloisters construction
Courtesy of Delray Beach Historical Society

Land auction during the 1926 "Land Boom"
S.E. 7th Avenue, Delray Beach
Courtesy of Delray Beach Historical Society

During the "Land Boom" of the mid-1920s—the "Roaring Twenties"—which included several years of Prohibition, land prices in South Florida accelerated almost hourly. A parcel of land that sold for $1,000 at 10 A.M. may have sold for $10,000 by noon and $25,000 by late afternoon. It was a crazy as the "High Tech" stock market explosion of the late 1990s. In one week alone, Mizner sold $26,000,000 of raw land, probably much of it under water. Certainly it was without streets, utilities, even access. In those halcyon days, land sales, like the stock market, required only 5% cash down payment. The balance of 95% was borrowed over years, usually from the seller. Such highly leveraged buying was a recipe for disaster. But the post-war euphoria was too intoxicating, and the momentum buying with skyrocketing "paper profits" made everyone drunk with joy.

Yet only a few years later, when the 1927 tourists didn't buy, the top-heavy market crashed suddenly. Millionaires became paupers overnight. Even the Mizner brothers went bankrupt.

Negative publicity in Northern newspapers following the devastating hurricane of 1926, promises not fulfilled (hotels didn't open on time), and a railroad embargo that stopped all construction were proof that the bloom was off the rose. The land-buying fever and skyrocketing land prices of 1924 to 1927 fell and real estate values crashed nearly two years before the stock market crash of October 1929.

As a result of all these events, the region went into a deep depression. It would take some eighteen years of the Great Depression, World War II, and a two decade influx of post-war newcomers to increase land values and the appeal of coastal southeast Florida, to even resemble the land boom of the 1920s.

Highland Beach, better known as "Jap Rocks" even into the 1960s, would find its fortunes intimately connected to those of its neighbors, Delray Beach to the north, and Boca Raton to the south. The two neighbor cities were totally different in their cultures, potential, and ways of life. The next twenty years would witness dramatic change for all three communities. Amazingly, land values of the 1920s did not return for forty years—the late-1960s. The impact of Addison Mizner and his Cloisters Inn would for many decades define the character of Boca Raton and, in significant ways, impact the fortunes and future of Highland Beach.

Highway A1A
and the
Hurricanes of 1926 and 1928

Once one has stood on the high dunes of Highland Beach, gazed on the magnificent waters of the Atlantic Ocean and felt its soft breezes on the face, it is not surprising that from the earliest days of the settlement of the Florida peninsula some 10,000 years ago these dunes have been looked on as the best nature has to offer. For the Paleo-Indians, the Tainos, the Tekestas, and later settlers, the views from the Highlands have been coveted as the best in the region. Even the barefoot mailman favored walking the dunes here rather than along the shoreline.

It is also no wonder that during the early years of the 20th century, the settlers decided the dune ridge was the best route to travel north and south. The ridge was always high and dry and there were excellent places to stop and rest without mosquitoes and sand gnats, and the views were always incomparable. As the area began to grow, the footpath along the dunes' ridge became a wagon path. The sand was soft and sometimes it was easy to get stuck, so the settlers spread gravel and crushed coquina stone along the path.

In time, an oceanfront road extended along quite a stretch of the coast. At first it was only within settlements, then the road was extended portion after portion, from house to house, until it connected the coastal settlements.

When the graveled path extended from the Boca Raton Inlet north to Highland Beach, the crude dirt road was named Beach Road. Seven miles to the north, in neighboring Delray, the one-lane path along the top of the ocean dune was referred to as Ocean Road, and during the mid-twenties' "Land Boom" it became known as Ocean Boulevard. In Boynton, another five miles to the north, the road was initially called Ocean Road, and during the 1920s had its name changed to Ocean Boulevard.

As the population of the region grew, property owners along the route, sometimes with assistance from the towns and counties, built additional increments of the dune road. In the booming 1920s, most of the settlements and towns from Palm Beach to Miami were connected not only by what is now known as Route #1 (Federal Highway) and Dixie Highway, its parallel corridor. They were also connected along the dune by a third corridor road, Ocean Boulevard in Delray, Ocean Road in Boynton, or Beach Road in Boca Raton, or whatever name the locals chose in that particular area, all now A1A. The principle exception was the locale of the Gulfstream Golf Club, north of Delray Beach, where the clubhouse and 18th fairway are built on the dune. There, Ocean Boulevard, in deference to the Vanderbilt heirs who built the club in 1926, the road was built just west of the dune where it is located today.

As late as 1909, the beach drive from Delray to West Palm Beach took up to five hours by mule wagon. Later, by automobile, the time was significantly reduced to less than three hours. In the mid-1920s, the county connected all the parts of the beach road and then reconstructed the entire route. In concert with the state's road building of the coastal highway in the Jacksonville to Daytona Beach section ("Buccaneer Trail"), Palm Beach County named it the same Highway A1A.

Since the first local settlement in 1895, the ocean dune route provided the most scenic vistas of coastal South Florida and was used as a powerful marketing tool by developers and speculators to promote sales of their lands at skyrocketing prices no matter where they were located, even if under swamps, to this day.

Ocean Boulevard, Ocean Road, or Beach Road, depending on where you were, offered the best leisurely scenic route. It also meant no one could build a house on the dune. The earliest "summer homes" near the ocean were thus built on the west side of the oceanfront road. And this was the way the oceanfront developed, especially in the Palm Beach County communities of Palm Beach, Lake Worth, Delray Beach, Boca Raton, had anyone at that time been interested, which apparently they weren't, even in Highland Beach, one of the most sparsely settled areas in the region.

Until the 1960s, most land east of the Intracoastal Waterway was deemed unattractive because it was so very wet most of the year, had hardly any accessibility, and too many biting bugs and other "varmints," alligators and snakes. Only on top of the dune ridge on the beach itself, was it dry, breezy, or bug-free much of the time, and of any appeal to the general public.

All this changed after the horrific storms of 1926 and 1928 hit the region. Some say Hurricane Andrew that hit mostly Miami and the Homestead area in 1993 was the most devastating natural disaster in the recorded history of Florida. To be sure, the losses, estimated as $30 billion dollars, were monumental. Also monumental was its impact on the insurance industry and premiums of coastal

Florida policyholders for many years. Thousands of homes in the heavily developed South Miami Kendall area were so badly damaged that their owners had to leave for months, some never to return. Ten years later, many homeowners continued to migrate some sixty miles north, and build new homes in South Palm Beach County.

The 1928 hurricane struck much of the southern portion of Florida, from the Florida Keys north into the middle of the state, as far north as Daytona Beach.

The damage done by the 1928 hurricane, as described by those who lived through it, including my family and other pioneer families, was far more severe in its destruction and loss of lives than the 1993 hurricane. Thousands of lives were lost in the 1928 hurricane, especially those African-American farm workers who were living in wooden houses south of Lake Okeechobee at the time the Lake's dikes broke. Hundreds of homes were destroyed. Beaches were washed away. And the entire region stayed flooded for weeks.

Yamato Colony fields after the 1926 hurricane
Courtesy of Tamotsu Kobayashi

Flagler's elevated island-hopping railroad, built on timber bridges across the Keys to Key West during 1914 to 1916, was completely destroyed by the extraordinary surge of the sea and the high winds. The surge of the sea, coinciding with extra high tides, compounded the storm's effect into tidal wave proportions. It was one of the severest in history. Hurricane Andrew which struck at low tide was violent yet small and fast-moving. However, it had no significant storm surge and was therefore not as devastating as the one in 1928.

My father's recollection of the damage done in 1928 was more graphic than anything else he ever talked about,

> "Son, you cannot believe how bad it was. There was no warning, not like today, no television, no reports on the radio, nothing. We really didn't know what to expect, although we built this house very strong in 1924 and it brought us through the 1926 hurricane. Now, that was our first bad hurricane, and as bad as it was, it didn't come close to the hurricane of '28. Thousands of people died because of the flooding, especially out in the 'Glades by Lake Okeechobee. It was terrible. Houses crashed all over and thousands of trees came down.
>
> I'm amazed that our two-story, four-bedroom house at 216 S.E. 1st Avenue, just south of Atlantic Avenue, stayed here. Yes, son, it rocked and rolled and creaked and shook. It was so loud. But we lived through it and, thank God, no one in the family—your mother, Ernie and I, and Zicky's family across the street—got hurt. So many other people lost their homes.
>
> Along the beach, almost all the beach road was swept away by the hurricane. Almost every bit of Ocean Boulevard was gone from Miami to Palm Beach, even farther north, up to Juno. The storm was like a big claw that reached out of the ocean, grabbed the dunes, and pulled them back out to sea. There were big fish everywhere. It ruined the area. And it ruined land values. I'm sure glad I built this house on this sandy ridge, and I'm glad we put the gas tank in the ground. I think your mother was the only woman in the area who could cook and had hot water for over a week.
>
> After one look at the beach, I never again wanted to live over there. The whole place, even to Federal Highway, was under at least three feet of water. Boats were everywhere. And the beach highway was gone. I mean it was gone. You couldn't drive to Boca Raton or Palm Beach along the beach after that. There were so many washouts.
>
> After the '28 hurricane, no one wanted to buy land here anymore. It took from 1928 until 1968—forty years—for land values to recover. And at that, it wouldn't have happened without central air-conditioning."

John Miller remembers A1A as "The Wash-out" road,

> "Prior to the 1928 hurricane, A1A was a small gravel road that

included a stretch from Delray Beach to Boca Raton. There was a section from the north city limits of Boca, or at 'Jap Rocks,' that extended north about one mile. This section was washed out by a storm, most likely the '28 hurricane, and later a sandy unpaved roadway ran up and down over the dunes. It was very difficult to navigate this stretch by automobile without getting stuck in the sand at least once. This section of A1A was then known as 'The Wash-out.'

From the north end of the washout, the existing road, still driveable, curved around sometimes on the dune and then turned to the west as it approached Delray. There was one point about two or three miles south of Atlantic Avenue in Delray where the dune was quite high. From the road at this point, one could look west and see a section of the Spanish River in its natural state. The river snaked through a swampy area between the coastal dune line and the FEC Canal (now known as the Intracoastal Waterway). Sometime between 1933 and 1935 the canal was widened and deepened and the fill was pumped into these swampy areas, erasing the Spanish River.

I remember my dad, Albert L. Miller, telling me that when he first arrived in Delray about 1909, he and other fishermen would travel south by boat, starting in the canal at Delray, working south, and then east to a point directly west of 'Jap Rocks.' Walking across the dunes, they were then able to fish at this favorite spot. It seems logical that there might have been a natural outlet there at some point in time.

In about 1938 or 1939, a new A1A was built from Delray Beach to Boca Raton, replacing the sandy, sometimes gravel, winding road. This was constructed west of the dune, away from the old roadbed. This new road was also built differently from conventional roads. Instead of a rock base, the new road had oil tilled and compacted into the soil until it became a hardened base. This remained until the 1950s when it was again redone.

West of 'Jap Rocks' was the small town of Yamato, settled by a group of Japanese farmers. They would cross the canal and frequently would be seen fishing the area. Hence, it was labeled the 'Jap Rocks' by the early Delray fishermen. It is unknown to me what the Japanese folks may have named the rock."

But, in time, the resilience of the frontier settlers, farmers, and even land-owners began to re-emerge. Throughout the weak economy of the Depression years, consolidation began to take place. Banks re-opened, Federal financial safety nets were put in place under President Franklin Roosevelt in 1933. Confidence was slowly returning, and, by the mid to late 1930s, parts of the Beach Road began to be rebuilt with a joint effort of landowners, developers seeking prime homesites, the counties and the state who sought to reverse the economic damage of the Great Depression by attracting once again, new settlers to the state of Florida.

A1A dune park where shamans foretold events

However, as portions of the ocean road, now known as State Highway A1A, connecting the southern tip of the state to the northernmost cities, sometimes meandering away from the ocean, were rebuilt, no one wanted to risk rebuilding the road on the vulnerable dunes between Miami and Palm Beach. Nature had yet to rebuild the dunes The inland landowners, in an effort to improve their land values, convinced the authorities to rebuild A1A on the lee side of the dune in places as much as some thirty feet below the dune ridge elevation. "It's safer from storms if we shift the road to the west 50 to 100 feet," they argued.

This pattern of rebuilding Highway A1A west of the old dune ridge road created an entirely new effect. It created homesites for the first time on both sides of the prestigious A1A. It created an avenue that would, in time, bisect what would become Highland Beach.

To this day, during the early years of the 21st century, the lands along the ocean dune remain the most cherished, most coveted, and most valuable lands in the Palm Beach to Miami sector of coastal Florida.

A Family Farming Community: Butts Farms

August Butts was a successful bean farmer in Ft. Lauderdale during the late 1920s. In 1931, his son, Harold, having just been graduated from the School of Agriculture at the University of Florida in Gainesville, came back home to help his father.

Harold Butts recalled, as I visited with him in his beachfront home just south of Palmetto Park Road,

> "My daddy had heard about the success of the Japanese up in Yamato Colony, and how they grew the finest beans in the region. So, he sent me up to Boca Raton to visit them and find out what they did to get such fine beans.
>
> They were really good farmers, Sandy. They actually grew beans around the pine trees and the thick palmettos like gardens. And they dealt with the wet land and droughts better than anyone did. I learned a lot from those Japanese."

By 1932, during the early years of the Great Depression, Harold Butts began locating and buying land west of "downtown" Boca Raton in the area now occupied by Town Center, at the intersection of I-95 and Glades Road. Butts Road is his namesake.

> "We only wanted to farm about 300 acres, but we had to buy another 1,000 acres just to protect our water. Our beans were easy to market because we were dedicated to growing the highest quality beans. Your father bought a lot, I mean, a lot of

our beans. Everybody at the Pompano Farmers Market knew your daddy only bought the best."

"How many acres did you finally accumulate, Mr. Butts?" I asked him that day, in his home on the dune overlooking the beaches.

"Well," he said, "we had to protect our water, and everything we grew sold at premium prices. Land was cheap then. So, we kept right on buying land until we finally ended up with more than 4,000 acres. I think we paid, on average, less than $15 per acre during the 1930s and '40s. With all that land and those crops to be protected, I had to devise a sophisticated water management system that would get rid of all that water during the rainy season, 'cause that could rot the plants. And when the droughts came, we had to have water to pump back into the rows. So, I put together a system of reservoirs, piping, and pumps. It was because of all that irrigation system that we could keep the bean plants wet enough to produce lush beans, never too dry and never too wet. 'Course, Sandy, I don't mean to say it always worked. But it did most of the time."

August Butts
Courtesy of the Boca Raton Historical Scoiety

The Butts family prospered for years, even during the Depression years, producing food for the nation as did many other farmers in the region. But, the Butts' farms, with their coveted irrigation system well in place, became nearly immune to the vagaries of the extremes of weather in South Florida long before the U.S. Corps of Engineers, the Lake Worth Drainage District constructed their systems of canals.

The Butts family continued its very successful farming operation, employing 350 to 400 workers during the peak farming season from October to May. The family provided their farm workers with their own stores, food market, movie theater, and housing. These lands became very, very attractive indeed following the years of World War II. But, they held on until the mid-1950s when an extraordinarily wealthy, diminutive man, a visionary, to be sure, came to town and offered $75 per acre for land valued at $50 per acre, more than five times what they paid for the land. They had reaped substantial profits from farming that land for more than thirty years. As a repeat of the mid-1920s "Land Boom," land was becoming too valuable to farm, and too attractive for developers. As a result, again, land prices began to escalate beyond anyone's sense of logic.

Still, the Butts family remained active locally, and with Harold's sister Myrtle's husband, Tom Fleming's financial acumen, the family became part of the local banking world. They donated land for church sites, St. Andrews School, charitable organizations, and even for the intersection of the Florida Turnpike. Boca Raton's growth projections were not then deemed adequate by the State of Florida, especially when, in 1950, the population of Boca Raton was only 992, most of whom worked at the Boca Raton Hotel or at the Butts Farms.

The impact of the Butts family has been very significant, especially in helping to establish the culture of the community through their generosity.

Even during the harsh 1930s, until the NATFA agreement of the 1990s, Palm Beach County provided more than 90% of all winter crops for the people of the United States, including corn, peppers, beans, cucumbers, cabbage, lettuce, carrots, eggplant and the like.

People of the coastal communities fished from the beaches or along the canal year-round. Everyone seemed to watch out for their neighbors in those days of the 1930s. There are many wonderful stories of farmers and fishermen with their truck beds filled with bountiful harvests driving along Atlantic Avenue announcing, "Vegetables here!" or "Want some fish?" I am told by those who lived through those years that "no one ever went hungry in Boynton, Delray or Boca Raton."

As Mr. Butts told me, "Sandy, we are like your family. We have maintained our trust in the Lord, sought His guidance, and, as it turned out, we blossomed where He planted us."

The Great Depression
1930-1941

During the decade of the 1930s, the terrible years of the Great Depression, summer seemed hotter, more humid, and longer in South Florida. Mosquitoes and gnats seemed bigger and more voracious.

During the years of Prohibition, which ended with the 21st Amendment in 1933, the beaches from Miami to the Boca Raton Inlet north to Palm Beach were favored destinations of "bootleggers" using boats to bring illegal whiskey from the Bahama Islands. The Canadian distillers, having to avoid the heavily guarded border with America, sought to deliver their liquor to major Northern cities and Florida winter resorts by way of Nassau, since the Bahamas were also a member of the British Commonwealth. Although this routing was highly complicated, the risk of the whiskey being confiscated was very low. Everyone knew the beaches of southeast Florida were virtually unguarded and the few residents were not particularly sympathetic with efforts to prohibit whiskey from flowing into Florida anyway. Most folks, especially the wealthy tourists seeking their favorite brands, ardently looked forward to the delivery of the high quality Canadian Club and Caribbean rum.

As a result, nocturnal visits by small boats crossing the sometimes churning Gulf Stream laden with Canadian whiskey and rum from the Caribbean islands of Cuba, Puerto Rico and the Dominion Republic became part of the way of life along the unpopulated coast of southeast Florida.

Here's how the system worked:

After crossing the ninety-some miles from Bimini to the Florida shoreline, the boat captain would follow the agreed plan by flashing his light in Morse code from the boat to the men waiting on the dunes. Given the "all clear" signal, the captain would steer his boat toward the flashing light and run his boat up the beach where his cargo would be unloaded into black sedans by the waiting men dressed in black suits, fashionable fedoras, and carrying guns. The workers would be guarded by two men with submachine guns, or "Tommy" guns. From there, the whiskey would either be driven to the hotels of Palm Beach, Boca Raton, Delray Beach or to the Boynton rail station where the men would be undisturbed as they loaded the liquor into rail cars destined for Chicago and Al Capone's operation, or to New York.

Sometimes, depending on the hour, the whiskey and rum would be buried in the dune on the lee side toward A1A until a time when the train schedule was a better fit.

Helen Long remembers her teenage friends who were Boy Scouts.

> "My friends would sometimes sit on the dunes at night like teenagers do, and being Boy Scouts, knew Morse code. They would watch the signals from the boat and learn where the boat would come up on the beach. They thought they were on the 'in,' and even though they knew where the whiskey was buried, they were smart enough not to fool with those bootleggers. But they did tell other older teenagers about the boats."

My father was a very busy produce broker those years. He later told me a story that shocked me at the time,

> "Sometimes, after loading hundreds of bushels of beans and other vegetables in rail cars at The Pompano Farmers Market, I would drive to the Boynton railway station as fast as I could, well after midnight, to supervise the loading of the fine tomatoes harvested west of Boynton.
>
> One night in 1931, I was loading the train cars with boxes of tomatoes, filling the cars to the doors. Up drove three big black sedans. Four men in dark suits and hats jumped out, swinging their machine guns all around. I got very concerned, but I just kept on with my loading. Then, other men got out of the car and opened the door of the rail car next to mine. It was full to the doors with hampers of beans and bushels of peppers.
>
> Some of them started unloading the car and threw the beans and peppers on the ground, hollowing out the car. Then, they started refilling the interior of the car with boxes of whiskey. When they were done, they took some of my tomato boxes and stacked them just inside the door to hide the whiskey behind the tomatoes. Then, they slid the rail car door shut, put the lock on,

recorded the car number, got back in their cars and drove off into the night."

Then, I asked a very naive question, "Dad, did you report them to the police?"

He laughed, knowing I had no idea how dangerous those times were, and responded,

> "Son, Boynton had one policeman in 1931, and he was home in bed, asleep. He wasn't stupid; he was outmanned. As for me, I was 29 years old, had a wife and two young sons at home depending on me, so, no, son, I just forgot what I saw. And that's why I'm still here."

The Depression years were, in some ways, beneficial, although times were extremely difficult. Many did not have steady jobs, and those who did worked for very small wages. As a result, people found it better to "tenant" farm. They would seek out a landowner, agree to farm a small portion, say one to five acres, and share the profits. The owner would provide the seed, fertilizer and tools. The "sharecropper" would provide the labor, often including his wife and children. In most cases, extra harvest and fish caught either at the beach or in the "canal" or streams would be shared. There was little or no capability to preserve foods and fish, so it would "go bad" in three days… "may just as well share it with the poor" the same day it was picked or caught. People tended to help one another all the time during those days because it was "crisis time" all the time. These were the years that affected so deeply the young people who would, starting in 1942, become an enormous military force and, as labeled by Tom Brokow, "The Greatest Generation."

Land west of what is now Military Trail, much of it inaccessible or under water, was available for next to nothing, mostly from the State of Florida or the county, which likely had taken back the land in foreclosure. It was very cheap in the 1930s. The prices were $2.50 per acre if you could drive to it by car or horse-drawn wagon, and $2.00 per acre if you couldn't.

Jimmy Love, from the pioneer Love family, told me,

> "Sure, it was cheap, but nobody had any money! We would have loved to have bought a bunch of land back then, but we didn't have the money. And if we had bought it, we couldn't have paid the dang taxes.
>
> Matter of fact, that's why the state and the county were selling it so cheap in the first place. They needed the tax revenue. The last owner couldn't pay the taxes, so the government took the land back. Now, the county was broke, but it owned lots of land."

Personal
"Jap Rocks" Vignettes

For most of the first half of the 20th century, the beach area commonly called "Jap Rocks" was thought of as a remote, desolate, area the locals went to for fishing, beach parties, and simply seclusion. No one seemed ever to be there to interrupt whatever it was you wanted to do. Only on Saturdays and Sundays, during the day, would the Japanese be there and almost always on or alongside the coral outcropping.

Those who did venture to "Jap Rocks" those quiet days following the "Land Boom" and "Crash" were usually young men who loved the beach, fishing or swimming.

"Bud" Priest
1937

Besides Eddie George, who was renowned for his powerful body and distance swimming in addition to his fishing successes, R.O. "Bud" Priest, Jr. and his friend, Bill Adams, Jr., really enjoyed their time on the beach at "Jap Rocks."

The two of them even built a self-styled hut on the beach just north of the rocks in 1937. Following is Bud's description of their adventure,

> "Around 1937, Bill Adams, Jr. and I built a palmetto hut approximately 12 feet by 16 feet on the back side of the beach at the weed line and original A1A, way beyond the high tide waves, because the beach was 250 feet to 300 feet to the water. The corner posts were cypress poles cut west of Delray and the

rest of the material was picked up on the beach where it had washed up. We used palmettos overlapped on the roof and sides. It was weatherproof completely. Inside, we made two single bunk beds, a table, and a couple of shelves to store canned food. Back then, we never saw people for weeks. If we did, they were honest and never bothered us or took anything.

When I left Delray in the late 1940s to go into the Navy, the hut was still there. The hut was built a short distance north of 'Jap Rocks' which had a deep channel on the southern outer edge. The channel was filled with fish coming in close to shore.

Our rowboat lay outside the hut. It was made out of any wood we found approximately 3 feet wide and 12 feet long. Cracks were stuffed with rags, and when we went fishing on the ocean, we would fill the boat with water. The wood would swell up and close the cracks. We always had a baling can. We would row out on a good day and bottom fish. The first reef was 85 feet deep, the second reef 105 feet and the third reef was 125 feet. The water was clear and we had a water glass made out of a lard bucket. We could see the fish biting the bait."

Chesebro palmetto thatch barn
Courtesy of Boca Raton Historical Society

Bud's recollection segued to another subject of the 1930s. He described the coastal area of "Jap Rocks" and its exposure to illegal whiskey shipments into southeastern Florida.

> "Bootlegging was very common. The bootleggers would run close to shore. If they were chased by hijackers or the law (Coast Guard), they would dump their load in the ocean. Somehow, the Boy Scouts who knew the Morse code knew where to find it. They would swim out, recover the bottles, all individually wrapped in straw so they wouldn't break, and take the whiskey, mostly rum, and hide it in the palmettos between original A1A and the newly traveled road. Our family had an old Indian friend named Mark Johnson. When I was about eight years old, he took me everywhere with him. Many of the times he would take me along to pick up some whiskey. As we were about to turn onto A1A, he would stop and make me lay down on the back seat floor of the car, in case he ran into trouble with hijackers, the law, or bootleggers. He'd pick up the whiskey, sell it or drink it."

From the first arrival of the settlers to the area in 1895 and thereafter, the locals were able to look to the beaches or nearby offshore for debris or shipwrecks to provide them with "serendipity" or unexpected good fortune.

For example, in 1911, the three-mast cargo sailing ship *Coquimbo* capsized off the beaches of Boynton. After staying aboard to protect his ship and its valuable cargo of lumber, the captain finally capitulated to the fierce waves and went ashore.

A Federal Marshall came to protect the ship and its cargo from thieves. He was authorized to auction off the lumber, most of which was purchased for nearly nothing by the residents of Boynton and used to build several houses, including the Boynton Women's Improvement Association's two-story building on the south side of Ocean Avenue, just west of Federal Highway. That's probably why the Boynton Women's Club, while much larger than Delray's, cost less. Most of the material was practically free.

The "Jap Rocks," Highland Beach area also benefited over the years from the same source of supplies. As Bud Priest recollects another instance,

> "Before 1926, a ship had capsized loaded with lumber of all sizes. I remember my father, with friends, load several large truck loads that were picked off of the beach, stored on his lot at 319 S.E. 3rd Ave. They let it dry out and used it in our house built in 1926."

Murder in Highland Beach
1937

My Uncle Carl Heyer who, in 1937, was living on Beach Road in Boca Raton, just south of where Palmetto Park Road today intersects with A1A, told me about an event that shook-up most of the locals in the region in the late 1930s.

"There was a beauty contest held in Miami Beach to draw national attention to the resort. There was, among the many opportunists, a man who pretended to be a Hollywood talent agent. He wooed two would-be starlets from the contest— remember, these were very difficult times, no one had any money, and a few dollars and promises of 'being in the movies' was very enticing to young people in a frontier area. The two naive girls joined the man in his car and they all headed north.

In a few days, word got out that the teenage girls were missing, and police were notified by telephone to be on the lookout. I got a call from Police Chief Brown because he knew I had a pistol and access to a car. We got together and drove north along Beach Road. Some boys had called Chief Brown and told him that they had found a young girl in their shack on the beach near 'Jap Rocks.' We went there as quickly as we could. We did find one young girl, bitten all over by mosquitoes and other bugs. She was dead. The other girl was gone. So was the man."

Here is the way Bud Priest corroborated this terrible story of kidnapping and murder that struck this very quiet remote area,

"In 1937, there was a beauty contest in Miami. A man, who said he was a Hollywood talent scout, lured two girls to go with him. They drove to Highland Beach and stayed in our hut for about a week, hiding out. The man killed one girl and kept the other with him at his side. They were later caught in Delray by the law. I don't know what happened to the hut. When I came out of the Navy in 1946, it was gone. I continued to fish at 'Jap Rocks' for many years thereafter.

In the early days, we traveled the beach road in a Model T Ford. We spent many a day and weekends on Highland Beach—big all night parties, fish frys and barbecuing, etc.

A1A only went south to the Boca Inlet. Mrs. Grace Weir owned five acres of land just north of 'Jap Rocks,' including where we built the hut, about in the 4500 or 4600 block of Highland Beach now."

Sam Ogren, Jr.

Another interesting character who also still lives in the Delray Beach-Boca Raton area is Sam Ogren, Jr., born in 1925. Aside from his travels, he has lived in Delray Beach all of his life. His father, Sam Ogren, Sr., has been recognized as one of the area's first and finest architects, and his son, Sam, Jr., continues as his father's successor designing local homes even today.

Sam Ogren, Sr., born of Swedish missionaries in China in 1899, came to South Florida during the early days and found a small seaside village with no architect. He began his career and soon became known for his exceptional work. A close friend and colleague of Addison Mizner during the "Land Boom" years of the mid-1920s, both were considered on a par, although Mizner's image became more prominent, likely because of the fact that he was developing "The Greatest Resort in the World." Sam Ogren, Sr.'s designs had the trademarks of Dade pine or pink textured stucco, barrel tile, and the popular pecky cypress details. His work included Delray's Sandoway East, the Seacrest Hotel (site of today's Marriott Hotel), and a prominent house on Bankers Row situated on the southwest corner of N.E. 1st Avenue and 2nd Street.

Seacrest Hotel, built in 1926
Now the Marriot Hotel
Courtesy of Delray Beach Historical Society

Sam Ogren's work was in demand at the time and, as his son recalls, "he was busier than hell." Among his other lasting designs are the Delray Beach High School, his first major project, built from 1925 to 1926, the adjoining gymnasium built in 1928, a variety of luxury homes in the region, and many commercial buildings that line popular Atlantic Avenue even today, including the outstanding Arcade Tap Room. The old high school is now the Crest Theater in Old School Square, renowned for its design, acoustics and historic importance.

It is difficult to tour the area and not often notice Ogren-designed homes and other important structures, a large portion of which are properly listed in the Historic Preservation Records.

When Sam, Jr. was young, he attended Delray Beach High School. He suffered from a serious case of asthma and its related impairments. During the 1930s, when little was known about treating this debilitating illness, Sam was told that if he would workout athletically, lift weights, and get focused on building up his physical capacity, he could overcome his asthma constraints. With the help of his father, who set up a room of pulleys fastened to the wall, he began what has become a lifelong, and now more than seventy-year regimen of physical exercise and muscle strengthening. During the late 1930s, a local character and very popular house painter, with one good eye and a limp, named Peewee Baggett convinced young Sam to get involved with Golden Gloves boxing that had a workout gym in nearby Lake Worth. Peewee became his coach for two years. Sam also went fishing on the beaches, a very popular pastime. He told me,

> "The best fishing was at 'Jap Rocks'—and I don't use that name in any negative way—that was its name from the early years because that's where the Japanese from Yamato Colony always went to fish. My close buddy Ed George, whose nickname was 'Horsie' because he was so darned strong and powerful, would go down with me to fish, swim, and catch turtles all the time. We rarely disturbed the mother turtles until after they had laid their eggs, and then we almost always released them. We were teenagers having a good time and we never ever thought of hurting them, although some people cooked them and ate them during the Depression for sure. Of course, catching turtles today is illegal and frowned upon by everyone.
>
> In the late 1920s, my dad needed work. None was here, so we moved to Milwaukee after the 'Land Crash.' But we only stayed two years since the early crash here happened two years before the October 1929 Crash. Ohio, like most of the North, was late getting hard hit by the bad economy. So, we came back to Delray and I went to Delray Beach High School. That's when I really got into fishing and water sports.

In 1942, when your brother Ernie and cousin Zicky and I graduated from high school, we all went to either Palm Beach Junior College, now Palm Beach Community College, or to the University of Florida. Since the war had started, we had to declare a military program either V-12 or V-5. I transferred to the University of Miami because it was nearby. I wasn't accepted into the Navy because of my history of severe asthma.

I remember during the late 1930s and early 1940s, especially before the war, we'd all gather on Friday nights in 'The Pines,' as we called one area along the ocean dune just south of Delray. It was a great place to take your date, a quiet place because nobody lived or even drove south of Delray till you got to Pompano in those days—only the teenagers. We roasted hotdogs and marshmallows over the fire that we built on the beach surrounded by stones we gathered. It was so much fun back then, very innocent, just groups of teenagers having a good time. That's not allowed anymore, is it? I remember the mosquitoes and the stinging sand gnats, especially if the breeze came out of the west. And the land crabs! They were big and fierce-looking too! Those were great times, for sure. The beach was empty then.

The war changed everything and we had to get serious pretty fast. Lots of people went to war and many decided, in those times, to get married first. After all, none of us knew what might happen. Many young men were getting killed everyday. Suddenly the world and our lives changed dramatically.

After the war, I found work where I could and came back to Delray Beach in 1950 and went to work for my father. I've been actively designing for fifty-two years now and will keep on as long as people want my work.

You know, those years fishing at 'Jap Rocks' were wonderful. It's now Highland Beach, you know! Those were the best years! I still go fishing, but now, with so many people here, I can't fish off the beach. I have to use a boat now, but I still have a lot of fun and still catch a lot of fish too, but not like those days at 'Jap Rocks.'"

"Meet you at the beach, Saturday noon, Sam. I'll get the truck and we'll go swimming and fishing at 'Jap Rocks,'" said Ed George.

"OK, Horsie," replied young, slender Sam. "I'll get Ken Davis, if Doc Davis will let him go too."

"OK, see you at the store."

The three friends spent most summer Saturdays swimming or fishing in the ocean. Sam had a bad case of asthma and found swimming and lifting weights helpful. Both became life-long patterns.

When they arrived at "Jap Rocks," they parked the small Ford pick-up truck near the dune on the shoulder of A1A in the desolate area, knowing there would be little or no traffic for hours. They ran down to the coral outcropping with their fishing gear.

Ed said, "Let's fish for awhile and see what's in the water. Then, we'll go find some turtles to ride. Tonight we'll get one after she lays her eggs."

Fishing was always good at "Jap Rocks." This day, there were four young Japanese hand-line fishing from the edge of the coral outcropping.

"Hi, Toshio," Ed yelled to his friend.

"Hello, Eddie," responded the young Yamato Colony resident.

Sam asked, "How's the fishing?"

"It's good, Sam. There's plenty for everyone. Come join us."

By the middle of the afternoon, all three had caught several snook, the great fighter, grouper, snapper, and one big jewfish, probably over fifty pounds. The sea was rich with delicious and mature fish in those days before dragnets and commercial fishing.

"I've had my fishing for today," smiled Ed to his friends. "I'm going for a swim. See you in a few hours, before dark."

Sam and Ken turned back to their fishing, casting their weighted bait into the choppy ocean waves, some over a hundred feet out.

"Got another one, Sam," yelled Ken. "I guess you could catch fish here all day and never run out of fish."

"That's right," replied Sam, "this place is the best. Delray's beach is real good too, but there's something about 'Jap Rocks' that's better than the other beaches."

Then, looking down the beach, Sam said to Ken, "Let's go join Eddie. Let's go catch a ride on a turtle. It's June, and the place should be full of loggerheads."

Like on other Saturdays or Sundays, the three buddies swam together. Of course, Ed George was the most powerful swimmer in the region and loved to swim for hours every day if he could.

"That guy," said Sam to no one in particular, "that guy," he repeated, "swims the length of Delray's beach, probably two miles each way, back and forth, everyday! I don't know how he does it. He's some kind of swimmer. Now he's going to catch a turtle, the bigger the better, even when they have barnacles all over them. Boy, can those things cut your chest. And the points on the rear fins. They can cut up your legs somethin' awful."

"But it's so great," Ken replied, "so much fun riding a turtle."

By dark, Ed had found and ridden a turtle from "Jap Rocks" out about a mile and then back, steering him as he held the top front edge of the turtle's shell with both hands, keeping his legs clear of the turtle's fins.

He then headed back to the beach to meet up with Sam and Ken.

There, on the dunes, they stood, waiting for the female turtles to appear, emerging from the lapping waves.

"There, Horsie, over there," said as he pointed toward the shoreline. "There's our turtle for the night."

"Yep," he replied, "we'll wait for her to climb toward us, lay her eggs, then put her in the truck."

"She's heavy, Ed," said Ken. "I'd say over 300 pounds."

Ed responded, lifting one side of the heavy turtle, "Yes, I'd say more, maybe 400 pounds. Step back. I'll lift her into the truck." Then, continuing, "Your dad can give turtle steaks to his patients."

"Yeah," added Sam, "ol' Doc Davis is probably the only doctor in the county who heals people's wounds, births babies, and gives them somethin' to eat."

"He sure has taken care of my family for a long time," said Ed. "From broken bones to ringworm to a burst appendix."

"How did you lift that turtle into the truck? It would have taken Ken, two others and myself to do that."

Ed just shrugged and stepped to the truck door to drive their booty back to town.

"'Jap Rocks' is like a cornucopia. There's always plenty for all of us. That is, of course, if we don't get greedy." Sam's voice trailed off as Ed pressed his foot against the starter and shifted into first gear.

Turtle hunt, 1922
Courtesy of Boca Raton Historical Society

Ernie Simon Remembers
1937

"The very sight of 'Jap Rocks' always brings to mind some of my fondest beach recollections. One of my earliest visits to that jagged landmark was as a young 'tenderfoot' Boy Scout in Delray Beach during the 1930s. Our Scoutmaster, Al Miller, determined that we could qualify for the coveted Fourteen-Mile Hike merit camping badge by walking along the beach from Delray to 'Jap Rocks,' camping there overnight, and then retracing our sore-footed paths back to Delray. Pretty neat—a prized merit badge for simply taking a casual stroll on the beach—in the middle of a very hot summer…at the height of the mosquito season…and carrying a backpack. Trudging along in the soft beach sand, each weary step became an ever-increasing challenge as we peered through burning, squinted eyes for the first sight of our ultimate oasis. Finally, there it was… 'Jap Rocks' in all its craggy glory, greeting each ocean wave with a splashy welcome.

After a refreshing swim, we built a fire and cooked our supper of hot dogs and beans. With tired bodies, we settled in around the fire, at last, for a good night's sleep. The gentle ocean breeze was very soothing and just strong enough to keep away the dreaded nighttime insects. Then, at about midnight, the wind died down and switched to the west. Immediately, swarms of gnats and bloodthirsty mosquitoes descended upon us with a vengeance. For the rest of the night we took turns burning seaweed to create a smoke shield from those fiendish visitors. Between the bugs and the smoke, there was little sleep. I kept thinking, 'Hurry, sunrise.' Thankfully daybreak brought relief. I can still picture how 'Jap Rocks' truly glistened in the early morning sun's rays. It was glorious. After a refreshing swim and breakfast, we broke camp and headed back to Delray Beach. The beach sand was hot, and my backpack was still heavy. But each step brought me closer to my merit badge—and completion of my Fourteen-Mile Hike encampment at my favorite beach oasis—beautiful, glistening 'Jap Rocks.'

Several years passed before my next memorable visit to the oasis-like 'Jap Rocks.' In those days there was no paved A1A roadway south of Seagate in Delray Beach, so access was limited. In fact, in the late 1930s, the end of A1A at Seagate was a favorite gathering place for teenagers after high school dances which ended about 11 P.M. There were usually three or four automobiles lined up in a semi-circle with their radios tuned to the big-band broadcast from the Hotel Roosevelt in downtown New Orleans. With beach sand on the roadway to provide a smoother surface, we enjoyed dancing under the stars until our midnight curfews.

After World War II and completion of A1A south of Seagate, we began our regular Saturday night beach parties at 'Jap Rocks.' Our group was usually about forty in number, and the menu was always the same: hot dogs, beans, and potato salad, each generously sprinkled with beach sand and washed off with beer and soft drinks. The initial step was to find a stem of sea oats strong enough to hold a hot dog over the huge fire without dropping it. The final step was to clean the hot dog of sand and ashes before eating. Occasionally, a giant sea turtle would crawl ashore to lay her eggs. We watched but never molested the turtle or her eggs.

My favorite beach party at 'Jap Rocks' was in 1955. It was basically the same group, the same menu and the same refreshments—even the same full moon. But there was one major difference. It was my first date with my future wife, Norma—a 'blind date' arranged by my good friend, John Ross Adams. That was the best beach party of all.

Although 'Jap Rocks' may no longer be available for Boy Scouts camps and Saturday night beach parties, for me it still remains that glistening beach oasis—that never-ending reminder of some of my most cherished memories."

Pristine Beaches of Highland Beach

Ed George
and the U.S. Coast Guard
1942

Area teenage boys had a lot of time on their hands during the warm, humid summers, unless, of course, their fathers put them to work. South Florida, in those days, was not a locale for corporations, industry or manufacturing. As a result, there weren't many jobs available. So, teens did what teens usually do when they don't have to work. They enjoyed themselves. There was really "nothing to do."

Until the 1970s, there was still a very small population in the southeast Florida region. In 1930, at the outset of the Great Depression, Delray Beach's population was only 2,433, and though small, it was clearly the commercial center of the South Palm Beach County, the busiest downtown between West Palm Beach and Ft. Lauderdale. Boca Raton's official 1930 population is recorded at just 320 persons, most of whom were employees at Addison Mizner's Cloisters Inn, now the Boca Raton Resort, which was for decades, Boca Raton's major employer. There is no record of any residents located in the area then known as "Jap Rocks," now Highland Beach.

During the years of the Great Depression, on weekends, local teenagers camped-out, fished, hunted, or went down to Ft. Lauderdale to the movies or to try to meet other teenagers. But mostly, they spent much of their time at the beaches and swam in the ocean unless they were working on the farms. The beaches were the favorite places to be during those very quiet summer days of coastal southeast Florida, especially at "Jap Rocks" because nobody else ever appeared except maybe the Japanese.

Ed George, Coast Guard swimmer
Courtesy of Mrs. Mim George

The more adventurous spent lots of time swimming or fishing in the ocean. The most notable teen was 19-year-old Ed George, whose family owned and operated the upscale men's clothing store on East Atlantic Avenue with *"A. George & Sons, since 1911"* printed on the front of the two-story wooden edifice.

Eddie, a strapping, tall, muscular young man was one of the strongest and best swimmers in the region. He spent day after day swimming in the ocean. "He was like a fish." It was as natural for him to swim out three miles on Saturdays as it was for him to run down the street. His strength and endurance became legendary.

By 1942, Ed George's swimming habits and powers reached the ears of the U.S. Coast Guard who hired him to swim offshore in the Atlantic to search for evidence of enemy submarines. Ed, who had had a tumor removed from his brain, was ineligible for military service. So, he served his country throughout the war as a singular, swimming patrol off the beaches from Boynton to Deerfield Beach.

Day after day, Ed would walk from his home on the second floor above the family store at the southeast corner of Fourth Avenue and East Atlantic Avenue, swim across the Intracoastal canal, walk to the beach, and, after doffing all his clothes except for his bathing suit, would step into the water and swim out several miles without goggles, without flippers, and with only a knife strapped to his muscular calf.

Once offshore, depending on the sea currents, he would drift south to Deerfield Beach, or north to Boynton Beach, then swim in and either catch a ride or walk back home. Sometimes, he would hitch a ride on a turtle swimming somewhere near where he wanted to go. Sometimes, he would run into a shark. Once, he had an encounter with a large hammerhead shark. He told me he had to dive to the bottom, churn up the sandy bottom into the shark's face, then stab and kill the shark. When he was certain the shark was dead, he dragged it to shore, pulled it up the beach, across Highway A1A, and then dragged it all the way across the canal bridge. As a teenage prank, he hung the twelve-foot shark by its tail on the city streetlight at the corner of Fourth and Atlantic Avenues.

After the weekend and a growing smell downtown, the police department called Ed's father and asked him to have Ed "please take it down because people were starting to complain."

Throughout the war, my brothers and I would venture over to my cousin Ed's house to see what he had pulled in from the sea. Often, it seemed, he had dragged lifeboats, boxes of German goods jettisoned by their submarines, even packages that they wanted found. In one box, there were actually cancelled tickets from the Delray movie theater, meaning some German sailors had come into town, bought movie tickets and gone to the theater. Imagine, Americans innocently enjoying the latest from Hollywood, sitting next to a World War II German naval officer, in Delray Beach.

Ed George was a living legend in the region. In due time, he married Mim McKennan who bore his children, all of whom cherish the unique life of their father.

World War II

From the 1920s to the 1950s, most of South Florida was a farming region. In Miami and the Homestead areas there were large potato and vegetable farms. Farther north, west of Fort Lauderdale, and in Pompano, there were large tracts of land planted in beans. Pompano was chosen as the locale of the State Farmers' Market, which was built in 1928. My father was, at age 26, the youngest charter member of the Market, and was on "the half-mile platform" everyday but Sunday during harvest season (from October until May) until his illness in the 1970s, nearly fifty years later.

Pompano had the largest concentration of green bean farms in Florida. Beans were so much a part of Pompano's life that its high school nickname was the "Pompano Beanpickers," a name that stuck until the 1960s when residential development consumed so much of the farm land.

From the beginning of Yamato Colony in 1904 and into the 1920s, the Japanese were very successful farmers. It is not commonly known that many of Yamato's colonists had never farmed before coming to South Florida. Some were businessmen, accountants, and store employees looking for a better life in America. Many left the farms during the harsh years of the Great Depression to find jobs or start companies in Miami. After Pearl Harbor, of the few Japanese who were still in the area, none was sent to California to the government internment camps. Among the last Japanese who stayed in the area was George Morikami. The Kamiya, Kamikama, and Kobayashi families continued to farm locally, but George Morikami would become the most remembered and cherished of the Japanese settlers. He symbolized the character, determination and grace of the significant Yamato Colony contributions to South Florida.

George, with whom my father had a close friendship from 1924 until their deaths in the late 1970s, came by the house every day at noon during the harvest season to do two things. First, George and my father would visit and sometimes have lunch together, and second, he and my father would lift the bushels of vegetables and hampers of beans from George's morning harvest onto my father's pick-up truck. My father would then drive George's harvest to Pompano to mix with his own. For that, my father charged George only a five cents per bushel brokerage fee, hardly a means of accumulating wealth. But they were close friends.

That is why it was so significant to our family when, on Sunday, December 7, 1941, George, who would normally have arrived in our driveway precisely at noon, smiling broadly as he walked to the house in his knee-high rubber boots, instead arrived at about 4 p.m., crying and yelling. He cried all day, asking my father rhetorically many times, "How could they do this terrible thing to America? How could the people of Japan, my homeland, attack the good people of America, my new home?"

They spent the entire afternoon and evening talking about this horrible thing that had happened. No one, including my father, could answer the questions in a way to help George understand. No one else understood either.

The next day, December 8th, President Franklin Roosevelt called on Congress to declare war against Japan. George again drove up our driveway in his pick-up truck filled with all his belongings to keep at our house. My brother, Roy, remembers watching and hearing George saying that he felt safe with us.

For nearly three months, the U.S. Government froze his bank accounts and placed him under virtual house arrest. He was broke, frightened, angry at Japan, and afraid that he would be arrested, and maybe shipped to the camps in California. For those three months, my mother and father kept him going. They fed George in our home, gave him money for food and his farming expenses and sold his crops at the Pompano Farmer's Market. "He didn't have his own money...even a dollar...to buy gas for his truck or his pump at the farm," my mother once told me. "Your father gave him money so he could continue to farm and drive."

My father and other farmers in South County, including Albert Machek, vouched for George before the Federal Government representatives in South Florida. They helped convince the government not to force him and other Japanese of Yamato Colony from their beloved farms and send them to California internment. The Japanese, especially George, were grateful to those friends for the rest of their lives. Few, if any, had to leave the area but they were watched and sometimes were under house arrest or, sometimes guarded each day by the FBI and the Coast Guard during the war years.

After the Pearl Harbor attack by the Imperial Navy of Japan, America went into a period of enormous shock. For the first time since the Civil War, the nation was faced with a frightening sense of vulnerability and began to realize that it was no longer insulated from the rest of the world. "Remember Pearl Harbor" became a national slogan.

Those who remember that infamous date can also relate to the nationwide trauma following the September 11, 2001 attack by airborne international terrorists who deliberately crashed U.S. commercial airplanes into the World Trade Center towers in lower Manhattan, the Pentagon in Washington, and a farm field in western Pennsylvania, killing thousands.

Both surprise attacks alerted the people and the government to the vulnerability of the nation and its well-being. "A Sleeping Giant" was what the Japanese task force admiral called America at the time. Perhaps that was a fair description on September 11th also.

Indeed, Americans had been quite complacent during the 1930s while ignoring the rise of Nazi Germany and the warlords then controlling Japan as they swept across Manchuria and China.

However, once the war was brought to the shores of America and its enterprise system was brutally challenged, the people mobilized. The nation accepted the challenge, and the "war effort" not only "jolted" the nation out of its complacency, but also out of the twelve-year-old Great Depression. Everyone was mobilized in some way.

While the war-building machine of America actually was located throughout other parts of America, coastal South Florida, soon became exposed to the impact of war.

The newly imposed "draft" of young men included those of Florida at the moment they completed their innocent years of high school. Boys from Boca Raton and Delray Beach attending Delray Beach High School went into the service immediately upon graduation, or reaching the age of 18, and they readily did so, often volunteering. It was difficult to watch sons and daughters leave home.

The war affected South Florida's residents in several ways. During 1942, the Boca Raton airport, part concrete runways, part grass, was confiscated by the U.S. Army Air Corps. The lands of Yamato Colony that abutted the air base were also confiscated. In short order, the airport became a major radar training base for the U.S. Army Air Force's personnel who came to be trained and then sent to air bases in Europe. Over the duration of the four-year war, more than 40,000 Air Force men were trained at the Boca Raton airport. Their presence taxed the local housing supply and caused the relocation of most of Boca Raton's African-American population to Delray Beach, Deerfield Beach, and Riviera Beach.

The Air Force cadets came to the area where radar was installed on planes destined for the war front in Europe. WASPS, the Women's Air Service Pilots, flew brand new planes from their manufacturing facilities in Fort Worth, Seattle, Wichita, St. Louis, and other centers to West Palm Beach. Those, including B-17s, B-24s, B-25s and the like, which would have radar installed were flown the twenty miles to Boca Raton. Once fitted and manned by newly trained personnel, most still in their teens, those planes would become the responsibility of the 23rd Ferrying Squadron based at Morrison Field, now Palm Beach International Airport.

My uncle, Col. Frank E. Heyer, commander of the 23rd, would then be in charge of delivering the new flight-ready planes to Africa or the Mediterranean, by way of the Caribbean island chain to Antigua then across the Atlantic. Sometimes, depending on need, his orders were to fly them north to Nova Scotia, then to England. "All very top secret," he would whisper to his young, eager nephews, with a smile.

Several enterprising Yamato colonists accumulated great tracts of land during the 1930s at very low prices, using all their earnings to buy land. Shiboh Kamikama owned more than 720 acres, 500 of which he ultimately sold during the 1970s for $2.5 million, perhaps equivalent to more than $20 million today. Although land prices in the region were low, the Japanese who wisely invested in land profited greatly. Unlike those on the West Coast, their property was not confiscated, except for the land needed for the Boca Raton airbase. As a result, those who had purchased raw land outside of Yamato Colony during the Depression years were able to hold them throughout the years of World War II, and profited greatly during the latter day land boom of the 1970s.

During the late 1930s, my father purchased a tract of land stretching from the north boundary of the airbase, now Florida Atlantic University, to where Linton Boulevard is today, and from Congress Avenue east to the FEC railroad. On that land, my family had about 300 head of cattle and two horses named "Daisy" and "Charlie" which my brothers and I would ride on Saturday or Sunday afternoons during the 1940s when Dad would take us to "the farm."

The cattle ranch or "farm" was totally fenced. In the middle of the land, the caretaker and his family lived in a small house and watched over the herd. The cattle invariably found ways of getting through the fences and roaming all over the area, including the U.S. Army air base. Too many times, the air base commander would call my father at home.

"Hello?" my father would say into the upright phone with the conical voice receiver, holding the earpiece to his ear.

"Mr. Simon," the deep voice at the other end would say in a most official sounding tone, "your cows are all over the runway and our planes can't take off. Would you please come get your cattle?"

"Of course," my father quickly reply, hanging up the ear part connected by the thick wire onto the u-shaped cradle. Then, to the family in the house, he would call out, "Boys, get in the truck. We have to go get those dang cows off the runways again."

I can't recall if my father would smile at the humor of this situation, or be really mad at the cows, or just do what he had to do. Anyway, off we'd go, all three remaining sons, and sometimes our cousin, Dudley Remus. I'm not sure how much I helped running down those cows in the fields or on the runways. I was only six years old. But to me, it was a really exciting adventure.

Sometimes, the cows would venture into town, chew the grass of lawns, walk through open doors, and once, I even chased a cow all the way through a house in Delray. It was pretty funny for me at that age, though I'm sure the homeowners had every reason to wonder why and how a full-grown cow came running uninvited into their house. Maybe it was an innovative way to deliver fresh milk.

Aside from that close relationship we had with the colonel at the base, our exposure to the war was provided by my brother Ernie who was in the U.S. Navy, and cousin Zicky who was being trained in Colorado as a waist gunner in B-17s.

Coastal South Florida got additional impact from the war by German submarines lurking very close offshore. Their mission was to sink as many Liberty ships as possible before they could get to England. These U.S. cargo ships, first loaded at New Orleans or Mobile with munitions, war materials, and foodstuffs, would begin their journey by sailing east to the west coast of Florida, then south, picking up a ride on the Gulf Stream, that seven knot current that would steer them around the Florida Keys and then north. The current was important to these Liberty ships because they could double their speed to 14 knots as they "rode" the Gulf Stream.

Since the Gulf Stream sometimes came within one to three miles of Florida's beaches in the Boca Raton, Highland Beach, Delray Beach region, German submarines could easily cruise between the shore and the Gulf Stream. Or, they could lurk just east of the Gulf Stream, perhaps three or four miles off shore. From that vantage point, the submerged U-boat would track the unwary cargo ships. Just when the unsuspecting Liberty ships crews thought all was safe—Boom!— torpedoes exploded at the hulls beneath the surface. On occasion, the bold submariners even attacked with their deck guns while surfaced.

By 1942, the presence of the U-boats offshore became a frequent reminder of the dangers of war. Aside from the cargo ships' crews, no one on shore seemed to be in imminent danger of land attack. But it was terrifying to see the Liberty ships burning and sinking so close to our town.

Tom Butts, my life-long friend whose family lived on the dune in Boca Raton, shared some memories with me of 1943 when we were both six years old.

> "One day, while sitting with my father on the terrace of our home between A1A and the beach, just south of Palmetto Park Road, we watched this big Liberty ship riding the Gulf Stream close to the shore when suddenly a German submarine surfaced very close to the beach. We actually saw the submarine come up out of the water, just like in the war movies. My father was upset, really angry. I was excited, and my mother got scared when we called her to come see.
>
> The submarine crew came out onto the deck and, after pulling the covers off the gun, started shooting the deck cannon at their un-armed, unwary prey. Boy, the cannon really pounded the cargo ship.

Then, after that, it went down a little, and then it shot a couple torpedoes at the Liberty ship. When it did that, the ship exploded.

My gosh, that big ship just exploded and exploded. It must have been carrying dynamite. My dad thought so, and got really mad because of the thought that maybe there were German spies nearby who knew this particular ship was carrying explosives or bombs. That was the most incredible sight I ever saw. And that day prompted my mother to demand that we move from the beach back to Ft. Lauderdale until after the war."

Quite exciting for a six-year-old! In 1943, the beach was a big part of our lives. We would all go down to the beach all summer, even during the war. Sometimes, on Sunday afternoons, we had family picnics, gathering around a fire on the beach where the family would have a cookout. My cousins, Dudley, Rodney and Carl, would be there. We'd swim, run on the beach, and just play. Sometimes, with our arms outspread, we would pretend we were American warplanes flying like those we saw everyday flying all over town as the radar operators at the Boca airport practiced their new skills.

The adults would also enjoy themselves on the sunny beach, visiting near the stone-encircled fire, while, I'm sure, someone from Civil Defense would be sweeping the ocean with his eyes, looking for ships or submarines.

I remember watching ships burn offshore Delray Beach. On shore, Civil Defense lookouts stationed at the Boca Raton Hotel, the Seacrest Hotel in Delray Beach, and along the beaches, near "Jap Rocks," would report any explosions to the local police. We would hear the city's fire department sirens wail an alert up and down the coast. Everybody in town would jump in their cars and race to the beach to watch or help if possible because flotsam, debris, and even wounded survivors would wash up on the shore. At night, car headlights were required to be taped over, except for a small slit of light. All streetlights were capped over so to eliminate the advantages to the submarine crews.

My Uncle Johnny Zaine and others in town who were too old to go to war served in the local Civil Defense. Most of their efforts were spent as lookouts. They would station themselves in the tower of the Seacrest Hotel, now the Marriott Hotel at A1A and Atlantic Avenue, and, armed with binoculars and walkie-talkies, scan the ocean's horizon for the stealthy submarines.

Eddie George, under orders from the Coast Guard, would swim out to the Gulf Stream, locate evidence of the Germans' presence, and bring it to shore, then to his home at Fourth and Atlantic behind the family store.

The U.S. Army Air Corps, based in Boca Raton, had other duties. Near the Boca Raton Hotel and Club there were eight covered docks. The government took over those docks and parked its boats there. Their "crash boats" were very much like the Navy's PT boats in that they carried and delivered torpedoes at high speed. Also, they had mounted two fifty-caliber machine guns on deck.

Tom Butts, again recalling his 1940s experiences, remembered,

> "I would ride my bike down to the Boca Inlet and wait for those 'crash boats' to head out looking for submarines. Sometimes, I'd be near the bridge and I'd hear their roar as they came in and out of the inlet one after another...one...two...three...four...five...all of them roaring out so fast. They told me that they could go up to forty miles an hour. Boy, were they fast. I could see the men at the machine guns. I could see the torpedoes. That was really exciting. They would patrol the shoreline looking for German subs from Pompano to Delray."

The Germans did succeed in sinking a reported sixteen Liberty ships off the beaches from Boca Raton to Boynton Beach between 1942 and 1944.

The years of World War II in South Palm Beach County witnessed a great deal of military activity. There were thousands of U.S. Army Air Corps radar trainees working at the Boca Raton airbase, German U-boats patrolling the sea lanes only a few thousand yards offshore and U.S. Coast Guard boats and torpedo planes seeking and destroying those U-boats. It was a frightening time to be sure, and it was a difficult time as many commodities were rationed, including eggs, sugar, beef, butter, milk, cheese, gasoline, and rubber. Those were needed to support our armed forces overseas. Local farmers produced as much as they could as a growing demand turned the area from a sleepy, Depression-era farming region into a huge producer of winter food supplies.

Spanish River:
Boca Ratones

To paraphrase a favorite Christmas saying, "Yes, Virginia, there really was a Spanish River."

For hundreds, perhaps thousands of years, coastal South Florida was mostly swamps. Actually, it was very much an extension of the Everglades all the way east to the ocean dunes. Of course, the evolution of the peninsula of Florida occurred over millions of years as waves of sedimentation and coral building took place and created, in succession, a "washboard" profile with slight ridges, alternating with valleys. For example, the easternmost ridge is the dune line overlooking the sea. Then, for a distance varying up to 1,000 yards, there was a wet low-lying area. This lowland swamp region is where Spanish River was located from north of Delray Beach south to Boca Raton until the East Coast Canal (later, the Intracoastal Waterway) was dredged deeper and wider into a straight-edged much larger waterway in the late 19th century, and again during the 1930s and 1940s. Ridges west of this low area included the north-south ridge where the FEC Railroad is located west to beyond Swinton Avenue and Dixie Boulevard. Then, the next low-lying area, where Congress Avenue is today, was mostly a swamp-like area, much of which was underwater until the 1970s when developers began filling in the lowest areas.

The "high and dry" land near Swinton Avenue was considered prime for homesites during the early years of settlement of the local towns because it was high and drained well, being "sugar sand." The ridge caught the breezes and had fewer mosquito-breeding water-logged areas. It covered much of the central part of Boynton, Delray Beach, and downtown Boca Raton. West of the Congress Avenue corridor were the dryer "pinelands" that reached in some areas as far as what is now known as the Rangeline or U.S. Route 441.

Spanish River, between the dunes and the Intracoastal diverted to the east, separated from the stream where the East Coast Canal was dug and built, near the south end of Lake Worth. It meandered southward to about 500 feet north of George Bush Boulevard, then flowed a bit southeast through the swampy area just east of what is now Andrews Avenue, then southward across Atlantic Avenue to between Venetian Drive and Gleason Street, meandering widely as it went south. It continued southward, curving snake-like along the east side of the present Intracoastal Waterway, sometimes coming very close to the east bank in the area of Highland Beach.

As it continued south, it finally rejoined the Intracoastal at a wide body of water within the very large watery, swampy region later known as Lake Rogers in northern Boca Raton. Its riverbed continued south into Lake Wyman, and finally into Lake Boca Raton.

Spanish River crossed Atlantic Avenue at about the spot where Gleason Street intersects, and where the high-rise Spanish River Inn is located. It was always a low spot between the Intracoastal Waterway and A1A. In the early years, when East Atlantic Avenue was a dirt wagon path, the four-foot wide stream was covered by wooden boards so that pedestrians and wagons could cross it.

East Atlantic Avenue, Delray Beach, circa 1905. Note the
wood boards in foreground covering Spanish River.
Courtesy of Delray Beach Historical Society

In 1933, when the Intracoastal was being deepened and widened, there came an excellent opportunity to fill the area that always flooded during the heavy summer rains. When fill was offered to the city by the dredge company at a very modest cost, the city representative told the company "thanks, but we do not need additional fill. What we have is adequate." Regrettably, as buildings covered the land, that area continued to flood during the rainy seasons, often staying under a full foot of water for days, year after year so that Atlantic Avenue east of the bridge was often virtually impassable. The city finally installed adequate drainage infrastructure in that area some sixty-five years later, during the 1990s, at an enormous cost of hundreds of thousands of dollars.

Linda Oxford remembers,

> "In 1933, my father, Fritz Friberg, was employed by Captain Anderson who was dredging the Intracoastal Waterway. Dad said that the muck and dirt from the bottom was placed on the banks of Delray, that Captain Anderson had extra fill and he contacted the city officials as to putting more dirt on the east side north of Atlantic Avenue. They said what they had was sufficient so no additional fill was used. That area still floods today."

Newcomers often ask, "How did Boca Raton get its name? I can't believe it actually literally meant 'Mouth of the Rat' in Spanish." Perhaps the following is an explanation. On historic maps of coastal southeastern Florida, there is a notation of an outlet of water that flowed into the sea. It had sharp rocks at its mouth. The location on those maps actually indicated that it was much closer to and just north of Miami and Biscayne Bay than to Boca Raton. One can only imagine how this mistake could have been made. Perhaps it happened like this during the Spanish Contact Period, circa 1610.

Sailing north along the Florida coastline on a Spanish galleon during the early 17th century, the captain stood on the deck near the railing with one knee bent and one foot on the hatch cover. Using his spyglass, he anxiously searched the shoreline for a place to take his ship to safety during a quick-forming summer ocean storm.

"There," he pointed. "Steer the ship to that opening. The maps say that there is a sharp-edged opening of water. Let us go there and see if there is a safe harbor for us before the storm comes upon us. It must be Boca Ratones."

"But, capitán," urged his officer, "Boca Ratones is farther south, not here. We are too far north."

"Perhaps, young man, but we have no time. We will enter the waterway and see for ourselves."

They quickly turned the ship directly west toward shore as the winds grew stronger from the southeast and the sailing vessel rode the rising frothy waves which were cresting very fast.

"Be careful at the wheel," roared the captain above the noise of the wailing winds. "Don't lose control. We are close. Drop anchor there and send a small boat in to see what awaits us," he ordered to his subordinate.

"Si, mi capitán," responded the assistant.

"If what you find is adequate for us to sail into, signal with the lantern so we can hurry before this storm breaks."

"Si, capitán," the assistant saluted crisply.

In a very short time, the boat reached the outlet and disappeared past the rocks beyond the dune. The impatient captain paced the deck, watching the churning, darkening clouds to the east.

"I hope 'Señor Imbécil' didn't get lost," commented the captain to no one. "His grandfather, a cartographer, got everything mixed up at Puerto Rico and San Juan back in Christopher Columbus' time. I hope stupidity is not inherited."

"There, capitán," pointed the lookout with one eye closed, the other looking through the long spyglass, "on the dune. The signal. See? It means there is safety. Shall I have the anchor weighed?"

"Si," yelled the captain to his lookout. "Have the anchor raised and let us sail slowly into the outlet. Quickly now."

As the small sailing ship entered the opening at the shore, the lookout pointed north.

"Hard to starboard," instructed the captain. "Into the lagoon. Drop the sails and anchor. We will stay here until the storm passes. We are safe," he called out with relief.

"Si, capitán," responded his officer with a proper salute.

The storm lasted into the night and beyond.

The next day, as the captain came up to the deck from his quarters, he saw the smiling faces of his crew.

"Capitán," one came to him excitedly, "look at the coconut trees, the fruit trees, and the crystal clear waters of this beautiful lagoon. This is heaven," he exclaimed.

"Well," responded the captain proudly, "I believe we have found the true Boca Ratones location. And this, in the name of Spain, I will call Boca Ratones Lagoon!"

"And what shall we name the river to the north that feeds this lagoon, mi capitán, so that we may have it drawn on the official maps for posterity?" requested the executive officer.

"Let me think of some really exciting name," replied the captain, as he rubbed his chin, staring into the distance, "…something we can easily remember."

"I know," said the officer. "Why not name it Spanish River so that the British can't claim the name?"

"Terrific," replied the captain. "It's kind of catchy…yes…Spanish River. That's it!"

And so, perhaps or perhaps not, this is how Boca Raton Lagoon got its name, and how the stream got the name Spanish River.

It is likely that the body of water now known as Lake Boca Raton carried the name Boca Ratones Lagoon for more than 300 years, until 1924 when Addison Mizner built the Cloisters Inn and must have decided, along with his brother, Wilson, that their marketing program would be more effective if it was named Lake Boca Raton, and not Boca Ratones. And since they were more concerned with selling their land than interpreting Spanish lore, they used Boca Raton. And now, as is fitting, Boca Raton uses his name "Addison and Mizner" in its marketing.

My three brothers and I were all born in Delray Beach. Ernie, the eldest, enlisted in the U.S. Navy after high school. The rest of us were too young.

Roy, the second eldest, was born in 1930. They both lived here with our parents through the Great Depression as youngsters, attended Delray Beach public schools, and graduated from Delray Beach High School, Ernie in 1942 and Roy in 1948. Roy obtained his degree in architecture from Georgia Tech and, following his military service in the U.S. Air Force, returned to Delray Beach. He associated with the respected firm of Kenneth Jacobson, Architect, and became extensively involved in the city's affairs and civic organizations. A civic leader for more than forty years, he was responsible for initiating many events that formed the foundation of the culture and helped shape the milieu of Delray Beach, including such town trademarks like the Delray Affair, the city's Winter Arts Festival, and the Pro-Am Benefit Golf Tournament at the Dunes Community. He has also designed many of the city's best and more prominent buildings.

In 1972, he was commissioned to design the Town Hall and public buildings of Highland Beach. Roy recently described to me the conditions of the region during those days of his youth when there were only about 3,000 people in Delray Beach and maybe 750 in Boca Raton.

"By the time I was nine or ten, I remember that we youngsters, who lived in this small seaside town, would go to the beach all summer. We would simply walk east across the sandy fields, the railroad…there were few homes then…and when we got to the 'canal,' we'd walk most of the way across through the mud. It was mostly swampland back then, not flowing water.

After we got across the canal, we would keep walking, maybe swim ten or twenty feet across Spanish River and walk the rest of the way to the beach. All of the Gleason Street area was swampland nearly to the dunes.

Until the WPA built a small bridge across the canal during the 1930s, we had to use the 'lighter,' where locals pulled ourselves, our horses and mules, and anything else across the canal. Even so, that area was mostly mud and swamp. As youngsters, it was actually more adventurous to 'walk' across the muddy canal. Back then, when our family drove to picnics at the Boynton Beach, Boca Raton or Palm Beach Inlets, we actually 'walked' across the inlets because they were so mud-filled. We used to find all sorts of sea life. We collected shells, starfish, sand dollars, sea urchins, and all sorts of goodies on the beaches back then. They were everywhere. It was a great time and place to be a youngster, sort of 'Huckleberry Finn.'"

During the war, the U.S. Government widened, deepened, and straightened the Intracoastal Waterway. I think they did that to provide a better and safer shipping route for supplies to the ports.

In the early 1950s, developers, envisioning upper scale homesites, began to change the area between the Intracoastal Waterway and the Atlantic Ocean which locals didn't really consider valuable land. It was very much a swamp right where Spanish River flooded the area most of the time, especially during the rainy seasons. Very quickly, the shoreline was lined with steel "sheet piling" to hold the land in place while work was done. Once in place, giant dredges and draglines excavated the waterway's bottom and east shoreline, lifting and placing the excavated soil gathered behind the pilings and filling in the land where Venetian Drive, Gleason Street, Andrews Avenue, and all those land areas north and south of Atlantic Avenue have small 'fingerlets' of boating waterways. Homes in this area were selling in the mid to late 1950s for twice the price of those west of the Intracoastal. Part of that was because each house east of the Intracoastal had to be built on pilings, wood poles, or concrete posts driven into the earth to hold up the heavy houses. Seawalls of concrete replaced the sheet piling used during the landfill operations. The south side of East Atlantic Avenue, east of the waterway, the "canal," was named Reid's Village after the developer of that tract. North of Atlantic Avenue, Robert Westerman developed waterfront home sites and waterway "fingerlets" as far north as the FIND (Federal Intracoastal Navigational District) spoilage area, just south of George Bush Boulevard. Those home sites sold at what was considered very expensive, $20,000, with homes sold in the $30,000s and $40,000s. Of course, those prices were more than double the average price of a home in America. Today, those home sites are bought at prices ranging from $600,000 to $1.5 million or more, with homes and land valued closer to $2-$3 million.

I recall when we designed and built the Waterway North condominiums at the Intracoastal just north of George Bush Boulevard. It was in 1982. We had "spot," or random, soil borings taken, and based on those engineering tests, we planned our costs based on a series of pilings about 35 feet deep.

As it turned out, we were astonished when several of the pilings were, seemingly endlessly, driven into the old Spanish River bed. As a consequence, I stood and watched piling after piling being driven into the ground. At 36 feet deep, it "disappeared."

As I sadly watched the pile driver sink the pilings into the mud, and watched the crew place another piling on top of the first, then watched a total of 60-70 feet of piling and thousands of dollars disappear, I thought of my development experiences in Atlanta where we didn't have to drive pilings "to China." Life got very complicated thereafter as costs skyrocketed over budget. Fortunately, most, but not all, of the pilings avoided the haunting presence of "old Spanish River." Such were the dangers of modern land developers over or near the old Spanish River bed.

An Interview
with
William Koch, Jr.

"There wasn't much to do here in the 1930s. The place was mostly sand and palmettos—and lots of farms. This was really a farming area."

Bill Koch, Jr. and his parents first came to visit Palm Beach County from Ann Arbor, Michigan in the mid-1920s when the local economy was booming. Interestingly, they had a summer home in Port Huron, the same town as the founder of Boynton Beach, Major Nathan Boynton. In Palm Beach, they stayed at the Royal Poinciana Hotel and, in the early 1930s, Bill Koch's father, Dr. Koch, built a house on the ocean in Delray Beach, just south of what is now George Bush Boulevard, a dirt two-lane road into the 1960s.

Bill Koch, well-known in the area and now in his early eighties, is in his 34th year as Mayor of Gulf Stream and remains robust and active. He and his son, Bill III, operate a real estate brokerage company on East Atlantic Avenue.

Still lean and tall, William Koch, Jr. remains a prominent citizen in the area and has extensive knowledge of South Florida, mostly from his personal experience. In addition to being Mayor of the Town of Gulf Stream for 34 years, which must be a record of some sort, Mr. Koch was on the original fund-raising board of the Gulf Stream Hospital Association from 1947 to 1957 which was raising money to build a regional hospital, now Bethesda Memorial Hospital. He continued to serve on the hospital's operating board in various capacities since its origins.

He told me as we visited recently,

"On Saturdays in the late '30s, my teenage friends, Hackney Allen, Jimmy Smith and I would go over to the polo fields in Gulf Stream and pick up a few of the broken and well-used polo mallets that had been thrown away. The wealthy polo-playing families like the Phipps and Igleharts, all 'ten goal,' the highest rating for polo players, played on their private fields for their own enjoyment.

We had a .22 rifle too. We weren't allowed to hunt along the beach in Delray then, so we drove down to 'Jap Rocks,' played and hunted on the dune and rocky shores there.

Nobody lived in between Delray and Boca along the beach. There was nothing there. The beach road was mostly gone on the dune, so we'd drive up on the dune and go hunting for rabbits, quail or snakes. There were lots of rattlesnakes on the dune, and the palmettos, sea oats and sea grapes provided plenty of cover for small game. So, we hunted nearly every weekend that we could get there. Other younger guys, like Eddie George, the Millers, and Ernie and Zicky Simon, would swim at 'Jap Rocks.' And we did too.

We used to swim under the rock overhang to spear lobsters. Spearing was legal then, and there were more lobsters than anybody could eat in those days.

There wasn't a Highland Beach then, and that whole area was open country. The county had just one constable to patrol all of A1A and South Palm Beach County.

The way we hunted was simple. We'd take the car down A1A south of Delray, and once we got out of town, one of us would drive and the other two would sit on the front fender, passing the .22 back and forth if we saw something—anything—move.

The ocean was on one side, the palmettos on the other, and when we could, we were on the dune, driving right along the top wherever it hadn't been washed out in the 1928 hurricane. Needless to say, we often got stuck in the sand. Where the new A1A was, we'd park the car and walk up the dune and hunt on foot. We used to get a lot of rabbits and quail on those Saturday afternoons. And we weren't the only guys doing it.

One Saturday, while we were hunting, the county constable caught us firing the gun.

'Y'all be careful now, y'hear,' he told us. And we'd promise we'd be careful. And since he knew all of us in the area and our parents, he drove on.

As another pastime, we'd get our polo mallets, sit on the front car fenders, drive down A1A to 'Jap Rocks' and play 'Crab Polo Games.' I mean, there were thousands and thousands of big blue land crabs that would cross A1A. And they were big—they were huge, and they were bright blue. They weren't like sea crabs that we eat in restaurants. They had big round bodies, not flat, and they stood their ground and opened their big claws when they felt threatened. They would spread out and snap those claws. I guess when their claws were spread out, some were more than a foot across. And they would scare the hell out of most people. So, we would go down to 'Jap Rocks' at night and, riding on the front fenders, wallop the crabs with the polo mallet. We would see hundreds of them and hit every one we could. And the car tires would run over some more. We had to be careful 'cause those claws blew out the tires sometimes.

That's what I remember about 'Jap Rocks' when I was a lad. There wasn't much to do. That area was really unsettled. Nothing there but wildlife and crabs, hunting with our .22 and fishing. Most wildlife in the area was small game like rabbits, quail, and all kinds of birds. And there were lots of all of these varieties of wildlife. There weren't many larger animals here during the '30s. Most had been driven away or killed. There were occasional panthers found west on some farms or in the woods near the farms along State Road 441 where they were scrounging for leftover food the farm workers would leave after they ate their meals in the fields.

During the late '40s and early '50s, it was really hot here, especially in the summer. And of course, there wasn't any central air-conditioning. There wasn't much in the way of storm drainage, either. There were places where water stood as prime breeding grounds of mosquitoes and gnats. They were so thick that they'd cover your arms solid. Nobody wore short pants then…didn't wear short sleeves much either. The stinging gnats and mosquitoes were "deadly" and everywhere. You didn't dare sit in the shade unless there was a strong wind or they'd drive you crazy. The area where Highland Beach is located now was the mosquito and land crab capital of Palm Beach County."

One of millions of one-foot wide land crabs
Courtesy of Highland Beach Archives

There was a place in Delray called Frog Alley, along Southwest Fifth Avenue. Its original name was Blackmer Street, named after an early settler from Detroit who chaired the six-person committee that renamed the town of Linton to Delray. He continued,

> "Well, the worst breeding place for mosquitoes was Frog Alley. It got its name because it was low-lying land that had sitting pools of water where mosquitoes bred every time there was a heavy rain."

Frogs, not being totally dumb, moved into this mosquito cornucopia, devoured as many as possible, leaving some for the thousands of buzzing four-winged dragon flies, and made that area their home and breeding grounds. You could hear frogs croaking all over town when it rained. Frog Alley was the source for all the townsfolk of a cacophony of rhythmic croaking by the thousands of happy fat frogs encamped there, joyously serenading the neighborhood and celebrating the latest rains as they devoured the latest crop of mosquitoes. Today, the storm drainage systems are so comprehensive and efficient that hardly any rainwater stands in the region like it did in the 1930s, and into the 1950s.
Bill resumed with his thoughts,

> "In the late 1930s, I remember a couple of houses were built on the beach in what is now north Highland Beach. One was the Collier family house."

I interjected,

"Yes, that's the same Collier family that settled in southwest Florida and owned most of Collier County."

Bill replied,

"Still do. They were very wealthy, and Mr. Collier was into racing cars, I remember."

I recalled,

"Yes, I remember that too. They had two sons, Sam, Jr. and Dick. Sam was one of my best friends in Delray Elementary School. 'Dickie' was a year or two younger, I believe. My cousin Rodney and I remember Sam's tenth birthday party. Mrs. Collier was really beautiful and very, very nice. She gave us all special beanie caps at the party. We were very close. Mrs. Collier and my mother were close too, and both were good friends of Mr. and Mrs. Forrest Lattner, who came from St. Louis every winter.

Bill resumed,

"Well, their house and one other, I recall, were the only two houses and a duplex between Delray and Boca in those days.

After graduating from Delray Beach High School in 1940, I enrolled at Rollins College in Winter Park. After a year of college, World War II intervened, and like most young men in America, I volunteered to fight in the war. I enlisted in the U.S. Army Air Corps. During the war, we flew 28 missions in B-17s and B-24s over Germany with the Eighth Air Corps, based in England."

World War II B-24 Bomber, piloted by William Koch Jr. 1944
Courtesy of William Koch Jr. archives

Bill was a recipient of the coveted Distinguished Flying Cross and Air Medal. Following his stint in the Air Corps, Bill returned to Rollins College to complete his education. As they say, there is no such thing as a coincidence, and Bill, still a lucky, young man, met a beautiful Rollins co-ed who caught his eye, Miss Freddie Sommer of Peoria, Illinois. They quickly fell in love. In 1949 they were married in the Rollins Chapel. After Bill worked in Milwaukee for nearly a year, they returned to Florida and resided on the beach in Delray Beach. He smiled and continued,

> "When I came back to Delray after the war, the area was really a busy farming area. The farms had all expanded to help feed the armed forces and Europe too. The Butts' farms were among the biggest. Marshall DeWitt was busy at the bank in Delray, and a son-in-law of the Butts family as was Tom Fleming. They both took part in running the farms. Rudy Blank had a large farm, I remember, and 'Cassie' Lyons had a big farm west of Boca Raton." (Butts Road in Boca Raton led to their farming village. Lyons Road is the location of that farm as is Clint Moore Road to the Clint Moore farm.)

> In the 1930s, Clint Moore, whose father had operated a big dredge business digging drainage canals in Broward County, moved up here and started dredging drainage canals west of town. He ended up buying and farming about 4,000 acres out by Route 441. I guess his land cost was pretty low back then, maybe less than $20 per acre. After I returned from Milwaukee, I bought into the Clint Moore Farm and became their partner. That's how I got started in the farming and land business.

> As development began to accelerate in the 1960s and 1970s, there was much activity and change in the area. In 1960, I was appointed to serve on the Palm Beach County Zoning Commission, when they took zoning in the county out of politics. At that time, Gulf Stream and Delray Beach residents determined to keep their communities mostly single-family. In fact, we asked the Gulf Stream beach residents to agree to downzone their land from multi-family to single-family and, although they may have given up future value, they agreed in order to retain the community culture.

> In Highland Beach there weren't many single-family residents, and those who came and bought tracts of land were from New York, New Jersey, and Chicago, Illinois where high-rise co-ops and condominiums were customary and enriching. So there was little resistance to high-rise zoning requests in Highland Beach in those days."

Visits by the
Rich and Famous

For years, very little was built on the ocean. Probably the first major development in South Palm Beach County was the Gulfstream Golf Club in Gulfstream, built in 1926.

Gertrude Vanderbilt and her brother, who spent the winters in Palm Beach, determined in the mid-1920s, during the "Land Boom," that "Palm Beach was getting too crowded." So, they looked south, to the northern section of Delray Beach, and purchased a large tract of land. Its boundary actually extended from the ocean to what is now Seacrest Boulevard, easily two to three miles to the west. On the dune, they built the beautiful, Moorish-style, Mizner designed, Gulfstream Club, including a fine golf course and clubhouse.

Gertrude and her husband, W.S. Webb, had a son, Jake, who is famous locally for his World War II escapades and his frequent visits to Bill Kraus's Arcade Tap Room in downtown Delray Beach. The Arcade was a favorite watering hole of the rich and famous who spent winters in Delray Beach. In those days, Palm Beach conservative elitists preferred that the Hollywood celebrities "not stay over in Palm Beach" even though some performed in the Royal Palm Beach Playhouse.

Jake Webb, easily one of the most fascinating characters I've ever met, recalled many memories to me during a four-hour videotaped interview. Jake started right in with,

> "Many really fun and famous people came to Delray Beach during the winter season, back in those days. There were lots of movie stars, famous golfers and, of course, Delray's own cartoonist colony.

Bob Hope, Bing Crosby, Joe Kennedy and his girlfriend Gloria Swanson and I would go to the Arcade Tap Room where we'd get together for drinks and dinner throughout the winter seasons during the 1930s and '40s. After awhile, we'd go for a walk down to Bob's Bar and Restaurant in your family's building, across the railroad tracks, and have drinks while Bing would lead us in singing. Boy, those were the winters."

During World War II, Jake got caught impersonating an U.S. Army Colonel in uniform and was nearly sent to Ft. Leavenworth Prison. Lucky for him, the Vanderbilts kept him out of jail. He always joked about his escapades. Actually, Jake was quite a local celebrity. He was generous and was always part of the town's community. He loved the New York Yankees so much that he sponsored a semi-pro team in Delray and named it "The Delray Beach Yankees." He even bought authentic Yankees uniforms directly through their manager, Casey Stengel. My brother, Ernie, who played on the team, recalled,

"Jake was a terrific guy, and spared no expense. There wasn't much money around, but he was getting monthly trust payments which he spent on all of us. He bought gloves, balls, bats, real baseball shoes, catcher's equipment, and he even drove us to away games. In those days, Delray had a baseball stadium with covered bleachers. The City Hall is located on that spot today. Homeruns into left field landed on N.W. First Avenue, if hit hard enough.

When the other teams north to Vero Beach and south to Miami got in financial difficulty, Jake, wanting to keep the league going, ended up buying those teams. And, in the end, I think he owned the whole league. It got to where he was cheering both teams at every game."

Movie stars joined the locals who were fun and comfortable with their presence, appreciating the respect they received for their privacy. Golfing celebrities also frequented Delray Beach during the winter, drawn by Toney Penna, one of America's most famous golfers, and one of Delray's most beloved citizens. He later moved to Jupiter Island in the mid-1950s. Among his friends who joined him at the Arcade Tap Room were Bob Hope, Perry Como, Kirk Douglas, Danny Kaye, Lon Chaney, Sam Snead, and Gene Sarazen, whose daughter, Mary Ann, now of Naples, was in my classes at Delray Elementary School. Dean Martin, Jerry Lewis and other great stars also came to visit.

Delray was a truly upscale winter season resort village that attracted the rich, the famous, and those who were both.

Delray resident Toney Penna, top golfer and designer,
entertaining the crowds in 1947
Courtesy of Delray Beach Historical Society

PART FOUR
1949 - 2003

Highland Beach Water Tower, 2002
Courtesy Of Highland Beach Archives

The Genesis of
Incorporated Highland Beach
Post-World War II into the 1950s

It was during the years following the end of World War II that events took place that would dramatically change forever the character, demo-graphics, geography, culture and architecture of Highland Beach, still called "Jap Rocks" by the locals. Most of the personnel stationed at Boca Raton's radar training base had left to return to their homes. There was a huge reduction of local activity for just a few years, as it turned out.

Very few people actually lived in the area, an unincorporated "county pocket," between Delray Beach and Boca Raton, east of the Intracoastal Waterway. Much of the coastal region of southeast Florida north of Miami and Ft. Lauderdale was a sparsely populated, pleasant and quiet beachside place to live, work, and raise a family. Most of the land to the west was devoted to farming vegetables, principally high quality beans, and later, gladioli. The quality of life for those who had chosen to live in the region between Palm Beach and Miami was peaceful and simple. While there were few restaurants, theaters, and other social places in the area, and few if any hospitals, what was in the area adequately fulfilled the needs of most residents. They chose the region for health reasons, or because they wanted to live and work in that milieu, during the temperate seasons away from the harsh, cold winters in the North. During the post-war period and into the early 1950s, few people came to the region to gain riches, to develop properties, to maximize profits, or focus on investments. That all came later.

Four years after the end of World War II, land development was dynamically growing in many urban centers in Northern metropolitan regions. Housing starts were exploding in New England, the Midwest, New York, New Jersey, and Pennsylvania.

The hot and humid Southland was still relatively undiscovered and unappealing. Air-conditioning was non-existent. Little real estate development was taking place in South Florida simply because there was no demand for housing of any consequence. It was too hot for too long during the year. The housing sector of southeast Florida was a non-starter. One could have said that the area was in a stagnation period or, perhaps, in a form of economic recession once all the military had left. The factors that would prompt significant demand for land and housing and shopping centers, a relatively new phenomenon, were not yet in place. But very shortly, they would be.

In 1940, only 723 people lived in Boca Raton, perhaps 30 in Highland Beach, 1,326 in Boynton Beach, and Delray Beach, the most developed of the area's towns, counted only 3,661. Ten years later, in 1950, Boca's population grew to 992, a respectable but not significant 37.2%, or 3.72% per year. Delray Beach, on the other hand, grew to 6,264, a whopping 72.3% during the same period, twice Boca's rate. Still, all of South Palm Beach County had few citizens, a miniscule total of only 9,798. Delray Beach, with its Midwestern flavor, and Boca Raton, a town of little appeal at the time were a farming area that provided few necessities. There were few inhabitants beyond the hotel workers and farm laborers, and hardly any activity. During the 1950s, Boynton Beach was nicknamed "Borington," Delray was labeled "Dullray," and since no one ever noticed Boca Raton, no one even bothered to give it a nickname at all.

Soon, however, central air-conditioning would arrive to make living quite pleasant in these tropical climes overcoming its mosquitoes, gnats, bugs, and the heat and humidity which was about 85% all summer. As a result, locals no longer had to rely on screened windows in which even the smallest hole would allow thousands of bugs into the house.

By the 1960s, new Federal VA and Social Security "transfer payments" delivered to veterans and others at retirement age would soon begin to flow into South Florida in huge amounts each month, providing an enormous influx into savings accounts and a stable source of capital just waiting to be tapped by those seeking wealth who, like moths to a flame, came a-courting. Consequently, all kinds of people began moving to the "Sun Belt" from the "Rust Belt." Retirees, service workers, construction workers, and opportunists began arriving almost non-stop. President Eisenhower's Interstate Highway System was being built across the nation, making long distance auto-travel much easier. Jet airplanes were speeding up the travel experience from New York to Miami and Ft. Lauderdale airports, bringing more and more people to South Florida. During the late 1940s and into the late 1950s, most of the growth and land development was taking place in Miami, Ft. Lauderdale and Pompano—all south of Highland

Beach. But interest was indeed rapidly moving north from Miami.

It was much cheaper to fly to Miami and Ft. Lauderdale from New York than to Tampa. It was also cheaper to fly from Chicago to Tampa than from Chicago to Miami. Interstate 95 connected New York to southeast Florida, and I-75 connected Chicago directly to Tampa, Sarasota, and Ft. Myers. These are the major reasons why southeastern Florida is so heavily populated with Northeasterners, and Tampa-Sarasota is more Midwestern.

There were very few people living within the so-called county pockets of unincorporated land, including what is now known as Highland Beach. Most had first come to southeast Florida on vacation, loved their winter season and the area, and chose to stay permanently or return yearly. Most came to retire.

Some purchased small parcels of land on which to build their winter cottages. In those days, most land parcels available were 100 feet wide and extended hundreds of feet from the beach to the Intracoastal Waterway and configured in a long east-west and narrow north-south shape. Those parcels in the north and south portions, still in the unincorporated county, were occupied by mostly small single-family homes, usually wood-framed, on the dune to maximize the ocean views and breezes. The settlers chose to be near the existing towns of Delray Beach and Boca Raton for shopping, convenience to bridges and, in time, to hook on to these cities' water and sewage lines. Before that, all had their own wells and septic tanks. It would have been very difficult to build a home, even a winter season home, on the west side of A1A during the 1940s and even into the 1970s because the land was so low, filled with swamp-land, thickly covered with mangroves and undergrowth, generally unstable, very hot, and thus undesirable. There was not equipment available in the area capable of moving earth like this or clearing such land. Worse, trying to exist on the leeward side of the dunes, with little or no sea breezes, and total infestation of mosquitoes, gnats, and large and abundant large crabs would have been so unpleasant as to make that choice borderline stupid. So, since those who came there were quite bright and knowledgeable, there were houses only on the dunes.

Most of the land from Boca Raton to Delray Beach and between the Intracoastal Waterway and the Atlantic Ocean at that time was owned by just a handful of people. Records indicate that from the late 1940s until the 1970s only three or four parties controlled the bulk of what is now Highland Beach land, mainly in the center of the town's three-mile boundaries. They owned or controlled hundreds of acres from the ocean to the Intracoastal in large parcels, all of which was unincorporated, virtually unzoned, and not served by utilities except for electricity. There were no sewer lines, no water, and no drainage. On the east side of Highway A1A, which bisected all the land tracts, was the Atlantic Ocean and its high beach dunes; on the west was the low swampland between the two-lane state highway and the Intracoastal.

Value of such land in the post-war years was still relatively very low. Land in Delray Beach was far more expensive than in Highland Beach at the time. In the late 1940s, an oceanfront lot in Delray Beach sold for $10,000. In Highland Beach, a parcel extending a few hundred feet from the ocean to A1A would sell for $5,000. In the 1950s, after incorporation, some parcels sold for $8,000 to $10,000. Other parcels, some 1200 feet deep, that extended to the Intracoastal sold for $20,000, depending on the location and quality of the land. In Delray Beach, at the same time, shallower homesites extending from the ocean to A1A were selling for $30,000. As a frame of reference, the average price of a home in America in 1946 was $4,500, far, far lower than today's average price of $185,000. In 1972, the average price of a home in America was still below $20,000, at $17,500.

It is very important to understand that there was little desire in the county government to spend large amounts of money to drain the mostly vacant, then unpromising lands east of the Intracoastal in unincorporated Highland Beach. There was no shortage of oceanfront land in the region from north of Palm Beach to Miami. Many desirable locations were still available.

Yet, there were those who invested in "Jap Rocks" because it was so lovely, quiet and serene. There were large tracts available and they were relatively inexpensive. And the area was nestled between its reputable neighbors. The few speculators who acquired most of the area of central Highland Beach saw, instead, great opportunity, and a future of development opportunities. Immediately to the north, was the commercial center of Delray Beach. To the south was the fabulous Boca Raton Hotel and Club. Both provided services and other amenities for these new residents. The single-family residents of Highland Beach had their solitude, something considered very desirable to those who located there during the late 1940s, and even during the quiet 1950s. But the next twenty years would be a period of extraordinary change.

—◄◙◙◙◙►—

An example of the diversity in families coming to coastal southeast Florida after World War II is the Mario Petruzzelli family. Mario, a language school-teacher at Atlantic City High School in New Jersey, earned $3,500 per year. Those were post-war years when salaries were still influenced by the economic climate of the Great Depression. The Petruzzelli family lived on the waterfront in Ventnor, New Jersey, as Mario, even then, preferred living near the water. Times were still very difficult for most Americans at the end of the war. Massive war material production seemed to cease immediately in 1945 causing many workers to lose their jobs. Teaching was still secure.

It was Christmas vacation of that year, when gas rations were ended, that the Petruzzelli family first came to Palm Beach County, Florida. Mario visited Delray Beach and Boca Raton, driving along A1A through what would become Highland Beach. Six months later, during the summer of 1946, he returned to the area with his sons, Frank and Al, and purchased a parcel of magnificent land with 200 feet fronting the Atlantic Ocean. It stretched some 1,200 feet west past A1A to the east bank of Lake Wyman and the Intracoastal Waterway. Most of his purchase was west of the highway with very rich soil and failing exotic fruit trees planted by the owners, which had been grown to provide fruit to the owners' health stores "back home" in Cleveland. However, the soil and plantings were already contaminated by salt intrusion and the trees bore no fruit. Thus, the owners were anxious to sell their nearly six-acres of land bounded at both ends by water. As in the preceding four decades, land was generally purchased in the area for use as a homesite or for farming, not necessarily for investment. At what was a fair price at the time, Mario Petruzzelli purchased his parcel for $34,000.

Then, in 1947, the Petruzzelli family purchased a small trailer for $300 in which they lived while Mr. Petruzzelli and his sons, Frank and Al, built a duplex and a cottage behind the trailer on the west side of A1A. Their land, very near the northern city limits of Boca Raton, was then in a county "pocket," that is, unincorporated Palm Beach County. There were few regulations in those days governing construction of one's home. For water, the family drilled a well into the ground some 300 feet west of A1A and 700 feet east of the Intracoastal. Because the land was bordered by the waterway and was so low, they found relatively clear water at just thirteen feet down. Typically, purification was not sought, but the orange, peat-colored water tasted so bad that they used buckets and buckets of limes to change the water's taste. "We just assumed water was water with nothing to worry about, not like today's pollution issues." The Palm Beach County health inspector noted that "you're still alive so the water must be okay!"

The same year, 1947, that Mario Petruzzelli placed his trailer and built his duplex, he also obtained a real estate license and opened his "sales shack." His move from Ventnor, New Jersey to South Florida was complete.

Al Petruzzelli, the younger son, was a friend of my brother Charlie and me at Seacrest High School. Back then, Seacrest, now Atlantic High School, had only 320 students—all white—and from Boca Raton, Delray Beach and Boynton Beach. It became a consolidated school in 1949. Students in the 9th through 12th grades from all three cities grew close. Of the 320 students, perhaps 10 lived in Boca Raton.

Al, who has been my friend since the early 1950s, shared his family story with me.

> "When we settled into our trailer, there was jungle all around us. The mosquitoes and gnats were terrible. We killed rattlesnakes. Bobcats and quail were in abundance; fish were for the asking. The water, the trees, and even the air were laden with salt. Air-conditioning didn't exist so windows had to be totally screened and covered. Not even a small hole in the screens could be allowed or the gnats and mosquitoes would swarm all through our trailer. Many plants and trees were unable to survive the salty air. Our clothes got sticky, and with the high humidity, salt penetrated everything. My mother was not in good health and

we did not have health insurance to help us with her medical expenses. So, in 1949, my father sold 125 front feet, the entire length of our land, at a loss, for $150 per foot. At the time, few people were buying land here. We struggled. It was hard in those days. Mom increasingly weakened and passed on.

In 1956, our property was annexed into Boca Raton. Had we been located further north, we would likely have been annexed into Highland Beach.

After I graduated from Seacrest in 1953, I went into the service. During college, I got my real estate license and sold 2,000 acres in Polk City. In 1959, I returned home and joined my dad in the real estate business. The timing was fortuitous. Within a decade the real estate brokerage business really got exciting in this area."

It was also fortuitous for Al that his father had chosen to locate his home and his real estate office right on the west side of Highway A1A where it stays as Petruzzelli Realty even to this writing some 55 years later, making their office something of a current "historical landmark" in this youthful region that honors such recent events unlike older Northern cities.

The Petruzzelli Realty office, so prominent in its location, easily pre-empted other such brokerage offices when prospective buyers came to purchase oceanfront or Intracoastal Waterway frontage parcels in the Highland Beach area. With demand beginning to escalate from the post-war late 1940s, a broker with intimate local knowledge and familiarity could be a valuable asset to his prospects. Being at the locale of some of the most valuable waterfront land in South Florida was of major advantage to this gregarious, likeable "hometown boy."

Land values for oceanfront land between Delray Beach and Boca Raton increased steadily and extraordinarily during the late 1960s through the end of the century.

"We watched values selling for $100 per front foot in the late-1940s triple to $300 in the 1960s. Then, as larger tracts extending from the ocean to the Intracoastal Waterway were bought for high-rise condominiums, the prices really skyrocketed."

Al, a very much-involved adviser, consultant and broker, availed himself wisely in many land transactions, sometimes selling the same parcel two and three times.

"During the boom beginning in the late-1960s, prices escalated to $500 per front foot. Then, in the 1970s, prices went even higher, as high as $1,000 per front foot. We really were amazed at the continuing escalation. We didn't see how it could continue and, sure enough, following the oil crisis years of the mid-1970s, prices began to level off and even slightly receded. During the early 1980s, with interest rates as high as 22%, prices went down, but not a great deal. We sold some parcels somewhat lower in those years. Still, that's a lot of money, to be sure."

The 1980s were significantly impacted by high interest rates and the Tax Reform Act of 1986 which almost devastated the commercial real estate market. American banks and especially Savings and Loans were in deep trouble. Some stopped funding their construction loans, causing building construction to slow down, and sometimes stop before they were complete. It took several painful years for the financial world to right itself. Some condominium developments in Highland Beach were not finished, and some sold off units at discount prices. Al added,

"Then, later when the whole world seemed to have huge amounts of money, beginning in the 1990s, expansion of Highland Beach development resumed at even higher prices. In the late 1980s, we were pricing land by the square foot and land cost per unit instead of by the length of frontage on the ocean or Ocean Boulevard/A1A. During the 1990s, prices for condominiums and luxury homes, even mansions, escalated from hundreds of thousands of dollars, and now for the first time, to the millions. We sold tracts in the range of the 'unbelievable.' We were now seeing land values in the range of $20,000 per front foot. It was amazing. But it was to get even higher. By the year 2002, prices had gone beyond reality, with some parcels selling as high as $40,000 per front foot, or $4,000,000 for a 100 foot wide lot, ocean to Ocean Boulevard.

Sandy, I've been selling land here for most of my life, over forty years, and I'm always surprised. I've probably brokered the majority of all the real estate sales of raw land during that period of time. I didn't broker many individual condominium sales because those were done directly by the developers. What continues to amaze me is that somehow virtually everyone from seller to developer to individual apartment buyer has made lots of money, either in profits when they sold—and often repurchased—to simply an enormous value increase in the value of their home. It's been an unusually wonderful place to invest as well as a beautiful place to live, not to mention the life-long friends I have made and enjoyed. As I stand here observing, I think that in the long term, allowing for some bumps along the way, in all likelihood it's going to continue to increase substantially in value."

In 1949, the owners within Highland Beach, twenty-one voters in all, came to the very significant decision to incorporate their collective lands into a state-chartered town and name it Highland Beach, reflecting their very high ocean dunes. The principal reason given is that they wanted to control their own water supplies separated from the politics of their neighbors to the north and south. Perhaps some felt strongly about the ease of obtaining high density rezoning without involvement of the county or the neighbors' politics as well. It wasn't a unanimous decision to be sure. Those folks whose homes abutted Boca Raton felt that they'd be better served if they connected to that city's utility system and stayed in the county. Since all Highland Beach lands were served with septic tanks and private wells, their individual locations influenced their opinions. Salination of their well water was becoming a problem. Moreover, the security provided by those cities' police departments was far more impressive than the occasional visit by a county sheriff's constable. Most of the north half-mile, named Bird's Beach after its owner, was vacant. The few others who lived in the north end felt the same way toward Delray Beach as those in the south portion did toward Boca Raton. Still, the bulk of the town's land in the middle was owned by a few investors and speculators who preferred having greater control over their promising land holdings than they would if they annexed into either city. For many years, it was more advantageous and less risky to deal with county government.

In brief, it seemed those at the opposite ends had different interests than those in the center: "Why would it not be better for me to simply hook onto Boca (or Delray's) water line? After all, it's just 100 feet away, and it will be years before we'll get our own system," voiced property owners at the ends.

Others had the opposite argument: "But we can always get water from either city if we want, and we think it's better for our long-term interests if we can control zoning and our own water," responded the three or four major central property owners.

The debate continued even after the town was chartered. Those two issues, zoning and water, stayed on the "front burners" for decades. The first Town Council members, earnest civic-minded individuals, much like pioneers, had to start with very little. They had no buildings, no staff, no police or fire departments, no utilities, no infrastructure of any kind. They hardly had a place out of the rain in which to meet.

Back in the 1930s, a few cottages had been built along the dune by some hearty souls. One of the groups of tourist cottages, named The Blue Waters Inn, was comprised of several simple one-room wood cottages sitting atop what would become an incredibly valuable ocean dune in a few years. To those in Delray Beach, the area would always be sparse and, in a way, desolate. The new town council decided to meet regularly in the home of Rudy Hertwig, manager of The Blue Waters Inn. He was the most experienced of the members and became the de facto Town Manager and host of the council meetings around his kitchen table. He effectively ran the town as its Manager in the Town Council manager form of government for some fifteen years. After all, there were not that many items on any given agenda at first. There were few residents and few newcomers arriving during that period. Most property owners simply wanted to be left alone. They cherished their homes, shopped and dined in Delray Beach or Ft. Lauderdale, and visited The Boca Raton Club. They looked at the ocean from their windows and open decks, and walked the beach. The only problem they faced was the increasing intrusion of salt into their private wells.

Indeed, the real issues that got the attention of the town council members were the issue of potable water and, in time, the issue of rezoning of the land owned by the three or four investor/speculators to multi-family use. They came from Chicago and the Northeast, intent on replicating their high-rise hotels, co-ops, and condominiums. Actually, few, if any, initially opposed that rezoning effort. Few understood what it meant. Growth meant progress in those early years. Those conditions are what prompted the central property owners to press for chartering the town in the first place. After all, they were quite a distance from their neighboring towns, and despite the expense of building a new water plant, trunk line, elevated tank, sewer lines, lift stations and the like, it would be worth it. Otherwise, they'd be at the mercy of "those towns' politicians" who were serving different agendas. They knew that at the least they would have to pay a significant surcharge over and above what citizens and property owners within the two neighboring cities paid. And who could tell how high that could go?

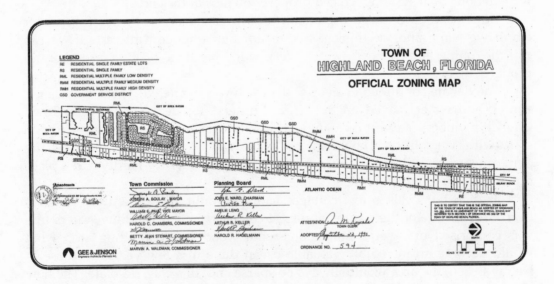

Official Land Zoning Map of Highland Beach
North-South is 2.9 miles
East-West is 600-2000 feet
Courtesy of Highland Beach Historical Society

In the end, water was the determining factor for that vital decision to incorporate, which would cause Highland Beach to become very different from its neighbors in many ways.

Even after the town obtained its charter on February 17, 1949, there were a few land parcels whose owners toward the north and south chose not to be within the original boundaries of the town. One such parcel was that 2,800 foot (more than one-half mile) oceanfront parcel adjacent to Delray Beach.

As the first year of being a legal town progressed, water was still the burning issue of the residents and landowners within Highland Beach. That issue was seriously addressed by the Town Council.

On November 3, 1949, under the leadership of Mayor Robert Totterdale, the first Town Council approved its first water plant bonds and began the construction of its first water plant. The town purchased a parcel of land on the west side of the Intracoastal, on which it would drill its wells, seeking to avoid any possibility of saline intrusion into their source field, had they been on the barrier island.

Even so, the town wisely negotiated supplemental inter-government agreements with both its neighbors in the event of pressure needs and sudden lack of raw water from the wells and the like.

Highland Beach's unique water tank

The Eypel family is a good example of the people who came to Highland Beach soon after its incorporation. In 1950, Arthur Eypel, now 56, and his parents, who had vacationed during the winter on Delray Beach's Nassau Street, decided to purchase two oceanfront lots for $18,000 in Highland Beach on which they would build their dream retirement home. In 1952, they hired respected Delray Beach architect, Richard Hanna and a local builder, Warren Reiff.

The Eypel home was built on the ocean side of A1A on one of the two lots at 3401 South Ocean Boulevard. One must note that the address remains based on being south of Delray Beach. Mr. Eypel decided to sell his second lot to his friend George DeBold for $9,000. In the fifty years since, each lot has increased in value to an astounding three to four million dollars. That means that its value has doubled ten times in fifty years, compounded at the rate of 15%, spanning good times and bad, while providing an extraordinary place to enjoy the finer things in life. But it wasn't always calm and serene for the Eypel family.

Arthur Eypel described the events of the mid-1950s,

> "We had only one major decision back then as we left our driveways for the day. Shall we turn right and drive into Delray for shopping? Or shall we turn left to drive to the Boca Raton Club for lunch? Life was simple, quiet and pleasant—most of the time!

> It was the 1956 hurricane that directly hit Highland Beach. I think they named it Betsy. Back then, we had only 24-hours' notice of hurricanes coming our way. Of course, there was no satellite information, no National Hurricane Center with hourly updates, and no 'Doppler' information. The only warnings were those that came from the hurricane hunters in airplanes flying out of Miami. At that time I believe they were using the four-engine propeller-driven Constellations.

> Betsy? I'll never forget it. We had heavy and unwieldy plywood shutters then, and the wind gusts would flip those sheets as we tried to install them over our windows, nearly tossing my father and me to the ground. The ocean got churning so violently that it literally became white from the unusually high, crashing waves. It was frothing, boiling! Then after a few hours of stronger and stronger winds, the highest waves hit. We battened down the house which, thank the Lord, was built really soundly. My mother filled the bathtub with water; we had canned foods and a small gas stove. The noise throughout the house became deafening. The trees were being whipped into submission. Our wind meter broke when it hit 120 mph. The hurricane seemed to last for days.

The day after it stopped, all we saw was destruction. There weren't many buildings in Highland Beach, but all the trees had taken a real beating. A1A was closed because of the fallen trees. The mangroves across A1A didn't have one little leaf left. All the leaves were gone. Our house had been sandblasted by the winds blowing the beach sand at such high swirling speeds. Because the eye passed directly over us, we felt a strange calm for about thirty minutes. When my father and I went out to look at the damage, the winds came back even stronger from the opposite direction. We lost our electricity and didn't get it back for two weeks. With all the trees down blocking A1A, the electric company had to wait. Of course, there weren't many people in Highland Beach so we didn't get top priority. When we looked at our once grassy lawn, it had more than a foot and a half of beach sand on top of it. It wasn't a pretty sight, especially to my parents. I was just a boy of ten at the time, and it was really exciting for me.

During the 1950s, lots of events were taking place in addition to 'Betsy's visit.' In 1952, there was one multi-family apartment structure built. It wasn't very tall, really. I think it was a co-op, like in New York.

The big issues then were annexation either into Boca Raton or Delray Beach, mainly because of the water issue. In the early years, most Town Council meetings were barely attended and were held in Mr. Hartwig's kitchen.

In 1957, some people came looking at the house next to ours. We later found out that they were Howard Hughes' representatives. They toured the house, wanting absolute privacy, looking for a place for Mr. Hughes to winter with his beautiful girlfriend. That was the most interesting thing that happened to me. I was young then and pretty impressed by their visit."

During the mid-1950s and 1960s, the Town Council decided to rezone much of the land, changing the earlier designations of single-family use to high density. The influence of the handful of non-resident investment owners of most land was very strong. Opposition was non-existent. They were owners who had already developed commercial properties in the Northeast, mainly New York and New Jersey. Their experience with high-rise hotels, motels and residential high-rise buildings convinced them to make certain their local land should also be able to maximize value and profits.

The overwhelmingly successful Levittown experience on Long Island, N.Y. during the late 1940s and 1950s, converting hundreds of acres of Long Island farmland into thousands of identical, inexpensive homes for returning servicemen, convinced Florida land developers that they should seek to maximize the value of their land investment and get in on the post-war building boom. At the time, this view was alien to most residents throughout the region because the only places in South Florida experiencing substantial development of housing and commercial land development were Miami and then Ft. Lauderdale. The Palm Beach County towns of Boca Raton and Delray Beach were still quiet towns where people farmed, kept shops, and catered to winter tourists. They were unaware of the "let's-maximize-our-investment-potential-as-soon-as-possible-syndrome." For many people, working in the area was profitable enough. Capitalism was really not the basis of life as it became later. After all, they did not want "to become like Miami or Ft. Lauderdale." They wanted the quality of their life to stay as it was.

As a result of the concerted efforts of the few larger landowners, a monumental decision was made by the Highland Beach Town Council. Serving the aggrandizing interests of the few, but larger, landowners, they rezoned most of Highland Beach, principally in the large central portion, and for the first time lawfully permitted high intensity vertical residential communities with up to an unheard of sixty dwelling units per acre. Delray Beach had a maximum of fifteen dwelling units per acre, and Boca Raton had fewer still. Gulf Stream was a very wealthy community to the north that, like Delray Beach, was mostly developed with single-family homes. They stayed that way, resisting higher-density development.

Extrapolation of this abnormally high density would prompt the prediction that Highland Beach would one day house an extraordinary population of 22,000 persons. It's interesting that today, some fifty years later, as a result of numerous and costly lawsuits whereby the town successfully fought developers in court to reduce the already zoned density and heights, the town, today nearly 90% built out, has just 3,500 year-round residents and just twice that number during the heavily populated winter season. It was quite a victory for the locals in the face of legal claims of "vested rights" by the few powerful developers who at one time owned more than half the town.

What was taking place in Highland Beach was, in many quarters, disdained by the people in neighboring towns. The efforts going on by the landowners and developers of central Highland Beach thus took place without much fanfare from the 1950s into the 1970s, while, to locals and most teenagers attending Delray Beach High School, "Jap Rocks" was just a place to fish, watch turtles lay their eggs, or take your date.

1954

The four teenage boys crouched on the dune watching the ocean's shoreline.

"Let's go down to the rocks," exclaimed Carl, youngest of the group.

"Nah," replied his thirteen-year-old brother. "We can see better from here. Let's wait 'til we see the first one."

The boys had driven down in Richard's converted Model-A Ford from Delray Beach where they all lived and went to Seacrest High School. They came this night because it was the first full moon since school got out, and they could watch the huge sea turtles emerge from the sea.

"Look! Over there," Carl said out loud as he pointed to the beach by the coral outcropping. "Isn't that a sea turtle?"

"Yes," replied his older cousin, Sandy. "That's a big one too. Must be a loggerhead for sure."

Richard, the most levelheaded of the four, knew more about the animal world than the others. He commented, "Yep, it's a loggerhead for sure. See the shape of her shell? The leatherback is smaller and the shell is shaped different than the green turtle."

"Can we go down to her now?" asked eleven-year-old Carl, anxious to touch the giant turtle.

"No," Sandy, fourteen, quickly said. "Let's wait 'til she starts digging her nest so that we don't scare her back into the ocean. We have to wait 'til she finds her spot."

"But it could take hours," Carl argued, lowering his head in a mock whine.

"Shhh," whispered Richard, "we have to wait. It won't take long."

"But it's already ten o'clock," responded the youngest, now agitated. "I'm supposed to be asleep by now," he yawned.

His brother, Rodney, shoved Carl's shoulder. "Take it easy, Carl. Mom knows where we are. We're safe here. Nobody comes here. It's just us and you can sleep late tomorrow. It's Saturday, you know."

"Yeah, but..."

"Shhh," Richard whispered to his close friend, Sandy, squatted next to him. "Why do we always have to be the ones who get the little tagalongs?" Then he smiled, watching the first turtle (Koonkah, perhaps?) slowly begin her trudge up the beach past the high-water mark, pulling and pushing with her strong flippers. "Here she comes," he whispered. "And look, there are two more coming out of the water over there. And there are some more coming close to the beach. See their heads bobbing in the waves? Boy, there're gonna be a lot of big turtles tonight!"

"Wow! Look at that turtle on the sand," Carl yelled. "It stopped, and now it's digging."

"Let's go down there," said Richard as he stood up and started walking down the dune toward the ocean, in line with the first turtle.

"Don't get near her head or her flippers. She can really hurt you," whispered Richard as they carefully stepped around the huge sea turtle. All four squatted on their

haunches on the sand behind the turtle. "I'll scoop the sand away so we can watch the eggs come out and drop into the hole."

"Look," Carl exclaimed, "look at the eggs. So many! They're so round and white—just like Ping-Pong balls. They look wet and slippery too."

"Yeah, they're soft though…so be careful," Sandy said as he placed himself closer to the turtle's tail. "Watch the eggs drop. I'll reach in and get some. Each of us can have four, I suppose. My cousin, Eddie George, said that they taste better than the eggs at home."

"Well, I think three each is enough," replied Richard, ever the conservationist. "We gotta let her have her babies, you know."

"But even if we don't get them, the raccoons will, or the seagulls or the 'possums."

After about twenty minutes of watching, Rodney whispered, "Let's go back over to the dune while she finishes. Then we can come and watch her cover her nest and walk back to the ocean."

"How long is that gonna take?" asked young Carl as he yawned again, having seen all he wanted to see.

"Let's go home now," Richard said. "It's late and I want to get these eggs in the 'fridge."

"Okay. It's nearly one o'clock."

They walked up to the dune carrying their eggs in paper bags.

"I love coming to 'Jap Rocks!'" Sandy yelled as they drove back north A1A in the roofless Model-A Ford. "During school, everybody comes here on Friday nights 'cause there's nobody here."

"It's cool at night on the beach. There's nobody here at all. The police are never around, and, aside from the gazillion crabs and, unless the wind is coming out of the west, the mosquitoes stay in the swamps."

"But I'd rather live in Delray," replied Rodney. "I mean, who would want to live down here all by yourself?"

"Me too. The only time anybody wants to come to 'Jap Rocks' is to see the turtles, fish, or come down for class picnics."

"Or," Richard smiled, "to come here with their dates and," he laughed, "watch the submarine races. Either they come here to neck or park in the pines nearer to Delray."

❧❖❦

And so that is how it was in "Jap Rocks," also known as Highland Beach, during the 1950s. At least to local teenagers.

If you asked someone, man or woman, who attended Delray Beach High School or Seacrest High School during the 1940s and 1950s, "What are your most happy memories of 'Jap Rocks?'" you will usually see a sly grin begin to form on that person's face as they recall their teen years in the area. You might hear responses like these that were passed on to me.

—

"When I was in high school back then, the favorite place to take your girlfriend to park and neck was on the dunes at 'Jap Rocks.' Nothing was down there. No one would disturb you, even the police, and you could look at the moon sparkle on the beach, listen to the ocean, or go down to the beach. Heck, we might even go for a swim y'know, sometimes we'd go skinny-dipping."

Another might respond, "Everybody goes to 'Jap Rocks' to fish," and with a broad smile would add, "and especially to park. There was nobody there, no traffic except for other high school couples. Hardly anybody even lived in Boca Raton, and all their teenagers attended school at Delray High or Seacrest back then."

Or, "I'd ask my date if she would like to go to 'Jap Rocks' to watch the 'submarine races' with me. That was a code name for parking that others, including parents, didn't 'jive.'"

"During the spring and summer," another would comment, "the big crabs were out in force crossing A1A, going from their Intracoastal Waterway shoreline homes to the ocean. Man, they completely covered all the pavement and they were huge! They would hold out those big claws and threaten humans and cars alike. They were big blue land crabs with round bodies and thick claws that, if they bit your tires just right, you'd have a blowout, a flat tire, pretty fast…maybe that's why later they came out with metal cables in the tires," he would laugh. "Actually, sometimes so many crabs would be killed that A1A would get seriously slippery."

—

I fondly remember our annual school class picnics. We always preferred "Jap Rocks." We could swim, watch the fish, play games on the sand, and, at sunset, build a fire to roast hot dogs and marshmallows.

But events were taking place in nearby Boca Raton, especially, and in Delray Beach which would significantly redefine the character, aesthetics, demographics and wealth of Highland Beach. The arrival of people like Arthur Vining Davis, Milton Weir and many others with big ideas, expansive visions and eagerness to put their wealth to work, would change the face of the area forever.

Beginning in the mid-1950s, a number of surreptitious events were taking place that would significantly and powerfully influence enormous change in South Florida, particularly in the communities of Boca Raton, Highland Beach, and Delray Beach.

In 1955, when I graduated from Seacrest High School, the regional high school that served students of Boynton Beach, Delray Beach and Boca Raton, there were no students living in Highland Beach. There were 92 students in my class, including only nine from Boca Raton.

Most of our class picnics were held on the beaches of "Jap Rocks" from sixth grade on. And most Friday nights, aside from football season, were spent partying in groups on the beach near the coral outcropping of "Jap Rocks."

We guys and our girlfriends all enjoyed the submarine races at "Jap Rocks," and like most everyone else, were totally unaware of Arthur Vining Davis' enormous land acquisitions, and what unbelievable change would come our way.

Arthur Vining Davis, the diminutive but visionary former Chairman of the Board of Aluminum Company of America, Alcoa, now extraordinarily wealthy from Alcoa's massive aluminum sales during the war began buying very large tracts of land in and west of Boca Raton and Delray Beach. He accumulated enormous tracts of property in the area, having witnessed the massive land development taking place near Miami. He lived in Coral Gables, a suburb, at the time. Among the large tracts of farmland acquired were most of the Butts, Lyons, Clint Moore farms and the Weaver Dairy tract.

⚊⚊⚊

Dodee Weir is a lovely, engaging woman whose family moved to South Florida from Toledo, Ohio in 1935. Her parents chose to locate initially in Coral Gables, next to Miami, during the midst of the Great Depression. Later, Dodee's family moved to Ft. Lauderdale where she attended and graduated from Ft. Lauderdale High School. Following graduation and, being as atypical as she is, she didn't go to college in Florida, but instead chose to attend the University of Alabama where she surely acquired her touch of a southern accent.

During her 1952 Christmas vacation, when she returned home for the holidays, her friends arranged a date for her with young, handsome Bill Weir. Sometimes events, chance meetings and timing dictate the course of certain lives. Attracted to each other almost immediately, Dodee and Bill grew closer and closer. By June of 1953, just six months later, they were married.

Milton Weir, Bill's father, was Vice-President of Real Estate at Gulf Oil Corporation. Accordingly, he had a wealth of knowledge when it came to site locations, growth area prospects, land management, and contacts.

Dodee commented,

> "My father-in-law was a visionary, a very intelligent, bright man. He knew real estate, and he was convinced that land should work for its owner, not the other way around. One day, he met

with Mr. Arthur Vining Davis as they traveled in the same circles and had many mutual friends. In time, they got to know each other. At some point, after many discussions, my father-in-law convinced Mr. Davis that he should do something with his land holdings in Boca Raton. Soon after, Mr. Davis, accompanied by Mr. Weir, visited the area to survey Davis' land holdings and to buy even more land. Mr. Weir acted as his paid consultant."

Milton Weir
Courtesy of Boca Raton Historical Society

Bill Koch remembers meeting with the two and brokering their purchase of certain lands in and west of Delray Beach.

At first, it occurred to Davis and Weir that Davis should approach the City of Delray Beach, the largest in the area, to determine if the town's leadership would be amenable to Davis developing a large residential community west of the city, utilizing its existing and more than adequate infrastructure to support his endeavors. During the mid-1950s, Delray Beach was still a small town of farming, tourists, and an attractive downtown shopping main street. Still, it boasted fewer than 10,000 residents and, in the words of the City Commission, 'wanted to stay small,' maintaining the status quo. Some say they even suggested that Davis 'take his plans to Boca Raton, thank you very much.' Actually, as it turned out, Boca Raton, with fewer than 4,000 people, was no more hospitable to 'Mr. Alcoa' than was its neighbor to the north. But it was much easier to buy very large land tracts

from just a few farmers than west of Delray Beach.
Dodee continued,

> "My father-in-law convinced Mr. Davis to put together a development company and start developing and marketing. As a result, Arthur Vining Davis, using the first two letters of each of his names, created the Arvida Development Company. In time, Arvida brought to the area experienced land planners, engineers, and MBAs as managers. Most were brought from the west coast, especially California, including graduates of such excellent schools as Stanford University. They began planning and developing the vast holdings of Mr. Davis west of Boca Raton."

The Fifth and Final Event:
The Building of Condominiums
Begins in the 1960s

By the early 1960s, Arvida's land acquisitions were nearly complete. The planning and rezoning of their massive holdings, most of which were in unincorporated Palm Beach County, west of Boca Raton, was accomplished. By the time he was through buying, Arthur Vining Davis had purchased the Boca Raton Hotel and Club, and the club's polo fields on which he developed the very luxurious residential waterfront community of the Royal Palm Yacht and Country Club.

At the time of Arthur Vining Davis' arrival, Boca Raton had a population of just 3,500 people, up from just 992 in 1950. The city ballooned to 6,961 by 1960. Delray Beach grew from 6,264 residents in 1950 to 12,230 by 1960. Not much was happening in Highland Beach. During the same period, in 1950, Highland Beach had just 52 residents. By 1960, the population had increased by a significant 25%, although the actual increase was only thirteen, bringing the total population of Highland Beach to just 65. It was still very quiet and unnoticed. But the upscale, pricey new Arvida developments were the foundation of Highland Beach's luxury future. New residents of 2003 are always amazed at these very low numbers from 1960 when compared to just forty years later.

Royal Palm and Yacht Club became Arvida's signature of quality and taste. Their marketing effort was directed toward attracting wealthy residents. Homes sold at then unheard of prices, and they sold very well indeed. To attract golfing aficionados, Sam Snead, one of the most respected professional golfers in the world, was hired to be the first club pro.

The Arvida marketing effort and distinct target population almost by itself identified Boca Raton and its neighbor Highland Beach as luxury retirement locales. It would take more than forty years for Delray Beach to separate itself from the identity of a low-cost retirement community brought about by the massive inexpensive residential developments west of that city. It would be the late 1990s before some people began to excitedly report, "We're so happy. We sold our house in Boca and bought in Delray Beach."

Milton Weir became Arvida's president and later the first member and elected president of Royal Palm and Yacht Club. His influence was significant and apparent in the early planning of Royal Palm. That community set the course of Boca Raton and Highland Beach toward excellent, expensive residential projects, quite in contrast to the large inexpensive projects west of Delray Beach and Miami.

While he had acquired excellent properties in the city, including the Boca Raton Hotel and the nearby waterfront polo fields, the bulk of his vacant land purchases were west of the city in the unincorporated county. His key purchases were the Butts' farms, Cassie Lyon's bean fields, and the Weaver family's 1,500 acres of land (where IBM later located). Just those three farms constituted approximately ten thousand acres. Almost all of his farmland purchases cost $75 per acre. With top-notch professional managers from southern California, he planned, developed, and marketed a new concept of "planned" luxury residential communities.

Some of Arvida's developments were for future offices, "employment or manufacturing" as they were then called. And others, large residential neighborhoods, were described as "recreational communities," including golf courses and giant clubhouses. Using professional marketing, communities like Boca West sold out very fast because of their low density, copious landscaping, high quality design and construction, and well-maintained open space. Low interest rates also helped, although much of Arvida's sales were to the wealthy who paid cash.

Delray Beach, in contrast, was visited upon by its initial new development to the west, several miles outside the city limits, on a different scale and much different quality. The initial high-density, eighteen apartments per acre retirement community of Kings Point, named after a Long Island, N.Y. community, was in striking contrast with Arvida's luxurious communities.

Boca West, a typical Arvida project, was developed at fewer than two homes per acre. These homes, in the early 1960's, sold for over $100,000. In contrast, much smaller manufactured apartments in Delray Beach's Kings Point sold for $9,999 to $14,995, creating a low-priced image of the city for decades. Hundreds of busloads of retirees were brought from Miami Beach to Kings Point. The average price of a home in America at the time was approximately $16,000. The early condominiums in Highland Beach during the same time period sold in the range of $50,000 to $60,000.

Most people in the area didn't really know that large tracts of land were being bought up by developers. Often, farmers continued to farm even after sale. Some local, prominent real estate brokers certainly were involved in the Davis purchases, including William Koch, Jr., Arthur Sprott, William Mitchell, and Eleanor Gringle, to name a few. Even if locals knew what was happening, it is unlikely anyone could have changed the massive transition from rural farming to urban and commercial. Davis's very large involvement began an almost revolutionary and unstoppable change in the milieu by removing tens of thousands of acres of farmland, woods, pinelands, and swamps, and replacing them with asphalt highways, shopping centers, subdivisions and condominiums. The conversion of the region was established. Future moratoria only frustrated everyone, enriched the lawyers, and caused hardships but did little to slow the massive influx of developers, builders and buyers.

Nationally, capital funding was becoming more and more available at attractive rates. Interest rates for borrowing to develop commercial and multi-family properties were attractively low. During the mid-1960's, I was in the commercial lending field. I can attest to the fact that apartment and shopping center loans provided by long-term lenders, including insurance companies, ranged at a low 6% to 6½%, a level that hasn't been reached during the following more than thirty-five years. During the summer of 2002, for example, lenders touted "refinance now, these are the lowest rates (6½%) we've seen since the '60s."

Florida cities were doing their best to attract investors and developers, continuing the pattern of the State of Florida marketing efforts since post-Civil War years. And come they did. Real estate developers, investors, speculators, and new homebuyers acquired as much land or residences as they could get, paying prices that seemed to increase by the day.

Even Walt Disney got into the act. While Disneyland in Anaheim, California was originally built on only 150 acres, Disney made sure that this time his company would reap even more benefits. By 1962, his company had acquired, almost surreptitiously, over 33,000 acres at a reported average cost of $600 per acre in Orange and Osceola Counties in Florida, southwest of the then quiet, central city of Orlando. Long after his company was buying, word got out and prices began to escalate. He also had to buy huge tracts of lowlands and swamps to contiguously configure his holdings. Ultimately, owners of the lands adjoining his theme park would also benefit, and, as they say in Orlando and Kissimmee, as well as in South Florida, "the rest is history."

By 1964, Disneyworld was announced to the galaxy. Over the next four decades and beyond, untold millions would be drawn to "sunny Florida," now not only for retirement, but also for the best entertainment and recreation vacations anywhere, specifically aimed at attracting families from across the nation and the world. There was great concern in southeast Florida that tourists would go only as far south as Disneyworld in Central Florida and not visit South Florida. Disneyworld was seen as a huge magnet that might, as a wall, stop tourists from venturing farther south.

However, despite Disneyworld, communities in South Florida were being swamped with rezoning petitions, site plan approvals, requests for utility services, and announcements of grand, enormous residential communities. Recreational neighborhoods surrounding pristine golf courses copiously landscaped with "instant forests" of Sabal Palms, Queen Palms, Royal Palms, and mandated Mahogany and black olive shade trees seemed to explode everywhere on former bean fields and tomato farms. Carpets of instant green lawns gleaned from sod farms near Lake Ocheechobee were trucked in daily. Colorful flags announcing "luxury models," and doublewide trailer sales offices hatched like turtle eggs all over coastal southeast Florida.

By the mid-1960s, the land-buying spree was on. Every open tract of land in South Florida seemed to be changing hands. Residents, farmers, and long-term investors could no longer resist what seemed like exorbitant offering prices by the developers swarming into the region. The paradigm had changed dramatically. South Florida shifted from a place of small cities, small farms and virtual villages to a place that begged for more, more and more real estate development. This surge resulted in attracting thousands and thousands of new people to the region. By 1970, Boca Raton's population had exploded to 28,500. In 1960, it had claimed only 6,961. Delray Beach was becoming intensely developed also. From its population of 6,264 in 1950, to 12,230 in 1960, almost doubling, it reflected an annual growth rate of nearly 7%. The city reached a population of 19,366 in 1970. Being located between these two fast-growing cities, Highland Beach was now being noticed by anyone interested in investing in Florida land as well as those seeking their retirement home, or both. During the explosive 1960s, the population of Highland Beach skyrocketed by an unbelievable 1000% to 624. Clearly, the culture of the area was changing from semi-rural Midwestern to urban, Northeastern. The whole of Palm Beach County was exploding in population, traffic, demands on infrastructure, and cultural shock. The county's population, mirroring Dade County (Miami) and Broward County (Ft. Lauderdale) to the south, doubled from 114,688 in 1950 to 228,106 in 1960. By 1970, its population increased further, nearly 50% to 338,993. It was confounding in many ways, and a very difficult and stressful time. Locals felt oppressed, saddened at the loss of their quiet milieu, and bewildered by the "in-your-face" culture that had arrived.

It would take years, actually decades, for the locals and the newly arrived to find ways to co-exist. Funny enough, it usually took only a few weeks of residency for a new condo resident to declare, "Six weeks I'm here, and already there's a condominium going up across the street. When is it going to stop?"

Developers of large-scale residential communities advertised on national television, that relatively new, now influential medium that had only just begun to be seen as "America's favorite pastime" during the late 1950s. Home models were installed in Grand Central Station in Manhattan by the New York developers who saw Florida fortunes just waiting to be harvested. People were coming once again, as in the 1920s, to South Florida to get rich. Many came to "start over," but most seemed to arrive seeking respite from the harsh, cold winters "up North." Grandparents and in-laws were sent to Florida so the children could do their best to "live their own lives." And some came, as they have been for more than two hundred years, to "get lost" in the crowd. And most did achieve their highest hopes.

It seemed like the entire population of New York and New Jersey was coming to South Florida. As the population continued to explode, and thousands of retirees descended with their own cultures and demands, its impact was growing exponentially. "All you can eat" restaurants went out of business; social conflicts erupted; claims of anti-Semitism were made by new retirees in Kings Point. New rules and regulations were made to respond to new demands and in response to a explosive growth in population.

One of those new laws of Delray Beach, the most impacted of the towns, was to prohibit fires anywhere, especially on the beach.

Summer 1960

"Boy, I sure do love the beach," laughed one of the young teenagers on Delray's beach across from the Seacrest Hotel. Then, as he looked to his teenage date sitting next to him by the small fire, she hugged his arm and whispered, "This was a great idea, coming down to the beach and having a wiener roast."

"Yeah," spoke the other teenagers, almost in unison.

"Hot dogs and marshmallows over the fire—couldn't ask for more. Boy, this is swell, guys," answered Sally. "Let's go for a swim. Last one in is a rotten egg," she giggled as she stood up to dash to the calm water's edge. "Come on, Stuart, race me to the water." Sally giggled as he started chasing her.

"We ought to go too, Betty Sue. Come on," urged Charlie, her date, "Let's go in the water, then roast our hot dogs."

"Well, I'm not gonna be a party pooper," Sue said as she laughed and raced in the soft golden sand to the cool ocean water.

After splashing each other, laughing, and sharing the wonders of swimming in the ocean at dusk, then embracing with hugs and long kisses, the foursome eventually waded out of the shoulder-deep water and walked back to their towels, which were spread outside the stones that circled the small beach fire. Distant sounds could be heard from another cluster of high schoolers laughing and enjoying the same beach pleasures farther down the beach. They all knew each other and, in their "not so innocent '50s" decade, were having fun on the beach. Friday nights were always the most popular for high schoolers. Some went to Delray's beach at the end of Atlantic Avenue, where the pavilion stood until the 1947 hurricane washed it away just like it did to the east half of A1A and all of Delray's beach only thirteen years earlier.

"How do, kids?" the policeman asked as he walked up to the clustered couples as they stuck hotdogs to the ends of Casaurina pine tree branches. "Y'all okay?" he asked them.

"Yeah, chief, we're okay," Stuart responded, "doin' just fine."

"Well," replied the police officer, "enjoy yourselves now because the Town Council passed a new law outlawing fires on the beach. Tonight's the last chance you're gonna get to have cookouts on the beach."

"Darn, darn, darn," replied Stuart, the self-chosen leader of the foursome. "Looks like too many old people are coming to town and making new laws."

"Yeah," replied Sally, "they're taking away all the fun again. Remember last year they passed a new law stopping us from throwing a football on the beach?"

"Well," Charlie responded with a smile, "that's 'cause Frank hit an old woman in the back with his football. Now, a ball with points can't be tossed on the beach anymore."

"Seems like the only thing we can do is join the others on Friday nights down at 'Jap Rocks.'"

"At least there aren't so many people down there, and they haven't put any rules there. At least not yet."

"Well," Stuart responded, "that's because hardly anybody lives down there. Just the Weirs, and they love kids. I mean, Mahlon and Joan act just like us all the time anyway!"

"Yeah," added another, "they're always fun people."

❧❖❧

Joan Battin Weir recently shared the following wonderful memoir with me about the Weir home near "Jap Rocks," and its location on land that was part of the historical route of the "Barefoot Mailman."

> "The beach bungalow at 'Jap Rocks' was built in the 1940s after World War II by Mrs. A. Grace Slane Weir. The builder was Stuart Weeks who was a local Delray Beach contractor. This wonderful beach home retreat was up on the bluff overlooking the ocean at 'Jap Rocks.' Also, the 'Barefoot Mailman's' route was a shell-rock road along this ridge. Grace built her home so that the original path was untouched and always remained part of the front yard. Grace was insistent that the path remained untouched to preserve a bit of history. You can still see it today. Grace's sons, Mahlon and Robin, were teenagers at the time. 'Jap Rocks' was a great spot for them to enjoy snorkeling, swimming and fishing with their friends. When the two boys were not spending time in the ocean, they were shifting through the white shell-rock of the road that the 'Barefoot Mailman' took on his

route back and forth from West Palm Beach to Miami, looking for Indian artifacts and treasures.

Mahlon called Delray Beach his home his whole life. We married and had a family. Our children, John Mahlon, Louise Vernice, and Melinda Grace had as much fun at 'Jap Rocks' as their Dad always did! Some of the kiddos' greatest hits were the big birthday parties and barbecues on the beach and at the edge of this historic road. We loved throwing these big events for our three children—always opening their hearts to welcome others. One of the favorite games was a treasure hunt in the 'tropical jungle' along the 'Barefoot Mailman's' route."

Land developers active in Dade and Broward Counties moved northward and scoured Palm Beach County by helicopter, photographing the flat farmlands available at alluring rates of as low as $200 per acre. It was an opportune time for large scale land developers looking for cheap, well-located, easy to develop lands.

Three such developers looking in Palm Beach County, who were originally from New York, New England, and New Jersey, came to Highland Beach. The very fact that they could purchase prime ocean to Intracoastal Waterway land already zoned at very high density, meant that they would not have to go through the costly rezoning battles that they were faced with in Pompano, Hollywood, and Deerfield Beach. Highland Beach stood out prominently from its neighbors as a place where a developer of condominiums "could make some real money." Here was prime real estate already zoned high-density residential, or, those parcels in the county pockets were easily rezoned by the county, ostensibly making it much, much easier and cheaper for developers. This was especially true during the 1950s. As a result, Highland Beach would become far more intensively developed with apartments than any other town in the area.

Much of the most preferred lands along the beaches were scooped up at prices that astonished their previous owners. One hundred feet wide lots in Highland Beach that stretched from the ocean Across A1A to the Intracoastal were now selling for $300 to $400 per front foot. During the quiet "not so innocent '50s," lots from the ocean to A1A now sold for $150 per front foot, or $15,000 per homesite.

In Highland Beach, much of the land was already "dressed in top hat, tails and white gloves," ready to be developed into "luxury high-rise condo-apartments," many at the astronomical density of 60 apartments per acre.

High-rise condominiums became very much in vogue. Certainly, this relatively new statutory housing concept imported, along with the co-op from New York City to Florida, enabled maximum use and profit from most any vacant parcel, particularly along the ocean dunes.

These behemoths, high-rise condominiums, veritable "vertical villages," were the *fifth and most devastating event* that spelled the final doom of the lifestyles of Native Americans, stretched side by side from Miami Beach to some fifty miles north through Ft. Lauderdale, Pompano Beach, Deerfield Beach and into Palm Beach County.

Retirees, now fully vested in Social Security and Medicare thanks to the "Great Society" programs of President Lyndon Johnson, television transmission of mass advertising to the enormous populations in the Northeast, jet airplane service to the three growing airports of Palm Beach (formerly Morrison Field of World War II days), Miami and Ft. Lauderdale, and especially, the universal availability of central air-conditioning at affordable costs, were the key factors that virtually "opened the flood gates."

Buyers, mostly Americans, came by the millions to South Florida. High-rise condos along the beaches were rising like mushrooms across the landscape from Miami to Singer Island. Supply could hardly keep up with demand. Without exception, all were advertised as "luxury" apartments, but most were built as inexpensively as possible, rendering maximum profits to the developers.

Even homebuyers got the fever. "Pre-development" described prices attracted speculators and homebuyers alike because, under those conditions, conditional contracts could be resold or "flipped" with great profits made with a nominal deposit, without risking even a large down payment. Some "flipped" contracts as a full-time occupation because there was always someone coming to town who wanted to "make money" too, and who would pay the asking price. Pre-development sales with minimum deposits allowed the developers to establish evidence of a strong market that they used to justify their construction loans from bankers.

The frenzy of the "Land Boom" days of the "Roaring Twenties" transformed South Florida into a "1920s déjà vu experience," now the "Roaring '60s" and "Explosive '70s" when the development of condominiums reached fever pitch. Highland Beach was very attractive and prime. Its location between the unique cities of Boca Raton and Delray Beach, just twenty miles from ritzy Worth Avenue in Palm Beach, served by three nearby international airports, made it deliciously appealing.

However, the residents of Highland Beach were becoming more aware of the impact that the zoning changes made during the early 1950s would mean to their cultured way of life. By the early 1970s, they took a stand. The Town Commission called on their attorneys to challenge the claimed "vested rights" of some landowners. Amazingly, just a few individuals owned or controlled the majority of all the undeveloped land in Highland Beach. The town went to court time and again for more than twenty-five years. Most often by settlement and victory, the town was able to bring the ultimate density down significantly. Today, allowable density is just six dwelling units per acre.

Culminating eighteen years of personal involvement, service, and leadership in the affairs of Highland Beach, including serving as a Town Commissioner from 1983 to 1986 and 1989 to 1990, Betty Jean Stewart was Mayor of the Town of Highland Beach from 1987 to 1989.

She and her family came from Chadsford, Pennsylvania and settled in Highland Beach during the hurricane season of 1966. In those days, the population of the town was still small. Mrs. Stewart kindly shared her recollections with me, providing a fascinating dimension to the early days of this newly incorporated oceanfront community.

> "When we moved here in 1966, the postal address for the town of Highland Beach was Delray Beach. Fire department services were provided by Palm Beach County's Del Trail unit and any volunteers in town. As younger men moved into the town they were asked to help, but all of them worked out of town and could not be available. Most of the volunteers were the motel owners who were here. A station house was built in 1967 for our fire truck. Later on, a tragedy happened when a very nice house at the south end of town burned down. The firemen were unable to attach the hoses to the fire hydrants. The wrench required to open the hydrants had not been returned to the fire station. That was soon corrected. There was no police department so this was handled by the county sheriff. We had wells for sprinkling and a public water supply and septic tanks for sewage. Building inspectors came from Delray for we had none of our own.
>
> Our beaches had an abundance of shells to be found and collected by the beach walkers. The beach itself was full of activity as small sandpipers, plovers, royal terns, and gulls scurried about in their feeding as ospreys flew overhead. Ghost crabs and sand fleas ran up and down the beach. Our friendly brown dog, Molly, spent her days walking up and down the beach with the walkers who came to know her and watched her digging for the ghost crabs until her nose was skinned pink. At night, we walked the beach watching the giant sea turtles dig their nests, and then weeks later see the hatchlings climb out in the moonlight. We would have eight to ten nests a summer on our beach area. At night, small red foxes, opossums and raccoons could be seen crossing A1A. In the morning, the road usually had many bodies of these animals who had been hit overnight.
>
> The ocean itself was a very rich environment in our area as we snorkeled to see the purple and blue parrot fish, the sergeant majors, baby jacks, rock beauty fish, angelfish, damselfish, puffers, squid, and sea horses. Many times, there were immature

fish swimming in the shallows of our 'front yard.' We could easily see them as we stood on the offshore rocks. Occasionally we had fresh lobster we speared among the coral rocks offshore for a special lunch. Our son took a very large octopus, which he found live on the beach, to school in a bucket so his class could see it and its inky flow. We had tried to keep it in a fish tank but it squeezed out of a very small hole in the metal lid and proceeded to enjoy its newfound freedom by venturing across our living room floor.

The Intracoastal area of mangroves provided nurseries for fish as an enriched habitat that resulted in an abundance of fish. Consequently, the shoreline teemed with fish. Fishing from the beach was great fun.

As we had moved here from a city environment, I was used to shopping in department stores. The closest department store to Highland Beach was in Ft. Lauderdale. Shopping for any household items, like sheets, bedspreads, furniture, clothing, etc. meant nearly a full day's round trip. Many miles were traveled in those years until other shopping areas came along, such as Pompano Shoppers Haven and the Palm Beach Mall. Some of our living room furniture came from Miami where more choices were available. Grocery shopping was done in Boca Raton via the Palmetto Park Bridge, and some was done at a store over by the Delray Beach post office. Our doctors and dentist were in Boca Raton, but others were in Delray. The two nearby medical centers were Boca Raton Community Hospital and Bethesda Memorial Hospital located in Boynton Beach.

A December, 1964 map of Highland Beach shows the platting of the Bel Lido, Highland Beach Drive and Boca Cove areas into lots and the ownership of the other sites before the land sales that resulted in the total changing of the town. One could not have foreseen all of the western water and tree areas soon to be destroyed.

As construction sites seemed to sprout up all over town, there was a noticeable increase in the noise levels as the cracking of the tree trunks by the huge bulldozers cleared the sites and great trucks carried the trees away. Dump trucks brought sand in from one end of the town to the other, day in and day out. These were followed by the grinding cement trucks. Changes were everywhere to be seen and heard. The small brown rabbits that were seen along the grassy areas of the road would soon be gone. The blue land crabs used to cover A1A in waves making it difficult to drive as they moved from the mangrove waters to the beach each year. They are now mostly gone from the town. We had not only migratory birds in our trees, but also spotted-breasted orioles, red-tailed hawks, robins, woodpeckers, night heron, whippoorwills, ibis, purple gallinules, great white heron, and a barn owl that I found. One of the last pileated woodpeckers stopped in our drive to eat on a dying limb of one of our trees a few years ago. He was about eighteen inches long and was about twenty feet away from our kitchen window; a rare close-up for us to see.

As some new condominium buildings went up, there seemed to be a growing concern as we looked at ourselves and other communities around us. Ft. Lauderdale, Pompano Beach, and the south end of Boca showed us intensive condominium development. Whereas, Delray Beach, Ocean Ridge and Hillsboro showed us the positive results of a mixed building plan. Comparisons gave us new ideas. We had an empty page on which to plan how the town would develop and look, if we wanted. The areas of undeveloped land would be developed, but with care it was hoped."

Through January of 1964, the pattern of governing the Town of Highland Beach had been for the commissioners to meet at the home of Mr. Hartwig as it had since 1949. Few, if any residents, though invited publicly, ever attended commission meetings, totally relying on their neighbors and political leaders. But this year would be different. As the population steadily grew as did the immediate region, the eligible voters list grew from twenty-one to seventy-six. Many newcomers demanded changes. Among them were several individuals who decided to challenge the status quo. As a slate of five, they filed to run against the sitting commissioners, led by Arthur Eypel, mayor since 1956, and Commissioners Arthur Jones, Mildred Nobel, Matthew Bertash and Milton Beekman.

Clem Hackman, motel owner and most prominent of the group, opposed Arthur Eypel for mayor. Statements by the new group were considered to be unseemly personal attacks on the integrity of the incumbents and, as a result, hard feelings developed within the community. The challengers announced, "We are going to look into everything done in the past outside the scrutiny of the public." These charges greatly offended the incumbents and their loyal friends. The town became polarized. It was a difficult moment in the evolution of this very small community. In March of 1964, seventy-six eligible voters went to the polls and elected the new slate of challengers. After a one and a half decades of doing things the old way, new Mayor Clem Hackman took over the political reins of Highland Beach, a very small, almost village community that had, since its incorporation in 1949, been a quiet, amicable albeit luxury, oceanfront community nestled in between Delray Beach and Boca Raton. For all those years, all were very friendly neighbors to the towns on either side. That is, it was amicable until June 1964. Only three months after taking office, Mayor Hackman threw down the gauntlet in the form of a harsh yet incorrect letter sent to residents in the county pocket between Delray Beach and Highland Beach. His letter was not well received by the political leaders of the city to the north, to say the least. Mayor Hackman, a relative newcomer to the area, wrote in a letter to the residents:

> "Dear....,
>
> We suggest that you take immediate consideration of the creeping annexation of Delray Beach. Their City Limit sign is south of the Outrigger Apartments, less than __ from your property.
>
> The Delray Beach tax rate is 12 mills (sic) plus one and a half personal tax or a total of 13.5 mills (sic) and going higher. Highland Beach is but 3, 4 and going lower. There is no personal property tax in Highland Beach."

Mayor Hackman was incorrect in quoting tax rates since Florida's statutory limit was ten mills, and Delray Beach or any other city had an intangibles tax. The fact was, Highland Beach enjoyed a valid agreement with its neighbor to provide a backup and/or emergency supply of water through the water main that connected the two cities. However, Mr. Hackman, apparently on a personal mission, went on in his letter, further insulting the leadership of Delray Beach, as his letter continued:

> "Our new $60,000 filter system gives us better water than the unfiltered Delray Beach water, and we are at this time serving you with water. By joining us, the premium you are paying will be eliminated."

Mr. Hackman, in his rather surprising letter, went on further in his attack on his town's neighbor, to say:

> "We have recently appointed a Chief of Police who has seven years of detective experience along with FBI fingerprinting and homicide schooling. He is a resident of Highland Beach who has joined our volunteer staff in assisting our community without cost.

Highland Beach is incorporated and cannot be annexed. Protect your investment by joining Highland Beach along with your neighbors to the south. Let us have your decision now before you are annexed into Delray Beach through the Florida law that makes it possible for you to be annexed without your vote."

Although Mr. Hackman's letter included many half-truths, incorrect statements, and misleading information, its intent was clear. Rather than seeking, as a good friend, to protect the residents he wrote to, the new mayor was, in fact, pursuing his own annexation program to the north. His letter went even further:

"Joining Highland Beach will enable us to improve our service. It will not effect (sic) your mailing address or telephone number. The property valuations are identical with those of the county. So get out your pencil and check the tremendous saving if you act now before you are annexed by Delray Beach.

Signed,
Clem F. Hackman, Mayor, Town of Highland Beach"

Mr. Hackman's abusive and arrogant presentation not only was a major cultural departure from the status quo, but it predictably raised the ire of the City Commission of Delray Beach who immediately voted to sever all ties with Highland Beach, including the water main that provided the residents of Highland Beach with water, interestingly blending with the "filtered" water of Highland Beach.

The Commission of Delray Beach, comprised of longtime residents and business leaders, included such prominent and beloved citizens as Mayor Al Avery, Roy Croft, whose brother "R.C." was the city's Chief of Police, Jack Saunders, who would later become one of the city's most revered mayors, George Talbot, and Emory Barrow. Mr. Hackman, a relative newcomer, had taken on the wrong group.

When Delray Beach responded by severing and plugging the water main at both ends, Mayor Hackman, amazing to everyone else, was quoted as saying, "I am surprised by the attitude taken by the council."

Others, as reported by *The Sun-Sentinel*, included Delray Beach Councilman George Talbot who said that he was "surprised at the action taken by Hackman" and suggested "Mr. Hackman had not correctly quoted the tax millage, and," he stated categorically, "there had been no efforts of 'forced annexation.'" Talbot went on to say, "It appears they don't want our water to contaminate their lines." Jack Saunders was quoted as saying, "We've leaned over backwards to help them out before. Now we are taking steps for our own protection."

But both communities' residents knew this event was in neither's best interests, and while Mr. Hackman had raised the "hackles" of his neighbors, a more diplomatic response was made by representation of Highland Beach. Mr. Arthur Eypel, former mayor from 1956 to 1964, was called on to negotiate a resolution. Within less than a month, the parties resolved their differences and, as Bob Holland, then City Manager, said, "Everybody here (in Delray Beach) seems to be happy with the way things have worked out."

Mr. Hackman, still unchanged, was quoted in *The Sun-Sentinel* after the agreement was reached, as saying, "I still don't know what stirred them up."

This has to be considered one of the most ludicrous utterances from a political leader in these parts.

Condominium Fever
of the 1970s
Another "Land Boom"

The condominium fever stretched into the early 1980s. Prices were escalating so fast that buyers "could hardly lose." Developers in the area fought endless legal battles with the Town of Highland Beach for approval of larger, higher and more intense condominiums. Residents feared their coastal town was becoming a "condo canyon."

Political leaders got into the act as the demand for more and more apartments continued to grow. Moratorium followed moratorium, lawsuit followed lawsuit. These were trying times for residents, town leaders, and developers.

Boca Raton announced it was placing a population cap on itself in a naïve and ill-advised tactic to stop the rampant over-development. They decided their "Best Resort in the World," as defined by Addison Mizner in 1924, should not only be the finest and a playground for the rich, but exclusive too by limiting its size. So, they limited its population to just 40,000 inhabitants.

The resulting responses were too predictable to resist. Lawsuits against the city by property owners flooded into the offices of the city's legal department. To paraphrase Prime Minister Winston Churchill, "they fought on the beaches, in the air, on the seas, and in the courtroom."

Legal fees paid by the City to defend its position exceeded one million dollars, not an insignificant amount for a small town during the 1970s. Additionally, as a result of the City Council's edict, *The Wall Street Journal* ran an opinion article, an "op-ed," declaring that Boca Raton, "that rich town on the beaches of South Florida," had declared a population limit. The response was unbelievable. Thousands of readers decided they had to move quickly to "get in the game," and flew, now by subsonic jets, to Palm Beach International and Ft. Lauderdale Airports to buy their piece of the beach in this "oceanside resort for the rich." Many came because they were already rich and wanted to be there; some *wanted* to be rich and raced to where the money and those with it were so that they could get some of it; and, some came hoping a little of it would find itself in their pockets.

Meanwhile, the Town Council of Highland Beach, under Mayor Lou Horton, in concert with the City of Boca Raton, pressed for state legislation to expand their political empires. Driven by the expert arguments of their lobbyist Mr. Don Reed, a Boca Raton lawyer, the legislature passed a bill during the 1972 session enabling Boca Raton to expand northward from its then north boundary at Twentieth Street to the C-15 Canal several miles north, reaching Delray Beach's south limits. This move greatly expanded Boca Raton's size to enable it to become the second largest incorporated city, second only to Jacksonville/Dural County. It also created a potential tax base of enormous economic benefit in later years.

Simultaneously, with the same enabling legislation, Highland Beach annexed northward more than 3,000 feet, or more than one-half mile, absorbing owners who also were in "county pockets" of unincorporated Palm Beach County. This land, shown on plat books at the time included the 2,800 feet of Bird's Beach. It also included, at the northernmost, the 300 front feet then owned by the Stephen A. Healy family who would in time file suit against Highland Beach when it purportedly changed the zoning of the property from the county designation of multi-family, in concert with its neighbors, to Highland Beach's single-family zoning.

The entire region, including Highland Beach, experienced enormous demands for housing, new developments and greatly expanded infrastructure. Many new east-west roads were built or widened, including such corridors as Palmetto Park Road, Yamato Road, Linton Boulevard, and Atlantic Avenue in Delray Beach. As a result, residents within the new, very large retirement and golfing communities to the west were then able to commute daily to the oceanfront communities and the beaches. Pressure was building from outside forces to widen A1A to four lanes. The town, led by Mayor Louis Y. Horton, strongly objected, successfully maintaining its intimate character. To this day, Ocean Boulevard remains a two-lane road, with relatively lower speed limits than comparable nearby north-south corridors. It has become a very attractive sightseeing route through a principally residential community. To be sure, the demands for widening A1A will likely continue and even increase in future years as the region continues to attract more and more residents and visitors. As resulting traffic increases, state and county traffic standards likely will be exceeded.

Besides attempts to widen the town's singular traffic corridor in the 1970s, during the same period, curbs to slow, sometimes even to halt further development, were instituted time and again. Zoning restrictions were extended regularly. For example, height limits on new condominiums were constantly sought. Even so, the town found itself growing too rapidly. The onslaught of new construction seemed endless.

The Town Planning Committee, appointed on August 3, 1971, was becoming one of the busiest review boards in the region, its staff's workload growing almost daily and requiring more space. That growth required that a new, much larger Town Hall be built. On January 15, 1973, work was started on the new edifice designed by popular Delray Beach architect Roy M. Simon.

Groundbreaking of new Highland Beach Town Hall
1972
Courtesy of Highland Beach Archives

A new town ordinance, passed in June 1972, was designed to protect mangroves. It required the submission of building plans, taking into account the presence of wetlands-loving mangroves the length of the town, though almost exclusively along the west side of Ocean Boulevard/A1A, east of the Intracoastal Waterway. Many changes related to the pressures of massive growth occurred during the years of Mayor Horton's leadership. In April 1974, Mayor Morton Gilday took office, picking up the baton from Mr. Horton.

New Highland Beach Town Hall 1973
Courtesy of Highland Beach Archives

Sometimes, in small towns, it is very exciting to have famous people come to town. In March of 1977, Carl Yastrzemski, the left field Boston Red Sox slugger and heir to Ted Williams' throne in Boston's Fenway Park, came to Highland Beach. He bought "Slammin" Sam Snead's oceanfront home. Now, the town, while losing a golfer, gained a famous baseball player.

On February 17, 1979, Highland Beach properly celebrated its 30th birthday. A "youngster" in the region, yet a formidable luxury residential community was still seeking to maintain its "small town" culture. And, in June 1981, the town gained another access to the mainland which was very important in providing an additional route off the barrier island in the event of hurricanes. That was the date the Linton Boulevard drawbridge in south Delray Beach was finally opened to the public after years of petitions, planning, public meetings, and construction. Now, Highland Beach residents had two means of emergency evacuation: Spanish River Bridge to the south in Boca Raton and Linton Boulevard immediately to the north in Delray Beach.

During the early 1980s in America, there was a plethora of cable "television preachers" broadcasting their well-intentioned messages across the land. Reverend Jerry Falwell of Virginia was competing with the PTL Club of South Carolina. Tammy Faye Bakker and her husband Jim were a couple who breathed the fear and love of God across America on their cable channel. During the course of their enormously successful fund-raising efforts, they built a huge colony in South Carolina. They were famous. They were passionate, they were widely popular in certain quarters and Tammy Faye with her abundant blonde hair and facial make-up became a national object of commentary and derision.

The famous couple purchased their $375,000 oceanfront condominium in Highland Beach in February 1973, claiming residence in a lofty resort community. There they enjoyed the same beaches others have coveted for centuries. Regrettably, during the late 1980s, Jim Bakker went to prison for various crimes. After costs mounted and the famous couple became infamous, their condominium apartment was sold in 1988 to a department store executive with Tammy Faye's beloved blue mirrors on all walls and cabinets included.

It was in the late 1980s that Palm Beach County began discussing the creation of an oceanfront public park at "Jap Rocks," inciting opposition among the residents of the town. They believed that this intrusion of outsiders would not only create traffic problems, but would also severely impact the value of their homes.

Now, it seemed that Highland Beach had a new and different issue to keep its leadership and residents concerned. The possibility of a county park on its coveted dune was almost more than some could bear. As a controversy, it joined the continuing dilemmas of water difficulties and the endless court battles with condominium developers.

Tom Sliney, Esquire

Tom Sliney, current attorney for the Town of Highland Beach, came to South Florida in 1967 to join his parents, then living in Boca Raton, after his stint in the U.S. Navy during the Vietnam War. That year, he became a practicing attorney in Boca Raton.

The late 1960s and early 1970s were the years when the major land development of the region began in earnest. Miami and New York developers had discovered Highland Beach. Tom's arrival was exquisitely timed to experience the initial legal battles that resulted from the rezoning efforts of some property owners in the northern portion of the town's limits as they sought to obtain town approval for multi-unit, high-rise condominiums in keeping with the already existing development of the central portion of Highland Beach. While they felt they had strong arguments, based on professed "vested rights," on their side, the town's existing residents and political leaders sought to limit the

intensity of and further development of the community. The town won those
initial battles and took on the owners/developers of the central properties
already zoned high density, up to 60 dwelling units per acre, seeking to reduce
that intensity. The northern and southern owners believed that since they were
zoned for multi-family development under County zoning laws, that even
though Highland Beach annexed their land, that fact should not deprive them
of potential wealth because the town sought to down-zone their lands. Even so,
the town's successful efforts to down-zone resulted in smaller, low-rise
condominiums instead of high-rise Goliaths.

Lou Horton was Mayor of Highland Beach during these years of trying to
prevent massive initial growth and numerous lawsuits. This was the legal
cauldron in which Tom Sliney, the young, new attorney, found himself embroiled
as he accepted his new position. While lawsuits were seemingly commonplace

Bel Lido development: Note Vacant Lands
1976
Courtesy of Highland Beach Archives

throughout all of southeast Florida as developers demanded rights to build as many condominiums as high as they could, their interests clashed head-on with the interests of existing residents, many of whom, ironically, already were living in such structures. Highland Beach had been sued since the late 1960s. And more lawsuits were yet to come. Perhaps there were times in those early days of his new career when he wondered if he had made the right decision.

By the early 1970s, there already were several high-rise condominiums built in the central area, including Highland Towers, Monterrey House and Penthouse Towers, built in the late 1960s. Since the properties characteristically were bounded on the west by the Intracoastal Waterway and on the east by the mean high tide line at the ocean, the first properties developed were typically configured long east-west, and narrow north-south, the most prime use of oceanfront and oceanview schemes. Thus, the configuration of those condominium towers was usually shaped in long, narrow designs on the dune, the east side of Highway A1A that not only bisected the town, but also the individual parcels. On the west side, the land was harder to develop. The marshes, thick with mangrove swamps, and the instability of the land created the need for costly sub-structures and foundations. Besides, the market place wanted the oceanfront locations and views. Balconies became absolutes in all the designs. New owners virtually "lived on the balconies."

When he arrived in town, young Tom Sliney found only a few single-family houses along the beachfront dunes. Most of them were located on the long Bird's Beach tract that had been sold off during the 1960s in parcels of 100 front feet. Some, like the Van Lennep and Healy families, purchased several parcels. In the Healy's case, they owned a total of three hundred feet at the far north end, next to Delray Beach. They were the first to seek to "break" the residential down-zoning of Highland Beach. Unlike Highland Beach, the neighboring towns of Delray Beach and Boca Raton had no real depth of land between the ocean and A1A, so, few homes, much less large condominiums, could have been built on the east side, on the dune. They also had existing single-family residents who resisted high-density towers. The surge of high-rise condominium building that moved northward from Miami had reached Boca Raton and Highland Beach, but did not impact Delray Beach and stopped when the recession of the mid-1970s hit the nation.

Still, Tom Sliney recalls the cultural milieu of Highland Beach, strongly influenced by its neighbor to the north as a "quiet, perhaps sleepy, community of Midwestern orientation when I came to Highland Beach."

From the early 1970s, Tom was almost totally occupied with real estate lawsuits in behalf of the Town of Highland Beach, reflecting the times of great demands by property owners to build maximum developments to optimize profits, driven with what seemed to be an insatiable demand for oceanfront apartments and homes. For a while, it seemed that Highland Beach, like Deerfield Beach and Pompano Beach immediately to the south, was in the vortex of this confluence of forces. When it wasn't the issue of more and more building permit requests, it was about water.

While the nation's economy went into a tailspin in the mid-1970s, the "oil crisis" and the stock market experienced what seemed to be a repeat of the October 1929 stock market crash, the fact is, residential development and sales along the ocean in the Highland Beach area appeared insulated from that debacle. But sales did slow and some projects failed. It did reduce the fever pitch, but didn't bring the local economy to its knees as it did in other regions of America. Once again, the wealthy segment survived the onslaught of weakness in the economy. Even Delray Beach, that pre-eminent "village-by-the-sea," comprised of more than 90% single-family residences at the time, did have a few high-rise condominiums, reaching thirteen stories, approved and built. They were almost exclusively on the east side of the Intracoastal Waterway, and most were developed by Charles Barr. However, those were comparatively few and scattered along the beach near the Intracoastal Waterway.

But, the legal battles of Highland Beach rivaled even those in Boca Raton. Tom Sliney's role was to represent the interests of his employer, Highland Beach, in opposing new zonings of high-density development. Even those parcels already highly zoned did not escape the legal challenges of the town. Almost every condominium was subject to a lawsuit, even those with declared "vested rights."

To his credit, search of the records indicates that Sliney's litigation record is enviable. In almost every case, Highland Beach was victorious in the courtroom, or, as it turned out, in many instances, lawsuits were settled in negotiation or on terms relatively satisfactory to the community.

The Town of Highland Beach was not exempt from the State of Florida's State Comprehensive Land Use Plan of 1975 which required every governmental body to plan the use of every parcel of land within its boundaries, with appropriate consideration of several key factors.

The law required every governing body, whether town, city or county, to develop a "Land Use Plan" with stringent requirements and parameters. Basic issues had to be addressed, including uses and consideration for residential, commercial, institutional, schools, transportation, drainage, environmental, and demographic issues. While the town of Highland Beach did not want any commercial ventures within its limits, and had absolutely no provisions for retail shopping—after all, nearby Delray Beach and Boca Raton had all the facilities and capabilities to serve the residents of Highland Beach—they did permit the only motel, the Holiday Inn, to be built. Yet, it is located on land zoned residential and thus is considered a "non-conforming use." That designation opens the door to interesting legal issues should its owners choose to expand it, repair significantly, or rebuild in the event of a fire, for example.

As for minority housing, it simply doesn't exist in Highland Beach. The state's Department of Community Affairs had to be convinced that the land was "simply too expensive" for low-income housing. Apparently, their arguments were convincing because there is no low-income housing in Highland Beach, and one can safely assume that there never will be. On the contrary, in 2002, Highland Beach was recognized as the eighteenth wealthiest town in America, placing it among those world famous locales as Palm Beach, Aspen, Grosse Pointe, and Beverly Hills. This is a revelation that certainly ratifies the decision of all those who chose to live in this land that would become such an urbane, cosmopolitan albeit residential community, including the ancient Paleo-Indians, Arawak, and the Tekesta, and even the Yamato colonists.

By the 1970s, of course, the Native Americans, with a totally different culture, were long gone. Even the few remaining Seminoles, some of whom, as recent as the 1950s, would often come from their camps west of State Road 7 into Delray Beach to shop had disappeared, moving deeper into the swamps of the Everglades in the far southwestern region of Florida.

The 1970s and the early 1980s were the most litigious and booming days during which fortunes were made by developers and speculators alike. Thousands had gotten their precious beachfront balconies, and South Florida had changed dramatically, perhaps forever. Most of those now living in Highland Beach came then to retire beside the ocean, and now walk the beaches, live in vertical villages or communities, and live the "good life."

In undertaking these legal battles, Highland Beach was able to significantly bring down the overall intensity of the town. From the early 1950s, when the central property investor owners, looking more to future maximization of the values of their lands through multi-family development, obtained extraordinary zoning, most retiree residents were looking for a quiet oceanfront home for retirement. As a result of those beneficial rezonings in the "early years of the new town," the projected population was projected to be 22,000 at build-out, and then projected to double by 2004.

As it has turned out, due in no small part to the efforts of the town's leadership, vision and tenacity the population of Highland Beach is now just 3,775. And while it was a quiet, sleepy community during the 1970s, it is now clearly an urbane, trés chic, affluent and quite cosmopolitan resort community that at this writing is attracting what has been labeled a wave of "mansionization," bringing to Highland Beach, and most of coastal South Florida, enormous single-family houses of tens of thousands of square feet and valued in the tens of millions of dollars.

As it has been said many times, residents are living organisms that never stop changing. And Highland Beach is no exception. Its quality of life exceeds that of most regions of America, and while almost exclusively residential, it relies on its neighbors for those "other necessities of life."

An extraordinary way of life is certainly true of the coastal South Florida communities who are where the money seems eager to flow, being coveted by those who can afford the very finest, the most opulent and the most comfortable.

These are not exactly the characteristics sought by the early residents, the Paleo-Indians, or the Spanish, or those who sought to start a new life.

As Tom Sliney observed to me one day,

> "I'm not sure there is another place on the East Coast with the quality of the continuous stretch of beach occupied by single-family homes, nor a place where more single-family homes have been torn down to 'build a castle.'

> First, Highland Beach transitioned directly from almost total vacant oceanfront land, sparsely populated, to high-density residential structures, without first having most of the land covered by single-family houses. It happened so fast.

> And, as a result of the high-density zoning placed on the land by the handful of businessmen, some of whom were hoteliers from New York, and in sharp contrast to neighboring towns, Highland Beach's pre-zoned land was an incredible opportunity for developers, like manna from heaven."

The residents of Highland Beach tried many times from the early 1970s into the late 1980s to limit its population. Moratoriums began in 1973, seeking to simply stop the building. In 1974, eight separate moratoriums were put into place. People wondered, "Is this any way to run a town? Or, is this a place I want to live in?" Lawsuits seeking to change, reduce the size, scale and height of new high-rises were filed, it seemed, almost monthly. Terms like "condo canyon" became commonplace when even residents angrily described their town. Zoning plans were continually updated. Efforts to prevent the State DOT from widening A1A to four lanes were continuous. The pressures of the times to "expand, build, expand" were unrelenting. The terms "growth" and "progress" erroneously became synonymous. As more and more trees were cut down, residents continued to seek remedies. The town appointed a Community Appearance Committee on March 14, 1975.

The intent was to utilize the same state-enabling legislation to begin, for the first time, to legislate and govern what some called "taste" or aesthetics. The purpose was to preserve the "charm" of Highland Beach. The same was happening in Boca Raton and Delray Beach. Much controversy erupted in all three communities because there were those who questioned the wisdom and objectivity of such quasi-governmental boards.

People continued coming to the area, with high-rise condominiums sold to those wanting retirement homes, and to those who hoped for a profit on resale. Florida had great appeal for many reasons, including the absence of an inheritance tax and liberal bankruptcy laws. Further, in time, the state government, placating the growing number of complaining senior citizens on fixed incomes, decided to increase the Homestead Tax Exemption from $5,000 to

$25,000. This caused great financial havoc for city and county governments whose principal tax income, ad valorem or property taxes, dropped suddenly and significantly. Also, Florida law allows the exemption of one's domicile from bankruptcy, without a limit, thus attracting those to the area who are heavily in debt, pouring all their assets into their home, and thereby shielding their wealth from their creditors. Legal, yes, and consistent with the new culture of aggrandizement coming on the scene. Yet, many honest and conservative people still found Highland Beach and neighboring oceanside towns very attractive.

Most of the new homeowners in Highland Beach during the following years were couples who had completed successful careers elsewhere, and determined that their senior years would be best served enjoying their balconies overlooking the turquoise waters of "the Highlands." Mrs. Gertrude Brownley, a cultured lady of Midwestern values, visited with me and shared her experiences.

> "I've been in this lovely town of Highland Beach since February 1973. We came here, having looked around the area, and chose Highland Beach as the place we wanted to retire. My husband loved to fish, and the town had a marina. We liked the condominium we selected, and bought our first in the Aberdeen Arms. We paid $49,000. When it first opened, I believe the pre-development prices were discounted to $44,000 and $45,000. We had never heard of condominiums in Cleveland, Ohio.

> There was a recession in those years and lots of developers were having a hard time. They enticed the first buyers by giving them two years of free maintenance fees. Some of the earliest buyers got two covered parking spaces. Then, it got so that many developers left town when their buildings wouldn't sell.

> In 1973, the Spanish River Bridge was built but the Linton Boulevard Bridge was not.

> There were good places to shop in the area, but you had to drive a good distance. Grocery shopping, for me, was best at Federal Highway and Spanish River. There was a Publix supermarket there. To go shopping for other than food, if you really wanted to go shopping, you drove north to Worth Avenue in Palm Beach or south to Bal Harbour near Miami or Fashion Square in Ft. Lauderdale."

I asked her about the notorious "Recreation Leases" of the 1960s and 1970s.

> "Oh, my. We had never heard of that before. That was terrible. Among the documents we signed when we bought, like everyone else in the Aberdeen and lots of other condominiums in the area built by those New York developers, was something

called a 'Recreation Lease.' We agreed to pay $120 per quarter to the developer just to use the pool. That's $40 per month, and there were 117 apartments. So, the developer was getting $4,680 each month, more than $56,000 each and every year, for us to use the pool, which we believed was free to the owners and our guests. But not so. I think the pool cost about $15,000 to build at the time. We were finally able to negotiate a deal with the developer to pay him $5,000 to invalidate the lease. But before it was concluded, we were forced to pay him $10,000. He was terrible."

Finally, after having worked its way up the courts, the Florida Supreme Court invalidated such "Recreation Leases," declaring them *unconscionable*.

To the best of the writer's knowledge, there are no such "Recreation Leases" being enforced in Florida at this writing.

The Fate of the Sea Turtles is Protected
1973

In 1973, the U.S. Government passed a federal law, the Endangered Species Act, which was intended to protect wildlife deemed in danger of extinction. The Act covered many animals and birds, including sea turtles, and outlawed the poaching and capture of turtles and their eggs during the egg-laying season. Severe penalties would be invoked. As a result, federal and local government agencies, seeking to limit poaching, and in an effort to educate and enforce undertook guided tours of the beaches during the summer season. Police and Sheriff Departments intensively patrol the beaches during the summer nesting season. At this writing, the penalties are as high as a $50,000 fine and five years in jail.

≈❖≿

The Fate of the Sea Turtles Changes
1980s

A group of twelve senior citizens stood on the ocean dune overlooking the coral outcropping, listening intently to the uniformed county officer from the Department of Natural Resources. "Isn't it lovely standing here on the dune in the sea oats and watching for the sea turtles to come and lay their eggs?" asked one elderly woman.

"Shhh," said the officer, "you'll have to be very quiet or you'll scare the turtles back into the ocean."

"Are we going to be able to watch them dig their nest holes and deposit their eggs?" asked another middle-aged man.

"Please keep quiet and listen to my instructions," ordered the officer.

A bit exasperated, another of the group whispered to her neighbor, "I thought this was going to be fun, but the officer is so official."

"Ahem," spoke the officer, mustering all the officious behavior he could, "pay attention and I will educate all of you about the nesting of giant sea turtles that occurs along South Florida's beaches each summer. Pointing to the shoreline, he continued softly, "Soon, at least within the hour, we should see loggerheads emerge from the waves and begin to move up the beach to dig their nests. We must be very careful not to interrupt their mission. Stay close to me."

He cleared his throat and continued, "In 1973, the U.S. Government passed a very important law to stop people from poaching turtles and their eggs." He cleared his throat again, seeking to quiet down his subjects who had responded to the newspaper ads that invited interested citizens and newcomers to join supervised groups led by officials from the county to properly observe the ritual of sea turtles coming to the warm, safe beaches to lay their eggs in peace.

"Now," he continued, "you will see the turtles emerge from the sea and, over the next several hours, many will be on the beach crawling, digging, laying their eggs, and after packing their nests, returning to the sea. After laying their eggs, many of them will actually pull themselves 10 to 15 feet to the side, fluff the sand, imitating the disturbance at the nest in order to create a faux nest to deceive predators. Mother Nature has placed wonders of instinct in the turtles to do what they must to preserve their species."

"Now," he added just before leading the group onto the sand, leaving the dune, heading toward the sea, "we must do all we can to help nature preserve these magnificent turtles, an important part of our wildlife. We must respect the turtles, avoid alarming them, never, ever touching them, stay quiet, whisper only, and stay away from the head. Do not, under any circumstances, reach for the eggs, take the eggs, or disturb the female turtle. I believe the fine, which will be enforced, is $500 per egg. Better you be satisfied with eggs from chickens. Any questions?"

During the waning years of the 20th century, Florida's coastal cities have been under state pressure and clamoring voices on behalf of protecting the environment to "do something" about the tragedy of turtle hatchlings confused by the lights onshore emanating from the lighted condominiums, streetlights, and homes. In their view, the newly hatched, endangered species would or could become extinct if the carnage of silver dollar sized hatchlings being run over by wheels of automobiles driving in the night along A1A didn't stop. Their claims have been that hatchlings, instinctively seeking the moonlit reflections on the white splashing waves, should by nature, be drawn to the ocean. But, with the thousands of new streetlights, lighted balconies of condominiums and the like, the citizens have become accessories to mass murder. As a result, coastal cities passed new regulations requiring streetlights, and the lighting of oceanfront condominiums and homes to become "amber," not white. Hundreds of thousands of dollars have been spent retrofitting streetlights and residential lighting over the years.

A question is begged: Is it true that the primary reason hatchlings would be so drawn by the lights that, in the case of Delray Beach, they would, with their tiny flippers, find their way through up to fifty feet of grasses, underbrush, tangled root systems, and elevated dunes, then crawl through a picket fence? And then, coming to a two-foot high concrete wall, climb that wall, fall down the other side, traverse some fifteen feet of grass and sidewalk, then fall six inches to the asphalt street? And finally waddle some ten feet, at least, into oncoming traffic to meet their untimely deaths? Perhaps.

Let's see if new lighting during the 1970s and 1980s is the culprit.

Newly hatched turtles have been emerging from their eggs deep in the warm sands of the beaches of South Florida for many years. Perhaps for millions of years. Usually six weeks after the giant female turtle returns to her birthplace and deposits her eggs, those silver-dollar size baby turtles dig out of the sand and, instinctively and hopefully, head down the slope of the beach sands to the water's edge where they will begin their life in the ocean. Very few ever even make it to the water's edge. Between the attacks of predators such as raccoons, opossums, terns and seagulls, a very small portion actually arrive in the water. And if they do, most quickly become dinner to underwater predators. In actuality, only about 1% ever live a full life or even ten years.

Regrettably, many hatchlings do become disoriented as they emerge from their nest. Instead of heading down the beach slope toward the sea as they should, many begin their early moments struggling up the beach to the dune where four-legged and air-born predators have a lingering opportunity. Some, in recent years, believe that disorientation is due to onshore lighting, causing the hatchlings to believe the brightness is the splashing, foamy suds of ocean waves hitting the beaches.

It may be interesting to note that at least on one occurrence, the hatchlings went the wrong way, long before there were lights on shore. They also went the wrong way during daylight hours.

Tom Butts told me this fascinating story,

> "In the summer of 1943, when virtually no one lived in the 'Jap Rocks' area now known as Highland Beach, my family would bicycle there from our home on A1A near Palmetto Park Road for Sunday picnics. I rode on a seat behind my mother. My sister, Jan and I would swim and play on the beach. We were about six years old. Then, after having had a wonderful family day, we would peddle home at dusk.

One Sunday, a loggerhead nest, near us, erupted with hatchlings. For some reason, the babies became confused and crawled west, up the beach, onto A1A instead of east to the sea.

My father quickly dispersed us. He went over the dune to A1A, my mother went to the foot of the dune, my sister went halfway down the beach, and I went to the water's edge. Daddy, stationed on A1A, caught the babies, tossed them to my mother who handed them to my sister, and she tossed them to me. It was my job to get them into the sea. We worked for quite a while until that evening.

I watched them swim until I was sure they had regained their bearings and were paddling earnestly into deeper water. They were safe again, away from A1A, the animals and the birds. Now they had to grow bigger to get past the fish waiting for them.

That was a day I'll always remember."

The pristine beaches of "Jap Rocks"
Courtesy of Highland Beach Archives

Highland Beach's Police Department Chief Anthony "Tony" Cervasio

Anthony "Tony" Cervasio is the third and current Chief of Police of the Town of Highland Beach. "Chief Tony," as he asked me to call him, first came to South Florida in 1982. At the time, he was contemplating retiring from his career and leaving his position with the Newark, New Jersey,¡ Police Department. He said to me during our visit in the spring of 2002,

> "I was driving down A1A in Palm Beach County and, liking the area very much, continued along the highway. When I came through Highland Beach, it occurred to me that 'Hmmm, this could be a wonderful place to be a policeman.' So, after checking into a motel for a vacation, I spoke to the Chief of Police of Highland Beach. He seemed like a really happy man, and made me feel very much at home. I thought, 'Is this what they call Southern hospitality? Or was it because I was like most of the policemen he had interviewed?' He informed me that eight of the thirteen men he had interviewed for a vacant position were retired policemen from police departments in the Northeast, mostly New York and New Jersey. So, I decided to apply for a position with the department, was hired, and joined the force in 1994. One year later I was named Chief of Police. I found out over time that former policemen from big cities like the idea of serving on the Highland Beach Police Department, similar I suppose to Delray Beach and Boca Raton, to get away from the hassle of big cities like Miami. It seems to work well both ways. Highland Beach is best suited for well-experienced, mature

police officers. The residents are comfortable with more seasoned officers than with young officers who may have a more youthful agenda.

I prefer, for Highland Beach, officers who have at least five years of experience, are mature, and don't see their time here as a stepping stone. We have a mature population who simply want a police department to assure as much as possible their security, safety and privacy as quietly as possible.

We moved on to another issue. I asked, "Chief, please tell me about 'Jap Rocks.'"

"Well, those rocks and the beach have been a favorite spot for fishing for many years, most of this century I'm told. First, the Japanese from Yamato Colony fished from the rocks, then, the locals from Delray Beach all during the 1920s, 30s and 40s fished here. There was a lookout tower south of the rocks during World War II used to spot German submarines. High school kids came every Friday night to party. It was pretty desolate here until the late 1960s, and teenagers like nothing better than to be away from adults, especially their parents at least one night a week. It wasn't until the population exploded in South Florida in the late 1960s and 70s that people around here began to drop the label 'Jap Rocks' and began to refer to this area as Highland Beach. It was about the time the teenagers found there were too many people coming here to enjoy their Friday nights on our beaches. So, we don't have any problem with them these days."

"And crime?" I asked.

"Well, sir, we've had just two major crimes since I came in 1984, both homicides. And, as is the case much of the time, both were by people who knew the victims. You can't stop that kind of crime. The two homicides were committed in the privacy of their homes."

"Robberies?"

"Fewer than five in eighteen years."

"Theft?"

"Same statistics. Actually, we're kind of unique, like an island in a way. There's really only one way in or out. To get out of town, the thieves have to travel on A1A. We can block them in either direction with our close inter-local departments in Boca, Delray, and the county who respond very fast to our alert. And we do the same for them. Our biggest problems could come from drivers speeding on A1A. It's a straight road, enticing a few speeders. It's certainly scenic, so a lot of our people drive slowly to see the sights. But sometimes people are in a hurry and drive well above the speed limit. We sure don't want to be known as a speed trap, but we have to keep it safe here. Highland Beach is a place where people like to simply enjoy their homes, their town, and their friends. They aren't very inquisitive about newcomers like most of South Florida. Al Capone came to Miami to 'get lost,' so it's our job to stay on top of all sorts of out-of-town visitors. We're always alert to newcomers.

Yes, we have to be vigilant all the time. South Florida is the closest point for our Caribbean neighbors to enter America. It's also a transient state unlike, say, Midwestern states. Our beaches, just like Palm Beach or Manalapan, are landings for runaway Cubans, Haitians and others from the Caribbean or Central America. The beaches have also been places where illegal drugs wash up after being dumped overboard. But, I'm told that during the 1920s and 1930s, this is about where bootleggers brought Canadian whiskey and rum from the Bahamas, making the ninety-mile run by boat from Bimini. Our dunes and beaches have been witness to so much over the centuries. Boy, if those dunes could tell us what they've seen…"

Highland Beach Police Department
Courtesy of Highland Beach Archives

The
Holiday Inn

The only commercial venture in the Town of Highland Beach is the well-located Holiday Inn at 2809 South Ocean Boulevard, Highway A1A. Situated exactly on top of the dunes in Highland Beach, with its restaurant overlooking the sun-bleached beaches and turquoise waters of the shallows of the Atlantic Ocean, this coveted resort is the envy of many hoteliers in the region.

The inn is situated on three acres of land on the beach and surrounded by wafting sea oats and grasses. As such, it is a witness to the abruptness of the oceanfront lands of Highland Beach that changed from a vacant stretch of beaches to very high-intensity developments almost overnight. Built on single family zoned land, the motel is unique.

Constructed in 1971, it initially had 81 rooms, but then, in 1974, was expanded by 34 rooms to its present 115 rooms amidst significant controversy. Ocean Properties, Inc., the current owners, purchased the property in the early 1980s. Since that time, they have completed extensive redesign and redecorating. It is considered to be a wonderful asset to the town and is the only hotel actually on the beachfront between Palm Beach and Boca Raton. Vacationers can dine in air-conditioned luxury and gaze on the waters of the beautiful Atlantic Ocean where the colors range from pale turquoise in the shallows to cerulean then a cobalt blue as the waters deepen past the sandbars. It will remain the sole commercial business in the Town of Highland Beach if residents prevail in their desires to maintain the quality of life they have had for at least the past fifty years.

Highland Beach Holiday Inn,
Note: Intracoastal Waterway in background
Courtesy of Ocean Properties, Inc.

St. Lucy Catholic Church
The Only Church in Highland Beach

As communities were established across America over the past three hundred years, there came a time when everyone's effort working in the fields, in their shops, and establishing homes in the new settlements was not enough. "Man cannot live by bread alone" became manifest in the spiritual needs of the people in their communities.

In neighboring Delray Beach, by 1894, when the local area was settled only by Afro-American ex-slaves and their families, that community had already built its first church. It was only after their church existed and their spiritual needs were being properly addressed that they petitioned the Dade County School Board for a schoolteacher. At that time, Dade County included what would later become Monroe, Dade, Broward, Palm Beach and Martin Counties. When the first white settlers arrived in 1895, Mt. Olive Church and School #4 Delray Colored were already established. Meanwhile, the white settlers who had left their Midwestern homes, mainly in Michigan and Illinois, arrived and devoted all their time building their new homes in their farming "village-by-the-sea." They cleared the wetland, removed the underbrush and palmetto, and they fought off the menacing mosquitoes, sand gnats and stinging flies from dawn to dusk. After a few years, many sent for their wives and children. When the women arrived, their loneliness nearly drove them to exasperation, frustration and tears. The ladies determined that their families' spiritual, social and emotional needs had to be nurtured. As a result of their determination, one of the first buildings constructed in the new settlement was a community building at the northeast corner of Swinton and Atlantic Avenues. It provided space for the first schoolhouse for the white children and some adults who could not read or write, and also served as a makeshift community church and social center. The first community church was soon built in 1902 on the southwest corner of the same intersection.

In 1904, as the community began to grow, two new churches were built. Trinity Lutheran would serve the large and growing population of German heritage. It was on the southeast corner of N.E. Fifth Avenue and First Streets. In those days, most of the Germans were first generation children of immigrants. As a result, sermons were spoken in German until World War I.

St. Paul's Episcopal Church was built the same year at the northwest corner of S.E. Second Street and Swinton Avenue. Soon, more and more churches were built as more and more people, mainly from the Midwest, settled in coastal South Florida. Most of them settled in Delray Beach because it was the most established community between Fort Lauderdale and Palm Beach. The Methodist and Presbyterian churches were soon built to serve the needs of the local Midwesterners.

Research into the records of Delray Beach's St. Vincent Ferrer Catholic Church provided a treasure of historic information relating to the local population of the Catholic faith. Vincent Giordano is considered to be the first Catholic resident, arriving in Delray Beach in 1905. By 1920, the first service was held for three families, winter visitors, at the O'Malley family home. Rev. William Nachtrab, who conducted the Mass, was the pastor at Sacred Heart in Lake Worth, the nearest parish some twelve to fourteen miles away.

As the Catholic community grew, so did their needs. In 1940, a group of women met in the Vincent Giordano family home on S.E. Sixth Avenue in Delray Beach and planned to establish a local church. The Delray Beach (movie) Theater, fifty feet north of Atlantic Avenue on N.E. Fifth Avenue, was offered to the Catholic community for their Sunday Mass. The first service was held there on April 15, 1941, shortly before World War II. Reflecting the sparse population of the area, the Delray Beach parish territory was defined as bounded from north of Boynton Beach, south to the city limits of Deerfield Beach, clearly including what would later become Highland Beach and all of Boca Raton. By 1949, the first temporary St. Vincent Ferrer Church was in Delray. Today, that structure is the Parish Hall. It had a seating capacity of 500, a substantial congregation, especially during the winter tourist season. To further reflect the enormous change in the local population of Catholics, in 1949, Bishop Thomas McDonough came down from St. Augustine to dedicate the new church. Later, due to continued growth, the local churches became part of the new Diocese of Miami. That year was, of course, the same year Highland Beach became incorporated. But Highland Beach had not followed the classic settlement scenario. It had no church of any kind at the time since most of the small population attended churches in nearby Delray Beach or Boca Raton.

By 1954, Father John Kellaghan, the visionary and initial priest of St. Vincent's since May 1944, determined there was sufficient need to build a school. The local children were then attending Sacred Heart in Lake Worth.

St. Vincent's grew significantly into the 1960s, filling the needs of the rapidly growing area's Catholic population who came from the urban centers of the Northeast. The population of Delray Beach, a mostly rural farming town of 6,264 in 1950, doubled in the next decade to 12,230, and grew to 19,366 in 1970. Boca Raton went from 992 people in 1950 to 6,961 in 1960 and then to an astronomical annual growth rate of 40% to 28,506 in 1970, surpassing Delray Beach's population for the first time. The burgeoning population growth convinced Bishop Joseph Hurley, Ordinary of the State of Florida, to create more parishes. On October 3, 1968, while driving A1A in Highland Beach, Bishop Hurley decided, almost on first view, to purchase a vacant parcel of land he had spotted and build a church there. St. Lucy's was created that day.

St. Lucy Church
Courtesy of Highland Beach Archives

Reverend Michael Keller, Founding Pastor, conducted services from a temporary chapel. In 1972, Archbishop Coleman Carroll dedicated a temporary church built under the supervision of Reverend Patrick Slevin. In 1974, Reverend Anthony Chepanis, the third Pastor, purchased the old rectory and the property behind it. The continuing growth of the congregation had to be addressed, and a new church and parish hall became a necessity. Because the land was almost totally covered in mangroves, it took four painful years to obtain the brutally difficult permits from the State Department of Environmental Resources and the Corps of Engineers. Finally, permission from the state and federal governments to expand the church was received in 1978. In 1987, nine challenging years later, the Most Reverend Thomas V. Daily, the first Bishop of the new Palm Beach Diocese, dedicated the renovated church. Very soon, however, more expansion was required and in December 1992, the Most Reverend J. Keith Symons dedicated St. Lucy Church, its Parish Hall and the new rectory and offices that exist today.

Churches are often established to serve an existing stable population of a particular faith, and sometimes they are established to serve the expected new residents of the faith. In fact, on many occasions, new churches by their very existence attract new residents to the area and serve the entire community. As a result of all these factors, St. Lucy Church became an immediate servant of the existing residents of faith, mostly as it turned out, of Irish and Catholic heritage. But St. Lucy Church is more than just a house of worship for those of the Catholic faith. It has, in many ways, fulfilled the spiritual needs of the entire population of Highland Beach simply by its existence and prominent location along the west side of Ocean Boulevard. Its architecturally dramatic yet pleasing design by Mr. E. N. Turano of Boca Raton, formerly of New York City, and its copious landscape, deeply set back from the main road, symbolizes the excellence, good taste, and harmony of the community. With a current membership of 600 families, approximately 25% of the year-round population, it overflows during the winter season with seasonal homeowners. The main intimate sanctuary seating capacity of 484 can be easily enlarged to accommodate 500 more parishioners by opening the rear Mosaic wall into an additional large room which can also be used for a variety of church functions. It is an oasis within a residential oasis of coastal South Florida, providing solace, a place of spiritual respite, soul nourishing peace and love for anyone who wishes to pray or simply meditate.

St. Lucy Church is the only house of worship in Highland Beach, as it has been since its founding in 1968. As this is being written, St. Lucy's is a spiritual anchor, a steadfast, diligent House of God with Reverend Gerald Grace, Pastor, and Reverend James N. Gelson, S.J. Parochial Vicar, serving the needs of the parishioners. It is clearly a vital part of the community of Highland Beach.

St. Lucy Church
Dedicated in 1987
Courtesy of Highland Beach Archives

The
Indefatigable Arlin Voress
The 1990's

It has been said that there are no such things as coincidences, and that events are merely the result of a confluence of forces that are sometimes beyond understanding. It is also believed that leaders oftentimes emerge exactly when they are needed.

Such could be considered the case when Arlin and Cary Louise Voress bought a home in Bel Lido, a luxurious single-family waterfront neighborhood in the south portion of Highland Beach in 1989. While they had first selected to retire in a residence purchased in Boca Raton in 1974, they later determined that they preferred Highland Beach and its waterfront community.

As the pressures increased on the town leaders, disagreements began to emerge within the citizenry as to where Highland Beach was going and what it might become. Some felt the leadership needed to address the integrity of their town and began seeking a different vision, one that would focus on the human needs of the residents. They also strongly believed that the town's house had to be put in order, particularly as to their independent water supply and treatment, and within the Town Hall itself. They felt strongly that those twin issues of constant court battles and other major Town Hall distractions were keeping them from their hopes to live in Highland Beach in peace and tranquility during their autumn years.

Among those dozen or so concerned citizens taking the lead were Tom Reid, Victor Hadeed, Gerald Golden, King Cayce and Leonard Bell. They diligently sought to define the areas that had to be addressed, then sought out among the residents those particular individuals with the appropriate qualifications, including business experience, diplomacy, capability, and knowledge.

Recognizing that the solution and preservation of the town's water supply was imperative and that the continuing court battles with deep-pocketed, determined developers were very expensive and sapping the town's financial strength, they began looking for the person who could advance their agenda for the betterment of the residents.

Arlin Voress's qualifications and background had not gone unnoticed and consequently he was asked to serve on the Water Advisory Board. After being so appointed, he drew on his education in Chemical Engineering at the University of West Virginia, his home state, and his forty-year career with Union Carbide, that major respected multi-national corporation. He was urged by fellow residents to bring this extensive background to bear on the outstanding and vital issues of Highland Beach.

Arlin and Cary Louise Voress had known each other since the age of five, and together they traveled to many places and confronted many challenges during his career. As a result, true to his wealth of engineering experience, Voress immediately proceeded to determine the facts of the town's water problems. He found that indeed in 1968, the Town of Highland Beach had built its first water plant and had bought twelve acres on the west side of the Intracoastal Waterway on which to locate its well fields rather than on the east side, too close to the sea and its salt water. It had later purchased a one and one-half acre parcel even farther west, nearly to U.S. Highway #1 in Boca Raton for additional wells away from the ocean. The wells, about 120 feet deep, were tapping into and withdrawing raw water from the subterranean Biscayne Aquifer. Voress, the new member of the Water Advisory Board, having extensive experience operating water plants, looked carefully into the situation and also found that not only did the town not have a proper state permit allowing it to draw from the aquifer, it was not reporting test results to the state. Private wells in town were rapidly becoming salinated. Further, since he also found there were no main water meters in the town, consumption information was unavailable and, in a word, the situation was simply "out of control."

He appropriately presented his findings and his recommendations which were delivered from the Advisory Board to the then Mayor Betty Jean Stewart and the Town Commission. Without proper permitting and test monitoring, the town was in violation of state laws and, because its current tests indicated increasing salinity levels, the state would have the power through the South Florida Water Management District to shut down the town's operation. Under Voress' leadership, the town properly and quickly responded. It began appropriate monitoring, obtained proper state permits, and watched over the increasingly alarming water test results.

To be sure, the town's explosive growth occurred over a very short period of years without deliberation and adjustments. Conditions were changing too rapidly for the town to monitor. It had literally expanded from a few dozen single-family houses with their own private wells and septic tanks to hundreds of very large multi-family high-rise condominium apartments. The explosive growth and its impact on water consumption was not correctly addressed. Many other issues commanded the attention of the not so experienced but concerned leadership. Mayor Betty Jean Stewart and the council members were convinced that there was much to do to protect the integrity of their community. Their neighboring cities were experiencing similar difficulties, the almost unbelievable population growth that was stretching all communities in South Florida. The town leaders took extraordinary action to address their extraordinary challenges. They called on the experience, wisdom and time of its citizens by forming five advisory boards to consider the plethora of requests for development and construction, work with the town's staff, and make recommendations to the mayor and council. As a result, on December 27, 1988, with Town Commission concurrence, Mayor Stewart signed Resolutions 548 through 552, officially creating the Planning Board, the Financial Advisory Board, the Community Appearance Board, the Code Enforcement Board, and the Board of Adjustment.

Arlin Voress and his colleagues on the Water Advisory Board rolled up their sleeves and went to work. They discovered that more than 60% of the town's treated water consumption was used just to irrigate lawns and landscape, while only 40% was used for human consumption and in households.

The alarming saline intrusion into the town's system and, as a result, into the Biscayne Aquifer was clearly due to several factors. First, there was a fairly serious drought during the first half of 1989. Even so, the towns and cities, including Highland Beach, continued to withdraw their usual volumes of water with no reduction in spite of the lack of rain. As a result, without replenishment by its normal rainy season, the over-pumping was acting like a vacuum cleaner, drawing seawater and its high saline content into the aquifer. Highland Beach was over-pumping and something had to be done. Steps were vital, and since Voress found such a high percentage of usage went to landscape irrigation, he recommended that the town simply reduce permitted days of sprinkling of landscape by at least one day per week. "Eureka!" The tactic worked, demand went down significantly, and the water problem had a solution without causing human hardships. At least for the time being.

By 1991, during Joe Boulay's term as mayor, the town had made good progress in its front burner issues. That same year, due to his diligence and capable leadership regarding the town's water problem, Arlin Voress, retiree, was elected to the Town Council.

But when Arlin Voress later became mayor, he found there were still remaining some five or six serious lawsuits against the town, with the most contentious and most complicated related to the so-called Hoffman tract, a 24-acre parcel on which the owner demanded protection of his "vested rights" to develop a large complex of condominium apartments. In fact, that lawsuit had been involved in the courts since the early 1970s. In 1974, an agreement was reached to allow the development of 840 apartments on 24 acres, or 35 units per acre. An integral pact of that agreement was a key requirement: the complex had to be completed within ten years, by 1984.

Bel Lido development
1963
Courtesy of Highland Beach Archives

Complications arose in the form of the enforcement of the Wetlands Act, a federal law prohibiting the filling, destruction or use of natural wetlands, including those on the Hoffman tract. As it turned out, the federal government did not issue to the developer the hard fought permit to fill the Hoffman wetlands for nearly six years of the ten-year allowance by the town. The developers then came back to the town and declared it was impossible to complete the project within the four remaining years. Later, the developer alleged that the then mayor had written them a letter allowing an additional five years for completion by extending the deadline from 1984 to 1989. The town commission cried "foul" and declared the letter was invalid by saying that the mayor could not unilaterally extend the deadline without the authority properly delegated by vote of the entire Town Commission. The commission members refused to endorse the extension. "Back to court, Mr. Sliney."

These were the years following yet another new federal law, the Tax Reform Act of 1986, much of which removed certain tax deductions or "tax shelter" benefits advantageous to real estate development for many years. "Artificial values" declared the pro-reform groups. "You'll lower the value of all commercial real estate by 40% and destroy values of real estate assets on which all lending institutions base their loans," declared the opposite "please don't do this" crowd. As a direct result of this new law, havoc and chaos in the capital markets and real estate industry prevailed for several years, impacting new and ongoing developments. It was especially exacerbated by the fact that the new law was made retroactive by nine months. Among the casualties of the impact of the law were most of the nation's savings and loan associations, multitudes of developers, private lenders, banks, investors, including doctors, dentists, attorneys, and real estate projects in process. Many failed because the borrowers could not continue payments as agreed under contract.

To deal with the catastrophic impact on the nation, the government, "in its wisdom," created the Resolution Trust Corporation, the RTC, which was to resolve the devastation. Billions were lost. The Hoffman tract was among those projects severely impacted by the long delays relating to the Wetlands Act and then, almost without warning, by the 1986 Tax Reform Act.

But the town was also a casualty of these events. It withheld building permits and got sued by the developers. It was during these years impacted by the new Act when Arlin Voress assumed the office of mayor. He was faced with the painful situation that indeed the RTC had taken over the lending institutions who had handed over to the RTC many projects, sometimes euphemistically labeled "assets," including the Hoffman tract. His courtroom adversary was now the Resolution Trust Corporation, which truly had "very deep pockets." They also had an incredible $30 million judgement that had survived the lost appeals. As even in wartime, billions were made by those who exploited the opportunities. The developer's award came to a whopping pro rata cost of nearly $12,000, including legal costs, per Highland Beach family. In fact, for the town, this most excruciating experience was also sobering. For years, the town had almost always succeeded in winning in court or through settlements with the developers. But this extraordinary situation, so costly, could impact the town for years, not only in its capital, but also in its efforts to bring the intensity of its housing stock from the previous high levels of 60 units per acre to much lower levels.

Mayor Voress, who assumed office after Mayor Joe Boulay resigned, in 1993, surely had his work cut out for himself in behalf of his community. But, he could not accept the possibility that the town would have to pay a total of $34 million in addition to permitting the 840 apartments sought by the developers.

In court, the developer had demanded damages from loss of development of profits of $30 million and 840 units sought at the outset, and sued the town. After all those years of battle, hundreds of thousands of dollars in legal fees and other costs, the town was now being forced to accept this very large project and pay a judgement of $30 million plus $4 million in legal costs claimed by the plaintiff. Voress, quite adamant, disagreed.

Highland Beach Water Tower, 2002
Courtesy of Highland Beach Archives

Mayor Voress, in keeping with his training and years of valuable business experience, created a plan that, if successful, would significantly reduce or eliminate the entire capital judgement on the town and, concurrently, reduce the court-approved 840 units. It would be quite a near miracle if the mayor and his town could pull it off.

Mayor Voress dedicated himself to resolving as best he could this remaining major litigation burdening the town. He put together a legal task team with as much political clout as he could since his opposite party was a quasi-governmental political agency that was part of the U.S. government. He sought support and counsel from the local district's congressman and both U.S. senators, one of whom declined. Then, not being successful in that sector, he turned to career colleagues in Washington. He marshaled the best Washington attorneys to represent the town, called on all his friends, associates and political powers to achieve at least a level playing field with the giant RTC. It truly was, in many ways, a David and Goliath encounter. The RTC was heavily armed with hundreds of attorneys, enormous capital resources and a public and government-supported mission. The $30 million judgement was reinforced by the developers winning appeals before the 11th Circuit Court of Appeals in Atlanta. Highland Beach, a town of perhaps 3,000 residents, albeit a wealthy community, had lost every battle in court. But, it is no exaggeration to add, they had not yet beaten Arlin Voress. He looked straight at me when he spoke,

> "You can't be intimidated and you can't give up. We found a way, and decided on a bold new approach. We argued the constitutional issues of the powers of the state, that is, state's rights versus those of the federal government. We re-petitioned the 11th Circuit Court of Appeals. This time we requested an 'en banque' hearing inasmuch the earlier appeal had been determined, as is often customary, by just three of the judges. The constitutional issues we raised were so important that the outcome could have had a powerful national impact on the RTC's core mission. It could have undermined their efforts across America. As a result, tension began to build at very high levels. All parties had a huge interest at risk.
>
> The town was backed against the wall with this expensive judgement against it, yet, my determination and conviction led to confidence. The developers stood to lose (or gain) tens of millions of dollars, and the Court of Appeals was placed in a position of determining an issue that could conceivably be reversed by the U.S. Supreme Court which of course they did not want. 'Checkmate.'"

We were all very focused and quite anxious as the parties and all those lawyers met outside the courtroom. All knew the previous verdicts could come tumbling down. Both plaintiff (RTC) and defendant's attorneys (Highland Beach) worked feverishly, sensing mutual benefit if a settlement could be reached. Fortuitously, while the judges were sequestered, in the eleventh hour so to speak, they succeeded in reaching an amicable settlement in the corridor outside the courtroom. Everyone, including the judges, breathed a sigh of relief. There was then no cause for a verdict."

In many ways, it was a win-win resolution. The town fought the good fight, but in the end, all parties had to compromise. The RTC and its purchaser/developer client would be allowed by the town to build just 50% of the original proposal, 420 dwelling units, and the town would be relieved of the $30 million judgement plus $4 million in plaintiff legal fees, and instead would pay $5 million. Mayor Voress, in his efforts, had fully removed 420 apartments from the town and eliminated $30 million in debt, nearly $12,000 per citizen of Highland Beach. That new project on 17 acres of the Hoffman tract would later become Toscana.

Toscana Ocean Club, 2004
Courtesy of Omega Development, Inc.

By the time Arlin Voress fulfilled his state mandated three-term limit in March 1999, many of the town's major problems were finally behind them. The water conflicts were solved, and the five to six costly lawsuits were either settled or completely adjudicated, and Arlin Voress could now go back to enjoying his retirement years with his lifelong friend, companion and wife, Cary Louise.

In the words of Leonard Bell, longtime civic activist and guardian of the town's historical legacy, Arlin Voress was the appropriate "Action Agent" for solving the challenging issues facing the town, including the lawsuits, the water problems, and the "unpleasantness" at Town Hall. "With determination, loads of experience and fortitude, he did so," resolving the "bricks and mortars problems" of Highland Beach.

In the eyes of the leading civic watchdogs, the town still needed its government to address the cultural and more intangible needs that continued to emerge in a constantly evolving social community. As Mr. Bell commented in retrospect,

> "After Arlin Voress had accomplished his goals, we knew the town needed to address our social and cultural needs and respect our history. And, after the incredible success of Arlin Voress, we knew we needed someone who was just as strong, as determined as he had been, yet focused on the intangibles. So, in 1998, we went to Tom Reid, who by that time was our Vice-

Mayor, and urged him to continue in leadership as Mayor. We also placed before him our support of his vision of what he felt our town must have. Delray Beach had recently gone through amazing success from its Visions 2000 in 1988 and 1989, and by financing its downtown renaissance and investing in new 'bricks and mortar,' so to speak. Later, in 1993, it held its Visions 2005 retreat which was focused on its cultural needs, neighborhoods and youth needs. Again, it was eminently successful. Thus, we felt we should, as citizens, do as they did by articulating our vision for a new cultural center and library—a place where our residents and visitors could gather, exchange ideas, learn, sit in quiet and tranquility, meet for group performances, enter discussions, use high-tech computers—and also be a home for our archives, of which we have many.

We found in Tom Reid a sensitive man who was committed to our community; very capable, amiable, and very much aware of our social needs. His vision, he assured us, was consistent with ours.

While Tom's personality was quite different from Arlin's, and his personal interests were not similar, it became clear from the outset that he embraced the same vision as ours, wrapped his arms around them, and became our next 'Action Agent.'"

Thomas J. Reid

A Visionary Mayor
In Pursuit of Excellence

Tom J. Reid, a powerfully built, imposing man, is diligent, determined, quick to smile, an extraordinary diplomat, and in many ways a "gentle giant." He is clearly a "people person." Mayor Reid described his background to me,

"I was born in Manhattan on October 21, 1930 in St. Andrews Hospital on 78th Street. From age six, I lived in a boarding school until the 8th grade, when I went to LaSalle Military Academy and graduated in 1948. I was eleven years old when World War II began. My entire youth was under the discipline of the Catholic Church. I was away from home all those years. I attended Manhattan College, a Catholic school, where I obtained my degree in accounting. My brother, Donald, another well-brought up Catholic boy, went on to Fordham University. Both of us were disciplined from birth through graduation in the parochial environs. We lived a cloistered, military lifestyle everyday. Of course, this was throughout the difficult Great Depression and World War II."

In 1951, Tom married and with his wife had three children: Thomas, Dona, and Richard. Even as a senior in college, reflecting his personal discipline of responsibility, Tom Reid created his own accounting firm, Thomas J. Reid Company, in Manhattan. His firm's work focused almost exclusively on preparing tax returns. To this day, after more than fifty-two years, Thomas J. Reid Company still provides tax accounting services.

> "I worked my way through college as a short order cook, theater usher…virtually anything to make a living. I was a fulltime worker while I was a fulltime student. These experiences made me who I am today, and while those were tough years, I learned so much. I'm a good salesman, a disciplined, honest man, a good husband and a good father."

Following jobs with Coopers Lybrand, Honeywell, and New York Life, he energized his company, and over the years, accumulated some of his more important clients, including 170 Coca-Cola franchises, and from 170 to 185 Seven-Eleven owners. He worked with perhaps as much as 1,500 different franchises in all five boroughs in New York City. When he remembers his clientele, he smiles his Irish grin and modestly comments, "I've kept busy all my life."

With his business almost exclusively tax returns, his busiest times of the year logically coincided with the tourist season in South Florida. So, ready to relax for awhile following the Internal Revenue Service deadline of April 15th each year, having remarried, he and his wife Ruth began coming to Delray Beach in May, 1979. They could manage to be away from New York at least eleven to twelve weeks each year. After several years of vacationing in the area, they decided that they wanted to live on the dunes of Highland Beach. As a result, in 1985, they purchased their current home in Highland Beach at Ocean Dunes. Although they paid a handsome price of $190,000 that year for the apartment, the Palm Beach County Tax Assessor reckons that today it is now worth $350,000, or nearly double their purchase price. Such a value increase over sixteen years reflects more than a 5% compounded value increase average per year while providing one of the finest living environments in America. He laughed as he described the summer Florida vacations he and Ruth enjoyed which always began just as most tourists and winter residents were returning North.

> "We were snowbirds in reverse. And yet, to maintain our Florida residency, we could not stay in New York more than six months in a given year."

Tom Reid's involvement in the civic, government, and church activities of Highland Beach began almost from the day he arrived in the town. Throughout their years in Highland Beach, St. Lucy Catholic Church in Highland Beach was and remains most important to Mayor and Mrs. Reid's daily life. At St. Lucy's, Tom works closely with its pastor, Father Gerald Grace, as the church sacristan. Ruth is currently treasurer of the Council of Catholic Women. After his morning hours at church, he is at the Town Hall each weekday three hours per day, with some days for thirty minutes if little needs to be tended to, and on many days, all day.

Tom Reid was elected to the Commission of Highland Beach in 1996. In 1998, he became Vice-Mayor, serving alongside Mayor Arlin Voress during those difficult years of major lawsuits, Town Hall problems, and solving the water issues. In 1999 when Mayor Voress completed his multiple terms, Tom Reid became Mayor of Highland Beach.

"When I became mayor following Arlin Voress and his success with the highly stressful RTC-Hoffman Tract lawsuit, as well as resolving the water crisis, I thought it would be simple. But, it hasn't been. There is much attention needed on many important issues facing our community. I inherited from Arlin the Hoffman development now known as Tuscana, and all its concomitant difficult ramifications. In addition, the remaining seven acres are still in debate for high-intensity development. It too has become, regrettably, a highly charged, problematic issue, and a very time-consuming affair for us.

Arlin deserves all the credit for saving Highland Beach's residents a huge amount of money, nearly $12,000 per residence, over $30 million, plus cutting in half the allowable development on the Hoffman tract. He did it himself. I give him all the credit.

His legacy also includes the new innovative water system we are now constructing which I must oversee. It is the 'R.O.' or Reverse Osmosis System which extracts water by pumping from new wells about 1,000 feet deep. We will no longer have to pump through shallow wells at about 120-150 feet deep from the Biscayne Aquifer. We'll be in really good shape when that's done next year. Now we are looking ahead."

Rarely does any officeholder, particularly a mayor or president of any given organization extend credit to his predecessor. It takes a strong individual to do so, and that reflects very well on the character and strength of Mayor Reid. It also takes a remarkable success story to deserve such applause. And Arlin Voress deserved and received a resounding applause of gratitude from the mayor of his town.

Mayor Reid continued,

"We must continue to deal with several important and complex, yet not so stressful, issues, like the county's proposed oceanfront public park at the rocks, 'Jap' or 'Yamato' Rocks, our new sewer system, redesign of the A1A State Road to allow bicycle paths on both sides, as well as the new Reverse Osmosis System.

Now we want to focus on bringing a new cultural center and library to Highland Beach. It will provide many things. It will preserve our historical legacy and artifacts of which we have a great deal. I envision a top-of-the-line cultural and enlightening center, a place for performances, high-tech computer capacity, the latest in preservation and use of information, and a place of tranquility for our citizens and visitors. It will be relevant and appropriate for our unique community. There is much to be done."

Because of his life long interest in archaeology, Tom Reid embraced the potentials of the importance of determining what had taken place over the many centuries along the high dunes of the community.

"The discovery of the Indian mounds—middens—on the ocean dunes of Highland Beach was a most exciting event in the history of our town. Even today we are finding more."

As a result of all his youthful learning, the archeological discoveries of the prehistoric Indian mounds meant more to him than to most people and have been the genesis of his passionate endeavors to ignite similar passion and support from his fellow residents

His passion for understanding and preserving the town's history was infectious. He convinced other residents and leaders, including Leonard Bell, Arlin Voress and other active citizens that these historical findings had to be considered uppermost in the town's priorities.

Tom Reid's love and interest in archaeology date back to his youth. When he was just a boy, his mother made sure that he and his brother visited virtually all of the museums in New York City, including the Museum of Natural History, the Museum of American Indian History, and the extraordinary art museums, including Frank Lloyd Wright's incomparable Guggenheim Museum. From these holiday and weekend visits over the years, Tom learned about archeology and Chinese art painting, both of which have become major parts of his lifelong interests. He comments,

> "I've always been interested in art. I am now a teacher of Chinese brush painting. My aunt, a master, taught me Chinese brush-painting and now I can teach others. I just completed taping 26-hours of television programming that I wrote, directed, and produced. I loved doing it so much."

He quickly became the driving force for the development of the proposed "Center of Enlightenment," the soon-to-be built Highland Beach Library. As a testament to his focus and active leadership, the citizens of Highland Beach voted to borrow $2 million toward the museum's construction. Another $100,000 was voluntarily contributed in a 1997 fund drive led by Reid's cohort, Leonard Bell, to expand the existing library. Even more impressive, grants recently have been obtained totaling $500,000.

It appears at this writing that soon after the completion of the Reverse Osmosis water plant construction, the new library will become a reality, endorsed by the whole community and the Town Commission. This new cultural center, to be located overlooking the beautiful Intracoastal Waterway, will be a testament to Mayor Tom Reid's passion, leadership and deep commitment to the community of Highland Beach, his home.

"I am committed to a grand vision of our town, including the new library and historical-cultural center. I love where I live and I am doing all I can to see that Highland Beach fulfills its promise. It will remain true to the quality of life our citizens expect and deserve. Together with the Highland Beach Historical Society led by Leonard Bell and our excellent Town Commission, we are moving into the 21st century, carefully, with wisdom and attention to our incredible history and promise of the future."

The Mayors
of
Highland Beach

Even before the Town of Highland Beach was incorporated in 1949, there were people who were considered de facto leaders of the growing post-war community then known locally as "Jap Rocks." Most people chosen to lead even now do so out of a sense of dedication to their community. But by that year, there were no residents of Japanese heritage, not even visitors who walked east along the Yamato path to "Yamato Rocks," nor were there any of Indian heritage. In fact, those some twenty-one known registered voters at the time were almost totally comprised of people who lived along the beach between Boca Raton and Delray Beach in an area that would become the Town of Highland Beach in fewer than ten years. There were no "pioneers" to whom residents could look to for counsel, wisdom or someone with that historic knowledge who could, with that knowledge, bond the people to the community.

Indeed, those who were elected initially to the first town commission would be chosen because of their knowledge of management, accounting, and hands-on capabilities to actually deal with the initial and future issues that would arise. No professionals were needed yet. The first group of leaders, H.H. Dubendorff, R.W. Hertwig (manager of The Blue Waters Inn), and J. Morrison Smith, led by Mayor Robert Totterdale and Vice-Mayor R.S. Weeks, assumed the unenviable and certainly gratis job of managing the small town's affairs.

In time, the need for a truly organized government became apparent as the twin issues of water and all that the word encompassed, and land use had to be addressed. At that time, each home had its own wells for water. There was no central system. By 1950, the population reached 52. By 1960, reflecting the almost explosive population growth of all of South Florida during the next few years, the count reached 65. And by 1970, with an astonishing annualized growth rate of 10%, the town's count came to 624. In 1980, Highland Beach reached a population of 2030, and by 1990, 3209. Neighboring communities experienced similar growth rates. Boca Raton virtually exploded during those years, increasing from just 992 residents in 1950 to 59,000 in 1990. All towns in the area needed but did not always get wise political leadership, yet they were faced with extraordinary demands beyond the experience, knowledge and capabilities of their political leaders.

Highland Beach was especially fortunate because of its small size, in spite of its growth rate described in percentages. Though small, its rapid growth taxed the capabilities of its leaders. Most of them had led quite successful careers in the corporate and government administrative sectors before retiring to Highland Beach and were experienced in such things. However, Highland Beach, almost from its start, came to face almost unheard of challenges of growth, legal disputes, and serious water problems. Most seemed insurmountable.

Unlike many other areas of South Florida, few, if any, new residents of Highland Beach came to "start over," make their fortune, or to "get lost." Rather, these people came with financially sound economic stability and simply wanted to "enjoy life." Most brought with them successful careers and sound thinking. They also brought with their silver hair volumes of wisdom. In this dimension, Highland Beach, while not having a perfect record by any means—does any organized human society?—has almost always been able to call on residents of integrity, sagacity, devotion and commitment to the betterment of their community. Recognizing the amazing 20-20 vision of hindsight, some decisions made can be viewed as terrible mistakes. Over the 53 years of incorporation, they have accomplished a good deal of success and, having had to face unfamiliar pressures of growth demands can hardly be criticized at this time. Essentially unpaid volunteers, one can be sure they all did their best, and while only a few left unpleasant debris, most have succeeded in their quest to maintain the quality of life for their residents. They all, for the most part, deserve acclaim for their love of community, their enormous hours of contribution, determination and, in the end, positive results.

The mayors and commissioners of Highland Beach: 1949-2002

Courtesy of Town of Highland Beach

OFFICE	1949	1950	1951
Mayor	Robert Totterdale	Robert Totterdale	Robert Totterdale
Vice Mayor	R.S. Weeks	B.C. Heaton	B.C. Heaton
Commissioner	H.H. Dubendorff	H.H. Dubendorff	J. M. Smith
Commissioner	R.W. Hertwig	R.W. Hertwig	R.W. Hertwig
Commissioner	J. Morrison Smith	J. Morrison Smith	Harry H. Pickwell

OFFICE	1952	1953	1954
Mayor	Robert Totterdale	Totterdale/Smith	J.M. Smith
Vice Mayor	J.M. Smith	J. Harmon	J. Harmon
Commissioner	J. Harmon	Roger Skillman	R. Skillman
Commissioner	R.W. Hertwig	R.W. Hertwig	R.W. Hertwig
Commissioner	Pickwell/Skillman	Mildred Nobel	Mildred Nobel

OFFICE	1955	1956	1957
Mayor	J.M. Smith	Smith/A. Eypel	Arthur Eypel
Vice Mayor	Harmon/A. Eypel	Eypel/Breckenridge	Robert Breckenridge
Commissioner	Mildred Nobel	H.F. Weber	J. Bond Winston
Commissioner	R.W. Hertwig	Mildred Nobel	Mildred Nobel
Commissioner	Skillman/Weber	R.W. Hertwig	Matthew Bertash

OFFICE	1958	1959	1960
Mayor	Arthur Eypel	Arthur Eypel	Arthur Eypel
Vice Mayor	R. Breckenridge	R. Breckenridge	Breckenridge/Turner
Commissioner	Mildred Nobel	Mildred Nobel	Arthur Jones
Commissioner	J.B. Winston	Matthew Bertash	Matthew Bertash
Commissioner	Matthew Bertash	Winston/Jones	Mildred Nobel

OFFICE	1961	1962	1963
Mayor	Arthur Eypel	Arthur Eypel	Arthur Eypel
Vice Mayor	James Turner	James Turner	James Turner
Commissioner	Arthur Jones	Arthur Jones	Arthur Jones
Commissioner	Matthew Bertash	Mildred Nobel	Mildred Nobel
Commissioner	Mildred Nobel	Matthew Bertash	Bertash/Beekman

OFFICE	1955	1956	1957
Mayor	J.M. Smith	Smith/A. Eypel	Arthur Eypel
Vice Mayor	Harmon/A. Eypel	Eypel/Breckenridge	Robert Breckenridge
Commissioner	Mildred Nobel	H.F. Weber	J. Bond Winston
Commissioner	R.W. Hertwig	Mildred Nobel	Mildred Nobel
Commissioner	Skillman/Weber	R.W. Hertwig	Matthew Bertash

OFFICE	1958	1959	1960
Mayor	Arthur Eypel	Arthur Eypel	Arthur Eypel
Vice Mayor	R. Breckenridge	R. Breckenridge	Breckenridge/Turner
Commissioner	Mildred Nobel	Mildred Nobel	Arthur Jones
Commissioner	J.B. Winston	Matthew Bertash	Matthew Bertash
Commissioner	Matthew Bertash	Winston/Jones	Mildred Nobel

OFFICE	1961	1962	1963
Mayor	Arthur Eypel	Arthur Eypel	Arthur Eypel
Vice Mayor	James Turner	James Turner	James Turner
Commissioner	Arthur Jones	Arthur Jones	Arthur Jones
Commissioner	Matthew Bertash	Mildred Nobel	Mildred Nobel
Commissioner	Mildred Nobel	Matthew Bertash	Bertash/Beekman

OFFICE	1964	1965	1966
Mayor	Eypel/C. Hackman	Clem Hackman	Clem Hackman
Vice Mayor	Turner/F. Bunn	Frederick Bunn	Frederick Bunn
Commissioner	Mildred Nobel	Arthur Jones	Mildred Nobel
Commissioner	Arthur Jones	Mildred Nobel	Harold Johnson
Commissioner	Beekman/Johnson	Harold Johnson	A. Jones/Wingle

OFFICE	1967	1968	1969
Mayor	Clem Hackman	Hackman/Horton	Louis Horton
Vice Mayor	M. Nobel/Bunn	Mildred Nobel	Nobel/Vedder
Commissioner	Laurence Wingle	Milton Beekman	Marshall McCook
Commissioner	Johnson/Beekman	Marshall McCook	Milton Beekman
Commissioner	Bunn/Nobel	Laurence Wingle	Clem Hackman

OFFICE	1970	1971	1972
Mayor	Louis Horton	Louis Horton	Louis Horton
Vice Mayor	J. Warren Vedder	J. Warren Vedder	Michael Dent
Commissioner	Clem Hackman	F.R. Jurish	F.R. Jurish
Commissioner	Milton Beekman	Clem Hackman	Leslie Joy
Commissioner	McCook/F.R. Jurish	Leslie Joy	Ruth Mumford

OFFICE	1973	1974	1975
Mayor	Louis Horton	Morton Gilday	Morton Gilday
Vice Mayor	Michael Dent	Michael Dent	Leslie Joy
Commissioner	Leslie Joy	Leslie Joy	Ruth Mumford
Commissioner	Ruth Mumford	Ruth Mumford	Robert Clark
Commissioner	Morton Gilday	Robert Clark	Harry Bauer

OFFICE	1976	1977	1978
Mayor	Morton Gilday	Morton Gilday	Louis Horton
Vice Mayor	William Hultz	William Hultz	Ruth Mumford
Commissioner	Ruth Mumford	Leslie Joy	Robert Clark
Commissioner	Leslie Joy	Ruth Mumford	Leslie Joy
Commissioner	Robert Clark	Robert Clark	Harold Storm

OFFICE	1979	1980	1981
Mayor	Louis Horton	Louis Horton	Louis Horton
Vice Mayor	Ruth Mumford	Harold Storm	Harold Storm
Commissioner	Harold Storm	Harry Bauer	Mary Louise Blosser
Commissioner	Harry Bauer	Peter Genovese	John Basso
Commissioner	Peter Genovese	Mary Louis Blosser	Edward Sullivan

OFFICE	1982	1983	1984
Mayor	Louis Horton	Louis Horton	Louis Horton
Vice Mayor	Mary Louise Blosser	Mary L. Blosser	Mary L. Blosser
Commissioner	John Basso	Harry Walker	John Basso
Commissioner	Edward Sullivan	William Paul	William Paul
Commissioner	Harry Walker	Betty Jean Stewart	Betty Jean Stewart

OFFICE	1985	1986	1987
Mayor	Edward Sullivan	Edward Sullivan	Betty Jean Stewart
Vice Mayor	Mary L. Blosser	Mary L. Blosser	Mary L. Blosser
Commissioner	John Basso	John Basso	John Basso
Commissioner	William Grier	William Grier	Robert Scholz
Commissioner	Betty Jean Stewart	Betty Jean Stewart	David Robinson

OFFICE	1988	1989	1990
Mayor	Betty Jean Stewart	Joseph Boulay	Joseph Boulay
Vice Mayor	John Basso	John Basso	William Paul
Commissioner	Robert Scholz	Doris Rome	Marvin Waldman
Commissioner	David Robinson	Marvin Waldman	Betty Jean Stewart
Commissioner	Doris Rome	Betty Jean Stewart	Harold C. Chambers

OFFICE	1991	1992	1993
Mayor	Joseph Boulay	Joseph Boulay	Arlin Voress
Vice Mayor	William Paul	William Paul	William Paul
Commissioner	Arlin Voress	Arlin Voress	David Augenstein
Commissioner	Arthur Eypel	Arthur Eypel	Arthur Eypel
Commissioner	John Rand	John Rand	John Rand

OFFICE	1994	1995	1996
Mayor	Arlin Voress	Arlin Voress	Arlin Voress
Vice Mayor	William Paul	William Paul	John Rand
Commissioner	David Augenstein	David Augenstein	Arthur Eypel
Commissioner	Arthur Eypel	Arthur Eypel	David Augenstein
Commissioner	John Rand	John Rand	Thomas Reid

OFFICE	1997	1998	1999
Mayor	Arlin Voress	Arlin Voress	Thomas Reid
Vice Mayor	John Rand	Thomas Reid	Michael Hill
Commissioner	Thomas Reid	John Sorrelli	John Sorrelli
Commissioner	David Augenstein	David Augenstein	Paul Kane
Commissioner	Michael Hill	Michael Hill	Robert Lowe

OFFICE	2000	2001	2002
Mayor	Thomas Reid	Thomas Reid	Thomas Reid
Vice Mayor	Michael Hill	Michael Hill	Michael Hill
Commissioner	John Sorrelli	John Sorrelli	John Sorrelli
Commissioner	Rachael Scala-Pistone	Rachael Scala-Pistone	Rachael Scala-Pistone
Commissioner	Robert Lowe	Robert Lowe	Robert Lowe

Population Figures

Year	Boca Raton	Delray Beach	Highland Beach	Palm Beach County
1895*	8**	120	N/A	N/A
1899*	N/A**	75**	N/A	N/A
1900*	16	150	N/A	N/A
1908	30	N/A	N/A	N/A
1910	N/A	250	N/A	N/A
1920	100	1,051	N/A	N/A****
1930	320	2,433	N/A	51,781
1940	723	3,661	N/A	79,989
1950	992	6,264	52***	114,688
1960	6,961	12,230	65	228,106
1970	28,506	19,366	624	348,993
1980	53,343	43,325	2,030	576,863
1990	59,000	47,181	3,209	863,518
2000*	65,000	55,000	3,775	1,067,000
2010*	N/A	N/A	N/A	1,262,400

Sources:

Boca Raton Chamber of Commerce Boca Raton, Boca Raton Historical Society, Inc., Delray Beach Historical Society, Inc., Delray Beach Chamber of Commerce, City of Delray Beach Planning Department, Palm Beach County Planning Department, State Library of Florida, a Division of The Florida State Department

* Designates estimates only. All other fiigures are U.S. Census.

** The hard freeze of 1898 caused many people to leave the area.

*** Census notes that Highland Beach was incorporated in 1949.

**** In 1928 the Palm County courthouse burned down and all records were lost.

Note: Population figures for Boca Raton, Boynton and Delray Beach are within the city limits only. Since the late 1960s populations adjacent thereto are nearly equal stated, effectively doubling the populations of each.

The Next Fifty Years
2003-2053

By the 21st century, most of South Florida had gone through extraordinary growth—from one of the least populated states of America to one of the most populated—from perhaps 20,000 people to fourteen million. It began the 20th century as one of the last frontiers in America to one of the most developed.

Highland Beach, as part of southeastern Florida, with its beckoning incomparable shorelines and pristine beaches became a mecca for those seeking a new home without leaving America. But this unique residential community witnessed its greatest change during the last half of the century, beginning with its charter in 1949. For most of those five decades, city had to deal with its water sources, and with the seemingly endless conflicts and lawsuits against those who coveted the locale for more and more intensive, high-density land development.

Town mayors and commissioners were called on during their retirement years when they had hoped to live in tranquillity, peace and serenity to deal with countless battles to maintain their visions of what they wanted their town to be. Surely, they did not seek financial reward. Salaries are often very low, ranging from $6,000 for commissioners to $7,200 for the mayor, per annum.

The commitment, tenacity and vigilance of the leadership, needing always to be focused on the long term, was difficult to be sure. But much was accomplished. And as a result, the citizens, visitors and neighbors now enjoy the fruits of their labors.

Yet, more needs to be done. Fortunately, and interestingly, the challenges that present themselves are of a different kind. In seeking to actualize those issues of importance in the years to come, it is significant that the town leadership, while recognizing there remains unfinished business, looks to the future with optimism and, ostensibly, with similar goals and an almost universal vision of what they want their town to be in the future. Now they are enjoying a sort of redirection.

By the end of the year 2003, Highland Beach is essentially 90-95% built out. There are few significant vacant parcels of land remaining that may be developed. In fact, aside from one or two such parcels, most believe future development will likely be limited to the same type of redevelopment going on in the neighboring cities that earlier had already achieved virtual build-out like West Palm Beach, Delray Beach and Boca Raton.

Ocean Grande Place, 2003

While most of Highland Beach residential structures built since 1960 have been high-density, multi-level, high-rise condominiums, there is a new trend that began in the late 1990s. Demand for large, luxurious single-family homes have become more evident in the community. An excellent example is Ocean Grande Place developed by Jeff Norman. These homes on smaller land parcels within intimate neighborhoods bring a lower density of six to the acre, mostly two stories tall. They are of opulent designs, abundant amenities, copious landscaping, natural preserve areas, and warm, tasteful architectural designs. Developed for families with children as well as for retirees, they are a departure from the past five decades of Highland Beach residential development. These single-family detached new custom homes have successfully sold at prices similar to the most expensive condominium apartments. Ocean Grande Place, a community of seventeen homes on four plus acres, opened in 1999 and sold out by 2001. The immediate success of Ocean Grande Place convinced many that higher quality, tastefully designed single-family detached homes would be an eminently successful alternative to penthouse condominiums in Highland Beach.

Bringing his Midwestern background of Ohio and its culture to the area, longtime local Florida resident Jeff Norman determined that a home unlike the multi-storied condominiums could be much in demand.

Ocean Grande Place, priced from $600,000 to $900,000 was so successful, Mr. Norman moved on to develop a second, more expensive neighborhood of twenty-two homes and named it Ocean Cove. This is a true luxury single-family detached community. Responding to the luxury marketplace, Ocean Cove, with homes of 5,500 to 5,800 square feet, are priced from $1.6 million to $3 milllion, comparable to the most expensive condominiums on the market. Ocean Cove, a project of 2003, will do much to offer luxury alternatives to penthouses atop nearby high-rise condominiums, perhaps bringing a smile to the early Tekesta residents.

Beachfront Manse, an example of recycling to
grander residences on the dune

Most opinion makers believe that future land development in Highland Beach, must come from the recycling of existing homes. Perhaps in the future, when economic requirements are satisfied, even the recycling of existing multi-family high-rise condominiums may occur. That means, the acquisition, destruction and replacement of existing structures by newer, more advanced, more modern homes and multi-family apartments. Purchasing a multi-million dollar home and replacing it with an even larger, more expensive residence has already become almost commonplace in the area, especially during the last decade of the 20th century, a period of almost unbelievable wealth, low interest rates and even international appeal.

The region still attracts thousands of new "settlers" and visitors mainly because of those same assets that attracted the Paleo-Indians, the earliest settlers. Those assets include the same warm winters, year-round temperate weather, beaches, the quality of life, personal freedom, and still, even in the case of the Town of Highland Beach, the highest, most stable ocean dunes along the coast. Highland Beach also has its own milieu that reflects the wealth, financial independence, and the mores, tastes and cultures of its residents. It continues to attract people of similar characteristics.

As a result, town leadership today is able to confidently turn its attention to the completion of their new water supply source, the innovative Reverse Osmosis wells and treatment facility, and resolution of the last remaining approvals of current development submissions.

Most Florida incorporated cities and towns use one of two options in their governance. In many cases, the mayor is the chief operating officer. In most others, the mayor and commission set policy, delegating the actual day-to-day operations to a professional manager. The latter form has come about as management needs have grown to such levels as to require professionally trained management. Universities and graduate schools today offer coveted degrees in public administration.

In November 1957, as Highland Beach found itself growing beyond the desires, and perhaps, capabilities of volunteer, retired citizens, the town commission adopted the commission-manager form of government. Most cities in Florida, thirty-one in Palm Beach County, have this style of government. Locally, the exception is West Palm Beach which departed from this form, opting for a "strong mayor" form during the 1990s.

Highland Beach, over its fifty-four year history, has had seven town managers, with Rudolph Hertwig being the first. Mr. Hertwig was also an elected commissioner. Ben Saag, the current town manager, began his tenure in January 1999. A native of Evanston, Illinois, he came to Highland Beach with his wife, Mary Anne, a third generation Floridian, and their four children, Rob, Stephen, Alex, and Matthew. Prior to his arrival in Highland Beach, Ben was the town manager of Dundee, Florida. A career manager, he received his Masters in Public Administration from Northern Illinois University. Many of the recent highly controversial events and issues described earlier were on Ben's "front burners" since his arrival. As Mayor Reid describes Ben's capabilities and contributions,

> "Ben has been a first-class manager for our town and makes my job as mayor so much easier. He is resourceful, well-informed and diligent. He serves our community very well and will be of great value as we tackle the major issues of the new millennium."

Once they deal with these unfinished issues, Mayor Tom Reid and the Town Commission seem in accord with their goals for the community in the coming years, goals that focus on two principle areas. First, as in the words of Mayor Reid, is "bringing to Highland Beach a state-of-the-art library and cultural center to serve the residents and their visitors." This "Center of Enlightenment" would include a high-tech center of the latest computer capabilities, quiet rooms, space for community meetings, concerts, programs, gatherings of all kinds, and, of course, a well-stocked collection of books, tapes, disks, DVDs, and research facilities.

He is joined by other members of the Town Commission. Michael W. Hill enjoys his position of Vice-Mayor, believing strongly that one should be involved in one's community. While a resident of Boca Raton, he was chairman of the American Heart Association for two years.

Mike and Shirley Hill met in Davie, Florida where she, then Shirley Smith, resided. He was living in Bushnell, Illinois, touted as "Home of the World's Finest Hammers." After joining Shirley in Davie, where they were married, they moved to Orlando and then Boca Raton. After a few years in Boca, they decided to move near the ocean to a residential community where they could also keep their beloved Yorkshire terrier, as many condominium associations did not permit pets. Thus, in 1989, they found their preferred community in Highland Beach, "that wonderful town on the ocean."

Continuing his strongly held view of participation in one's community, he responded favorably when former Mayor Joe Boulay urged him to consider filing for election to the town commission.

As a result, Michael Hill was elected to the Highland Beach Town Commission in 1997, and became Vice-Mayor in 1999. In his words,

> "Highland Beach is a wonderful town, and I want to make it the greatest place to live in all of South Florida. We have a wide diversity of home values, and a broad spectrum of traditions and cultures. Still, many people see their individual condominiums as their community. I believe it would be best if the residents consider all of Highland Beach to be their community rather than just their own condominium or neighborhood. I am excited about the prospect of building a larger library with meeting rooms, places for our residents to gather, involve themselves in the latest technologies if they choose, a place for performances

and discourse, and perhaps including large terraces overlooking the Intracoastal Waterway. Already, our library at Town Hall is bringing our people together, so much so that it is becoming a very active place.

I would join my fellow commissioners in even more beautification of our town, preserving the remaining open spaces and habitat for wildlife, especially our magnificent water birds. I believe our residents agree and want to become involved in the preservations of our beaches, our dunes, and the annual nesting places of our treasured sea turtles.

I know that if our people and its commission agree on this vision, we can accomplish those goals under Mayor Reid's leadership."

Town Commissioner John Sorrelli agrees.

"We have been through a lot of lawsuits seeking to preserve our community's quality of life. Now, with most of those behind us, we can look to a future with a new library, a cultural center, and growing community participation."

Commissioner Robert Lowe, who came from Poughkeepsie, New York, and finally moved into his Highland Beach home in 1981, has similar priorities. His response was,

"We must first complete our new water plant and wells. Then, I will work hard to help bring a new library and cultural center to Highland Beach. My vision is that it will be a two-story facility. As I see it, on the first floor will be the library, meeting rooms and other facilities. On the second floor will be a high-tech computer facility for our residents to attend computer classes where they can learn everything they wish, from using the Internet to graphic design. Our residents deserve the finest, and that's what I intend to help bring to our community.

We need to involve the public, that is, the town itself in the cleanliness and maintenance of our beaches and dunes. We have one of the most beautiful stretches of beaches in Palm Beach County, which is something I want to make sure all our citizens protect, enjoy and preserve.

We are going to be dealing with 'residential recycling' in the years to come, and must remain vigilant to those ramifications."

Commissioner Rachael Scala-Pistone, who has lived in Highland Beach since coming with her family in 1977, and has been a commissioner since 2001, strongly supports that same goal of a new library and cultural center and, in addition, feels strongly that attention, funding and financial resources should be directed toward preserving the natural environment of the town. She told me,

> "We must especially protect our beaches as a haven for nesting turtles so that they may continue the odyssey of their primal ancestors. That also means protecting the coral rock outcropping so unique along our beaches."

Perhaps especially grateful for her concern would be Koonkah, the season's first turtle to arrive to provide sustenance to the early Paleo-Indians and nearby residents over the centuries. And as for the coral rocks, the favored place of sentries, lookouts, swimmers, and fishermen who would now look back and smile. Among them would be the Japanese colonists of 1904 at Yamato who first named them "Yamato Rocks." And later the residents over the century who affectionately named them "Jap Rocks" as in "let's all go down to 'Jap Rocks' and catch some fish, picnic on the beach, or see a turtle—'Jap Rocks' is the best." Commissioner Scala-Pistone adds,

> "We really must preserve our precious natural resources including our beaches, the dunes, those remaining open spaces and wildlife, and our water. We enjoy a wonderful way of life because of our natural assets, and so we must be vigilant in protecting them."

It is apparent that Mayor Thomas Reid can look to his fellow commissioners to support his visions of seeking, by way of preserving the legacy of the town's fascinating history, its natural assets, its environment, and the new cultural-library facility. As he often has said,

> "Highland Beach has nearly all the capabilities and facilities of large cities. Now, as soon as we complete our new water treatment plant we will fulfill another vital need for our citizens with this new library and 'Center of Enlightenment.' We have the good fortune to live in Highland Beach and, we will work together to somehow improve our paradise."

For many centuries, people living on the ocean dunes of Highland Beach have enjoyed the highest quality of life available anywhere. Plentiful food, whether from the lands or from the prolific sea, attracted the first peoples. As new arrivals came, the area continued to fulfill their changing needs, their different cultures and tastes. The almost irresistible appeal of the beaches, the sea and its cooling breezes has never been lost. The ability to continue providing the best, the most attractive amenities available continues to this day. And with the strong leadership throughout the ages succeeding in that effort, the future appears secure, unequalled, and very bright indeed.